Economics for Everyone

Economics for Everyone
website: www.economicsforeveryone.com
e-mail Jim Stanford: author@economicsforeveryone.com

Economics for Everyone

A Short Guide to the Economics of Capitalism

Jim Stanford

Illustrations by Tony Biddle

Pluto  Press

LONDON • ANN ARBOR, MI

First published 2008 by Pluto Press
345 Archway Road, London N6 5AA
and 839 Greene Street, Ann Arbor, MI 48106

www.plutobooks.com

British Library Cataloguing in Publication Data
A catalogue record for this book is available from the British Library

ISBN   978 0 7453 2751 8   Hardback
ISBN   978 0 7453 2750 1   Paperback

Library of Congress Cataloging in Publication Data applied for

10   9   8   7   6   5   4   3   2   1

Illustrations by Tony Biddle, Perfect World Design
www.perfectworlddesign.ca

Designed and produced for Pluto Press by
Chase Publishing Services Ltd, Fortescue, Sidmouth, EX10 9QG, England
Typeset from disk by Stanford DTP Services, Northampton, England
Printed and bound in Canada by Transcontinental Printers

*Dedicated to the hard-working people who produce the wealth
– in hopes that by better understanding the economy,
we can be more successful in changing it.*

Contents

Part Five: Challenging Capitalism

Acknowledgements

This book had its genesis in an on-line course in basic economics for union members, that was jointly developed by my union (the Canadian Auto Workers, CAW) and McMaster University in Hamilton, Canada. As that project unfolded, I began to imagine that our efforts to teach economics in an accessible but critical way could have wider applications in other trade union and social change settings. I thank my colleagues David Robertson (at CAW) and Wayne Lewchuk (at McMaster) for their cooperation, support, and patience on that initial project – and for their outstanding commitment to developing worker-friendly pedagogy in this and many other subject areas.

Other colleagues at CAW played essential roles in this project. I am very grateful to our leaders, Buzz Hargrove and Jim O'Neil, for their support of my role as a union economist, allowing me to take on a range of issues and projects that go well beyond the immediate bread-and-butter work of the union, as well as for their generous support of this book. I received first-rate administrative and research support from Kristine Vendrame and Kathy Bennett.

Early enthusiasm from Bruce Campbell at the Canadian Centre for Policy Alternatives (CCPA) was crucial to getting the project off the ground. Several CCPA staff played important supporting roles, including Kerri-Anne Finn and Erika Shaker, in developing both the book and the Economics for Everyone website. I also thank Emira Mears and Elaine Hutton for assistance with design.

An equally enthusiastic and quick response from Roger van Zwanenberg at Pluto Press spurred me to imagine a wider, international audience for this work. I thank him and his colleagues (including Judy Nash, Robert Webb, Ray Addicott, and Tracey Day) for their timely, supportive, and high-quality contributions to editing and production. I also thank Nick Gomersall for putting me in touch with Pluto in the first place.

Excellent comments on draft chapters were provided to me by many people, including: Donna Baines, Grant Belchamber, Bruce Campbell, David Goutor, Brendan Haley, Marc Lavoie, Marc Lee, Malcolm Sawyer, Mario Seccareccia, Scott Sinclair, J.M. Stanford, Yvonne Stanford, and Don Sutherland.

Tony Biddle's awesome illustrations and road maps add immeasurably to both the educational and entertainment value of this book. I thank Tony for his interest in this project, for his timely and first-class work, and for all the other ways that he devotes his considerable artistic and political talents to the cause of social justice.

Most of my research and writing on this book took place when I was a visiting researcher at the Australian Council of Trade Unions (ACTU) in Melbourne, Australia. I thank the ACTU for their generous hospitality. The warm welcome I received from Grant Belchamber, Nixon Apple, Pat Conroy, Don Sutherland, George Koletsis, the Australian Manufacturing Workers Union, John King, John Wiseman, and Adam Game made the year as enjoyable as it was productive. The Australian labour movement's historic and successful "Your Rights at Work" campaign, which I experienced first-hand during my time there, is an outstanding example of how fighting back does make a difference.

Nobody develops their ideas in a vacuum, and I owe an intellectual debt to the many passionate, principled, and rigorous economists who have taught and influenced me over the years: my free-thinking professors at the University of Calgary, Cambridge, and the New School; my colleagues in the Progressive Economics Forum; and my soulmates in the broader community of heterodox economists (special mention to the late David M. Gordon, Tom Palley, Dean Baker, Malcolm Sawyer, Steve Keen, and the late Andrew Glyn).

My final and most passionate gratitude goes to my immediate family: Donna Baines, Maxine Baines, and Thea Baines. Their support while working on the project was invaluable. But I am even more thankful for sharing with me their energy, hope, and passion for life, and their determination to build a better world.

Introduction
Why Study Economics?

Never trust an economist with your job

Most people think economics is a technical, confusing, and even mysterious subject. It's a field best left to the experts: namely, the economists.

But in reality, economics should be quite straightforward. After all, economics is simply about how we work. What we produce. And how we distribute and ultimately use what we've produced. Economics is about who does what, who gets what, and what they do with it.

At that simplest, grass-roots level, we all know something about the economy. And so we should all have something to say about economics.

Moreover, because we interact, cooperate, and clash with each other in the economy (even Robinson Crusoe didn't work alone – he had Friday around to help), economics is a *social* subject. It's not just technical, concrete forces like technology and productivity that matter. It's also the interactions and relationships between *people* that make the economy go around.

So you don't need to be an economist to know a lot about economics. Everyone experiences the economy. Everyone contributes to it, one way or another. Everyone has an interest in the economy: in *how* it functions, how *well* it functions, and in *whose interests* it functions. And everyone has a grass-roots sense of where they personally fit into the big economic picture, and how well they are doing (compared to others, compared to the past, and compared to their expectations). This is the stuff economics should be made of.

Unfortunately, in my view, most professional economists don't think about economics in this common-sense, grass-roots context. To the contrary, they tend to adopt a rather superior attitude in their dealings with the untrained masses. They invoke complicated technical mumbo-jumbo – usually utterly unnecessary to their arguments – to make their case. They claim to know what's good for the people, even better than the people themselves do. They take great pleasure in expounding theories that are counter-intuitive and puzzling to the rest of us. They present themselves as interpreters of a mysterious realm which average people cannot hope to comprehend. And since they study things that are measured in billions or even trillions of dollars, their sense of importance grows – in their own eyes, and in others'.

That's why we see economists on the television news every night. We almost never see anthropologists, biologists, social workers, nutritionists, or architects on the nightly news. Perhaps we should hear more from those other professions, and less from the economists. Their advice might actually be more important to our long-term economic well-being than that of the economists.

Nothing better exemplifies economists' know-it-all attitude than debates over free trade. Conventionally trained economists take it as a *proven fact* that free trade between two countries always makes both sides better off. People who question or oppose free trade – unions, social activists, nationalists – must either be acting from ignorance, or else are pursuing some narrow vested interest that conflicts with the broader good. These troublesome people should be lectured to (and economists love nothing better than expounding their beautiful theory of COMPARATIVE ADVANTAGE*), or simply ignored. And that's exactly what most governments do. (Ironically, even some conventional economists now recognize that traditional comparative advantage theory is wrong, for many reasons – some of which we'll discuss in Part Four of this book. But that hasn't affected the profession's near-religious devotion to the doctrine of free trade.)

Worse yet, the arrogance of economists is not value-free. Outside the academic world, the vast majority of professional economists work for organizations with a deep vested interest in the status quo: banks, brokerages, corporations, industry associations, and governments.

Inside academia, meanwhile, most economists (though certainly not all) are wedded to a particular, peculiar version of economics – called NEOCLASSICAL ECONOMICS. This kind of economics is as ideological as it is scientific. It was developed in the late nineteenth century to *defend* capitalism, not just explain it. And it still goes to great lengths to try to prove a whole portfolio of bizarre, politically loaded, and obviously untrue propositions: like claiming that merely owning financial wealth is itself productive, or that everyone is paid according to their productivity, or that unemployment doesn't even actually exist.

---

* Throughout the book, terms highlighted in SMALL CAPITALS are defined in the on-line glossary at the book's website, www.economicsforeveryone.com.

Whether in universities or in the real world, therefore, most economists fully believe that competition, inequality, and the accumulation of private wealth are central, natural, and desirable features of a vibrant, efficient economy. This value system infuses their analysis and their recommendations. Outside of academia, it is reinforced by the fact that most economists are directly employed by organizations which have benefited mightily from the current, lopsided economic system.

I think we need a more democratic economics, a more grass-roots approach. I think we need an economics that's not based on abstract assumptions (like the other-worldly theory of PERFECT COMPETITION, which we'll explain in Chapter 11), but instead starts from the concrete circumstances of average people's lives. We need an economics for everyone.

My approach is not motivated by an "anti-expert" mentality. I would not want to be operated on by an untrained medical student. And people who make important economic decisions, and give important economic advice, should be formally trained in economics.

But debates over economic issues are not technical debates, where expertise alone settles the day. They are deeply *political* debates, in the broad sense of that word: distinct groups of people have distinct interests, they know their interests, and they naturally work to promote them. This occurs everywhere in the economy – and economics shouldn't pretend that it doesn't.

A hard-working labourer has very different economic interests from a red-suspendered currency trader. And the labourer has as much to say about economics as the trader. (In fact, in hard economic terms, the labourer almost certainly produces more real value than the currency trader – despite the enormous sums of money passing through the trader's computer every business day.) But the elitism of economics disempowers and silences the voices of non-experts.

My main goal with this book, and throughout my career as an economist, has been to encourage non-experts – workers, union members, activists, consumers, neighbours – to develop their natural, grass-roots interest in economics, by:

- Studying the economy, and learning more about how it functions.

- Thinking concretely about their personal role and stake in the economy (rather than abstract indicators like gross domestic product (GDP), stock markets, or foreign exchange).

- Recognizing that the economy embodies distinct groups of people with distinct interests, and that economics itself reflects those distinctions and conflicts. Economics is not a neutral, technical discipline.

- Being ready to challenge, when necessary, the way "expert" economists explain the economy and (even more dangerously) tell us how to improve it.

The economy is too important to be left to the economists. Ordinary people have valuable economic knowledge – knowledge that's usually ignored by the experts. More importantly, the analysis and advice of the experts is all too often compromised by their position in the economy they are telling us how to manage. Everyone has a stake in the economy. Everyone has economic interests they need to identify and protect. Learning about economics will help them understand where they fit into the bigger system, and help them fight for a better deal.

> **Watch Out!**
>
> "The purpose of studying economics is not to acquire a set of ready-made answers to economic questions, but to learn how to avoid being deceived by economists."
>
> Joan Robinson, British economist (1960).

An economist may tell you that your job depends on the central bank raising interest rates to control inflation (in the long run, anyway). An economist may tell you that free trade will increase productivity and hence increase incomes (although you may lose your job in the process). An economist may tell you that eliminating unions and minimum wages will make society richer (although, just as with aerobic exercise, it might hurt at first ... no pain, no gain!).

Never trust an economist with your job. Learn about economics yourself. And make up your own mind about what might protect your job – and what might destroy it.

A society in which ordinary people know more about economics, and recognize the often conflicting interests at stake in the economy, is a society in which more people will feel confident deciding for themselves what's best – instead of trusting the experts. It will be a more democratic society.

Capitalism: the economy we know

So far, we've been speaking very broadly about "the economy." But in fact, this book is about the workings of a particular kind of economy, called capitalism. "Capitalism" and "the economy" are not the same thing – even though many economists pretend capitalism is a natural, permanent state of affairs, and hence the *only* economy. However, there were other economies that existed before capitalism. And I tend to think there will be other economies that come after capitalism, too.

Capitalism has particular features and forces that need to be identified, just to understand how it works. This is true regardless of how you feel about capitalism. Just to understand what's happening in capitalism, we need to identify and study its crucial facts:

- Most people have to work for others, in return for a wage or salary.

- A small proportion of society owns the bulk of wealth, and uses that wealth in an effort to generate still more wealth.

- Competition between companies, each trying to maximize its own profits, forces them to behave in particular, sometimes perverse ways.

It seems bizarre, but conventional economists mostly ignore these central facts (with the partial exception of the third). They don't even use the word "capitalism." Instead, they call our system a "market economy." The fact that a few people own immense wealth, while most people own almost nothing, is considered accidental or even irrelevant. They claim, incredibly, that the economy would be

I once attended a dinner speech given by the Secretary-General of the Organization for Economic Cooperation and Development (OECD) (the "club" of developed capitalist countries). He was promoting the concept of "economic literacy." He argued that if more people in society understood the fundamentals of economic theory (like supply and demand, competition, and free trade), then they would go along more readily with policy "reforms" implemented by their governments – even if those reforms were painful.

As an example, he referred to the dramatic (and successful) protests that occurred in France in 2006 against government efforts to weaken labour protections. These changes would have made it easier for employers to fire workers, especially young workers. If the French understood that these seemingly painful "reforms" actually make the

▸

labour market function more "efficiently," he argued, they wouldn't have protested.

This kind of "literacy" sounds to me more like brainwashing than education.

During the question period, I took issue with the OECD chief's assertion that the French do not understand economics. Compare France to the US – usually held up as the prototype of an efficient, flexible, market-driven system. On average, French workers work 300 hours per year fewer than Americans (that's seven extra weeks off per year). Yet they produce just as much value added with each hour of labour as Americans. Unemployment is higher in France – yet most unemployed French receive more income (from social benefits) than millions of *employed* low-wage Americans. As a result, the French have enough money, and lots of time, to eat in restaurants, make love, and attend protest demonstrations (not necessarily in that order)!

In America, meanwhile, there are almost 9 million *employed workers* whose incomes leave them below the official poverty line (which is still based on the standard of living in 1964). Their hard work is not taking them far. Yet in a recent survey, an incredible 39 percent of Americans indicated either that they were already in the wealthiest 1 percent of society, or else believed that they soon would be there.* The mathematical impossibility of this bizarre worldview has not (yet) undermined the American myth of "upward mobility" – a myth which inhibits hard-working, poor people from standing up and demanding a better deal.

Ironically, later in 2006 the OECD itself published economic evidence indicating that employment protection laws (like the French regulations) have no visible impact whatsoever on unemployment rates.

So who really understands economics? I think it's the French protestors. *Vive le France*!

* Survey conducted by Time/CNN, cited in Andrew Glyn, *Capitalism Unleashed: Finance, Globalization and Welfare* (Oxford: Oxford University Press, 2006), p. 179.

exactly the same whether capitalists hired workers, or workers hired capitalists.

These central and unique features of capitalism impart particular kinds of behaviour and motion to the economy. They explain why capitalism is *dynamic*: flexible, creative, and always changing. They explain why capitalism is *conflictual*: with ongoing struggles and conflicts between different groups of people. They explain why capitalism is *unstable*: exhibiting periods of growth and prosperity, followed by periods of stagnation and recession.

Economists who ignore the key features of capitalism will be less able to understand and explain how capitalism actually works. So purely from a scientific perspective, it's important to be frank about what we are dealing with.

Of course, economists of all political stripes carry political baggage. I certainly do. It's impossible to name and analyze capitalism without passing judgement on it. (Conventional economists pretend that the "positive" science of describing the economy can be separated from the "normative" practice of evaluating and trying to improve the economy – but this phony distinction has never been very successful.)

Capitalism has been immensely successful, on many criteria. It ushered in the industrial era, and the prosperity (for some people, but not everyone) that came with it. It ruthlessly undermines old-fashioned restrictions and taboos, and probes endlessly to find new ways of generating private profit (some of which are socially useful, some of which are not). It harnesses immense energy, creativity, and discipline from many of its participants.

On the other hand, capitalism has obviously failed to live up to many of its promises. Billions of the world's people endure hardship, poverty, and premature death, even though humanity possesses abundant wealth to abolish these afflictions. Vast resources – like the talent and energy of hundreds of millions of unemployed and underemployed individuals – are chronically misused or wasted. The natural environment is deteriorating rapidly in the face of the profit-maximizing, cost-shifting imperatives of private profit; global climate change is the latest, most catastrophic symptom of this failure. And even on its own terms – the rapid investment of private capital to generate profit – capitalism may be running out of steam (something we will discuss in Chapter 12).

I am critical of capitalism's failings – but I am also respectful of its flexibility and its staying power. I am utterly convinced that there are many obvious changes that would help the economy meet human and environmental needs, without breaking fundamentally from the underlying logic which drives the whole system. I also believe that it is ultimately possible to build an alternative economic system motivated directly by our desire to improve the human condition, rather than by a hunger for private profit. (Exactly what that alternative system would look like, however, is not at all clear today.) We'll consider these criticisms of capitalism, and alternative visions, in the last chapters of this book.

But quite apart from whether you think capitalism is good or bad, capitalism is something we must study. It's the economy we live in, the economy we know. And the more that ordinary people understand about capitalism, the more well-being they'll be able to extract from it.

The organization of this book

This book has five major parts, which cover the following subject areas:

1. **Preliminaries** The first part of the book defines the economy, and identifies the unique features of a capitalist economy. It also provides some historical background. We discuss how capitalism emerged and evolved, and also how the study of *economics* emerged and evolved. In both cases, we highlight the conflicts and controversies encountered en route to the present day. I believe that studying economic history and the history of economic thought is an inherently subversive undertaking. It refutes the assumption that capitalism is "natural" and hence ever-lasting, and the related claim that economics is the neutral, technical study of that natural, ever-lasting economy.

2. **The Basics of Capitalism** This part of the book studies the core activities and relationships that make up capitalism. First we discuss *work*. Broadly defined, work (or human effort) is the essential ingredient that drives everything in the economy. But we don't work with our bare hands; we must work with tools. We have to make those tools, and (in capitalism, anyway) someone owns them. Most work in capitalism is undertaken by employees who are paid wages or salaries for their efforts. But much work also occurs without any payment, inside households, as people care for themselves and their family members. We describe this basic economic "circle," in which profit-seeking investment initiates production, generates employment, and allows people (supplemented by unpaid work at home) to support themselves.

3. **Capitalism as a System** After introducing these basic, core relationships, Part Three describes how the capitalist economy functions as an overall system. It describes competition between firms; the determination of overall investment; the determination of overall employment; the distribution of income; and the relationship between the economy and the natural environment.

4. **The Complexity of Capitalism** Apart from the basic relationships between private companies, their workers, and households, there are other important players in modern capitalism. We introduce these players and what they do in Part Four. We start with the monetary and financial system. The financial industry itself is not inherently productive, but it plays a crucial role in facilitating investment and distributing profits. We also introduce government and its diverse, often contradictory economic functions. And we start to describe capitalism on a global level: globalization, foreign trade, capital flows, and economic development. The smaller, simple "circle" we described in Part Two of the book now becomes a lot bigger and more complex.

5. **Challenging Capitalism** Once we've described capitalism as a complete, global economic system, the final part of the book evaluates capitalism: both its successes, and its failures. It considers ways in which capitalism could be reformed, to more effectively meet human needs and protect the natural environment. And it starts to imagine completely different ways of organizing the economy in the future.

Building an economic "map"

The book describes an economy of gradually increasing complexity – starting with the simplest relationships within an individual company, shifting our focus to the interaction between companies, and then considering the roles of the environment, the financial industry, government, and globalization.

To portray these increasingly complex relationships, we provide a series of eight economic "road maps," illustrated by Tony Biddle. The maps use simple visual icons to identify the major players, and connect the dots between them. By the time we've explained our "big circle" at the conclusion of Part Four, this map will be a very handy tool for finding your way around capitalism. Like any map, it will help you locate where you are – and figure out where you want to go.

The Economics for Everyone website

The overarching goal of this book is to make economics accessible and even entertaining for non-specialist readers. That's why we've kept the book short, used plain language, illustrated it with Tony Biddle's awesome cartoons, and avoided (wherever possible) the use of academic-style citations and references.

For those who want to continue their study of grass-roots economics, however, we have provided additional information and resources. These are posted, free of charge, at a special Economics for Everyone website, generously hosted by the Canadian Centre for Policy Alternatives (Canada's major progressive think tank):

www.economicsforeveryone.com

The following materials are available at the website:

- **Instructor resources**   We hope that unions, community groups, schools and colleges, and other organizations will use Economics for Everyone as a teaching resource for grass-roots economics instruction. To this end, the website includes a sample 13-session course outline (based on material in this book), lecture slides for 13 lectures, and 13 sets of hands-on, entertaining student exercises. The book and the web-based materials thus constitute a ready-made teaching resource. With them, any progressive organization can undertake to offer basic instruction in economics to its members, without any formal prerequisites. (We also encourage instructors to supplement these materials with local information and resources.)

- **Glossary**   Every term in this book that is highlighted in SMALL CAPITALS is defined in an on-line glossary that can be accessed from the website.

- **Background statistics**   To keep the book as readable as possible, we have avoided using too many charts, graphs, and tables. For specific topics on which additional background statistics (from a selection of countries) may be interesting to readers, they are provided on the website. Wherever this calculator symbol appears – ▣ – the website includes simple statistics (cross-referenced to the relevant chapter of the book) that help to illustrate the point being made.

- **"How-to" guides**   The website includes short guides to help readers locate and interpret key economic data and statistics, such as GDP statistics and corporate financial reports.

- **Other supplementary materials**   The website also provides a list of suggestions for further reading (including links to organizations which undertake progressive economic research and education), and a complete list of sources for the data and citations included in the book.

- **The E4E blog**   Through this blog discussion, I will answer questions, report on public events and reactions to the book, and provide updates addressing current economic issues and controversies.

It's up to you

Your impressions, responses, questions, and suggestions are invited and appreciated. They will help to refine and improve this work for future editions and applications. Send your feedback to author@economicsforeveryone.com. Within the constraints of my paying job (as economist for the Canadian Auto Workers), I will endeavour to respond to every query.

If there's a simple, overarching theme running through this book, it's the idea that people have to fight for whatever they get from the economy. Nothing comes automatically, via the magical workings of supply and demand. Rather, it comes to them through motivation, organizational strength, political influence, and power. Knowing this basic fact of economic life, and identifying where and how to fight for a fairer share of the pie, will allow you and your fellow unionists, activists, and neighbours to make the most of economics.

In this sense, it really is up to you: to take your grass-roots knowledge of the economy, and translate it into economic action, and economic change.

A Note on Sources and Citations

To keep this book as readable and uncluttered as possible, we have dispensed with most of the formal references, source notes and citations common in academic books. Most of the statistical information contained in the book (including graphs and tables) was obtained from standard public sources (national statistical agencies, or international organizations like the United Nations and the Organization for Economic Cooperation and Development). Specific sources for this data are provided in the on-line list of sources, available at the Economics for Everyone website. Similarly, most direct quotations listed in the book come from classic, well-known sources; specific publication details for these quotes are also reported in the on-line source list. In many places, the text of the book refers to research findings or conclusions supported by the broader economic literature; specific sources supporting these conclusions are also listed in the on-line source list.

The exceptions to this approach are the few instances where I have referred to data collected or analyzed originally by other researchers (rather than data from standard public sources), or where I have repeated quotations from a secondary source (when another researcher located and reported the original quotation). In these cases the other researcher's work must be acknowledged, and formal citations are provided in the hard-copy text.

Any readers with additional questions regarding sources and citations are welcome to contact the author directly.

Part One

Preliminaries

1

The Economy and Economics

Take a walk

The economy must be a very complicated, volatile thing. At least that's how it seems in the business pages of the newspaper. Mind-boggling stock market tables. Charts and graphs. GDP statistics. Foreign exchange rates. It's little wonder the media turn to economists, the high priests of this mysterious world, to tell us what it means, and why it's important. And we hear from them several times each day – usually via the monotonous "market updates" that interrupt most news broadcasts. Company X's shares are up two points; company Y's are down two points; the analysts are "bullish"; the analysts are "bearish."

But is all that financial hyperactivity really what the economy is about? Is economics really so complex and unintelligible? Should we trust the "experts" with it all? Maybe we should find out what's going on for ourselves.

Forget the market updates. Here's a better way to find out about the economy – *your* economy. Take a walk. And ask some questions.

Start at the front door of your own household. How many people live there? What generations? Who works outside the household, and how much do they earn? How long have they been working there? How long do they plan to keep working, and how will they support themselves when they retire? Who performs which chores inside the household? Are there any children? Who cares for them? Does anyone else in your home require care? Do you own your house or apartment, or do you rent it? If you rent it, from whom? If you own it, how did you pay for it? What shape is it in?

Now walk through your neighbourhood, and the next neighbourhood. Are the homes or apartments all roughly the same, or different? Does everyone have a home? Do most people have jobs? What sorts of jobs? Are they well off? Can they comfortably pay for the things they and their families need?

Watch your neighbours going off to work, school, or other destinations. How are they travelling? In their own cars? On public

transport? Walking? How much money, time, and physical space is devoted in your neighbourhood to "getting around"?

Is there a school in your neighbourhood? A hospital? A library? Who pays for those buildings? Who works there? How do those facilities compare with the private homes and businesses around them? Are they newer, or older? Nicer, or shabbier? Is there a park in your neighbourhood? Is there anywhere else a person can go without having to pay money?

Are the streets clean? If so, who cleaned them? Is the air fresh or smoggy? Are there any parks in your neighbourhood? Can people in your neighbourhood safely drink the water from their taps? How much do they pay for that water? And to whom?

Walk through the nearest shopping district. What kinds of products are displayed in the windows? Were any of them produced within 100 miles of your home? Elsewhere in your country? In another country? Can your neighbours afford most of what is on display? Are they usually happy with their purchases, or disappointed? Do they pay with cash, bank cards, or credit cards? Can they afford what they buy?

Now walk to a local bank branch and see what's happening inside. Compare what you see (deposits, withdrawals, loans) with the activities you read about in the business pages of the newspaper (leveraged buyouts, financial speculation, foreign exchange). Which matters more to day-to-day life in your neighbourhood?

This is a good time to stop at a café. Pull out a pencil and paper. List your approximate monthly income. Then list how much of it goes to the following categories: rent or mortgage (including utilities); income taxes; car payments or public transport passes; groceries; other "stuff" (merchandise); and going out (entertainment). Can you comfortably pay your bills each month? Do you regularly save? Is your income higher than it was five years ago, lower, or about the same? If you had a little more income, what would you do with it? If you walked back to that bank and asked for a loan, would they give you one?

Apart from the places we've mentioned (schools, stores, and banks), what other workplaces are visible in your neighbourhood? Any factories? What do they produce, and what shape are they in? Any professional or government offices? Other services? Can you see any office buildings from your neighbourhood? Who works there? Can you guess what they do? Imagine the conditions in those offices (spaciousness, quality of furnishings, security, caretaking), and compare them to conditions inside your local school.

Have any new workplaces opened up recently in your neighbourhood? If so, what do they do? Did you see any "help wanted" signs posted in local workplaces? What kinds of jobs were they advertising for?

Now you can return home. Congratulations! You've done a lot more than just take a stroll. You've conducted a composite economic profile of your own community. It has no statistics, charts, or graphs (though you could add those if you wish, with a bit of work at the local library). But just by walking around your neighbourhood, you have identified the crucial factors determining economic affairs in your community:

- **Work** Who works? Who works inside the home, and works outside the home? Are they employed by someone else (and if so, who?), or do they work for themselves? How much do they get paid? Is it hard to find a job?

- **Consumption**   What do people need to stay alive? What do they want, to make their lives better? How do they pay for it all?

- **Investment**   Private companies and public agencies must invest in maintaining and expanding their facilities and workplaces, or else the economy (and your neighbourhood) goes quickly downhill. Who is investing? How much? On what types of projects?

- **Finance**   Most economic activity (but not all) requires money. Who creates and controls that money? Who gets to spend it? What do they spend it on?

- **Environment**   Everything we do in the economy requires space, air, and inputs of natural materials. Is the natural environment being run down by the economy, or is it being sustained?

These are the building blocks from which the most complicated economic theories are constructed: work, consumption, investment, finance, and the environment. And they are all visible, right there in your neighbourhood.

Don't ever believe that economics is a subject only for "experts." The essence of economics is visible to everyone, right there in your own 'hood. Economics is about life – *your* life.

What is the economy?

The economy is simultaneously mystifying and straightforward. Everyone has experience with the economy. Everyone participates in it. Everyone knows something about it – long before the pinstripe-wearing economist appears on TV to tell you about it.

The forces and relationships you investigated on your walk are far more important to economic life than the pointless ups and downs of the stock market. Yet our local economic lives are nevertheless affected (and disrupted) by the bigger and more complex developments reported in the business pages.

At its simplest, the "economy" simply means all the work that human beings perform, in order to produce the things we need and use in our lives. (By work, we mean all productive human activity, not just employment; we'll discuss that distinction later.) We need to organize and perform our work (economists call that PRODUCTION).

And then we need to divide up the fruits of our work (economists call that DISTRIBUTION).

What kind of work are we talking about? Any kind of work is part of the economy, as long as it's aimed at producing something we need or want. Factory workers, office workers. Executives, farmers. Teachers, nurses. Homemakers, homebuilders. All of these people perform productive work, and all of that work is part of the economy.

What do we produce when we work? Production involves both goods and services. GOODS are tangible items that we can see and touch: food and clothes, houses and buildings, electronics and automobiles, machines and toys. SERVICES are tasks that one or several people perform for others: cutting hair and preparing restaurant meals, classroom instruction and brain surgery, transportation and auditing.

Where do we perform this work? Productive work occurs almost everywhere: in private companies, in government departments and public agencies, and in the home. In cities, in towns, on farms, and in forests.

Why do we work? We must survive, and hence we require the basic material needs of life: food, clothing, shelter, education, medical care. Beyond that, we want to get the most out of our lives, and hence we aim for more than subsistence. We want a greater quantity, and a greater variety, of goods and services: for entertainment, for travel, for cultural and personal enrichment, for comfort. We may also work because we enjoy it. Perversely for economists (most of whom view work solely as a "disutility"), most people are happier when they have work to do – thanks to the social interaction, financial well-being, and self-esteem that good work provides.

How do we distribute, and eventually use, the economic pie we have baked together? In many different ways. Some things are produced directly for our own use (like food grown in a garden, and then cooked in a household kitchen). Most things we must buy with money. We are entitled to consume certain products – like walking down a paved street, listening to the radio, or going to school – without directly paying anything. Importantly, some of what we produce must be re-invested, in order to spark even more economic activity in the future.

So when you think about the "economy," just think about work. What work do we do? What do we produce? And what do we do with what we've produced?

The economy and society

The economy is a fundamentally *social* activity. Nobody does it all by themselves (unless you are a hermit). We rely on each other, and we interact with each other, in the course of our work.

It is common to equate the economy with private or individual wealth, profit, and self-interest, and hence it may seem strange to describe it as something "social." Indeed, free-market economists adopt the starting premise that human beings are inherently selfish (even though this assumption has been proven false by biologists and anthropologists alike).

Economics Matters

"The mode of production of material life determines the social, political and intellectual life process in general."

Karl Marx, German philosopher and economist (1859).

"It's the economy, stupid."

James Carville, political advisor to US President Bill Clinton (1992).

In fact, the capitalist economy is not individualistic at all. It is social, and in many ways it is cooperative. The richest billionaire in the world couldn't have earned a dollar without the supporting roles played by his or her workers, suppliers, and customers. Indeed, our economic lives are increasingly intertwined with each other, as we each play our own little roles in a much bigger picture. That's why most of us live in cities (where the specialized, collective nature of the economy is especially visible). And that's how we can interact economically with people in other countries, thousands of miles away.

The economy is about work: organizing it, doing it, and dividing up its products. And at work, one way or another, we interact with other people.

The link between the economy and society goes two ways. The economy is a fundamentally social arena. But society as a whole depends strongly on the state of the economy. Politics, culture, religion, and international affairs are all deeply influenced by the progress of our economy. Governments are re-elected or turfed from office depending on the state of the economy. Family life is organized around the demands of work (both inside and outside the home). Being able to comfortably support oneself and one's family is a central determinant of happiness.

So the economy is an important, perhaps even dominant, force in human development. That doesn't mean that we should make "sacrifices" for the sake of the economy – since the whole point of the economy is to meet our material needs, not the other way around. And it certainly doesn't mean that we should grant undue attention or influence to economists. But it does mean that we will understand a great deal about our history, our current social reality, and our future evolution as a species, when we understand more about economics.

What is economics?

Economics is a social science, not a physical science. (Unfortunately, many economists are confused on this point! They foolishly try to describe human economic activity with as much mechanical precision as physicists describe the behaviour of atoms.) Economics is the study of human economic behaviour: the production and distribution of the goods and services we need and want.

This broad field encompasses several sub-disciplines. Economic history; money and finance; household economics; labour studies and labour relations; business economics and management; international economics; environmental economics; and others. A broad (and rather artificial) division is often made between MICROECONOMICS (the study of the economic behaviour of individual consumers, workers, and companies) and MACROECONOMICS (the study of how the economy functions at the aggregate level).

This all seems relatively straightforward. Unfortunately, the dominant stream in modern economics (NEOCLASSICAL ECONOMICS, which we'll discuss more in Chapter 4) makes it more complicated than it needs to be. Instead of addressing broad questions of production and distribution, neoclassical economics focuses narrowly on *markets* and *exchange*. The purpose of economics, in this mindset, was defined by one of its leading practitioners (Lord Lionel Robbins) back in 1932, in a definition that is still taught in economics courses today:

"Economics is the science which studies human behaviour as a relationship between given ends and scarce means which have alternative uses."

Embedded in this definition is a very peculiar (and rather dismal) interpretation of economic life. Scarcity is a normal condition. Humans are "endowed" with arbitrary amounts of useful resources. By trading through markets, they can extract maximum well-being from that endowment – just like school kids experience greater happiness by trading their duplicate superhero cards with one another in the playground. An "efficient" economy is one which maximizes, through trade, the usefulness of that initial endowment – regardless of how output is distributed, what kinds of things are produced, or how rich or poor people are at the end of the day. (This curious narrow concept of efficiency is called ALLOCATIVE EFFICIENCY.)

As we'll learn later in this book, by defining the fundamental economic "question" in this particular way, neoclassical economics misses many important economic issues related to production, innovation, development, and fairness.

I prefer to keep things simple. We'll stick with a much broader definition of economics: the study of how humans work, and what we do with the fruits of our labour. Part of this involves studying markets and exchange – but only part. Economics also involves studying many other things: history, technology, tradition, family, power, and conflict.

Economics and politics

Economics and politics have always gone hand-in-hand. Indeed, the first economists called their discipline "political economy." The connections between economics and politics reflect, in part, the importance of economic conditions to political conditions. The well-being of the economy can influence the rise and fall of politicians and governments, even entire social systems.

But here, too, the influence goes both ways. Politics also affects the economy – and economics itself. The economy is a realm of competing, often conflicting interests. Determining whose interests prevail, and how conflicts are managed, is a deeply political process. (Neoclassical economists claim that anonymous "market forces" determine all these outcomes, but don't be fooled: what they call the "market" is itself a social institution in which some people's interests are enhanced at the expense of others'.) Different economic actors use their political influence and power to advance their respective economic interests. The extent to which groups of people tolerate economic outcomes (even unfavourable ones) also depends on political factors: such as whether or not they believe those outcomes are "natural" or "inevitable," and whether or not they feel they have any power to bring about change.

Finally, the social science which aims to interpret and explain all this scrabbling, teeming behaviour – economics – has its own political assumptions and biases. In Chapter 4 we'll review how most economic theories over the years have been motivated by political considerations. Modern economics (including this book!) is no different: economics is still a deeply political profession.

Measuring the economy

GROSS DOMESTIC PRODUCT (GDP) is the most common way to measure the economy. But beware: it is a deeply flawed measure. GDP adds up the value of all the different goods and services that are produced *for money* in the economy. GDP is thus one measure of the total value of the work we do – but only the work we do for money.

In the private sector of the economy, GDP is based on the market prices of everything that's bought and sold. In the public and non-profit sectors, it is based on the cost of everything that's produced. In both cases, statisticians must deduct the costs of the many inputs and supplies purchased in any particular industry, from the total value produced by that industry. (This is so that we don't double-count the work that went into all those inputs.) In this way, GDP is designed to only include the VALUE ADDED by new work at each stage of production.

An obvious drawback of GDP is that it excludes the value of work that is *not* performed for money. This is a highly arbitrary and misleading exclusion. For example, most people perform unpaid chores in their households, and many must care for other family members (especially children and elders). Some of this household work can be "outsourced" to paid cleaners, nannies, and restaurants (the richer you are, the more you can outsource), in which case it is included in GDP. But if you "do it yourself," then it doesn't count! Volunteer work and community participation are other forms of valuable, productive work excluded from GDP.

This phony distinction has big consequences for how we measure the economy. Unfortunately, things that we measure often take on extra importance (with the media, and with policy-makers), purely

Table 1.1   GDP and Human Well-Being

Country	Human Development Index Rank (HDI)	GDP Rank	GDP Rank – HDI Rank*	GDP per Capita (US$)	Life Expectancy (years)	Educational Attainment Index†
Norway	1	4	3	38,454	79.6	.99
Iceland	2	5	3	33,051	80.9	.98
Australia	3	14	11	30,331	80.5	.99
Ireland	4	3	–1	38,827	77.9	.99
Sweden	5	16	11	29,541	80.3	.98
Canada	6	10	4	31,263	80.2	.97
Japan	7	18	11	29,251	82.2	.94
US	8	2	–6	39,676	77.5	.97
UK	18	13	–5	30,821	78.3	.97
China	81	90	9	5,896	71.9	.84
India	126	117	–9	3,139	63.6	.61
Human Development "Over-Achievers":						
Uruguay	43	62	+19	9,421	75.6	.95
Cuba	50	93	+43	5,700	77.6	.93
Armenia	80	112	+32	4,101	71.6	.91
Madagascar	143	169	+26	857	55.6	.66
Human Development "Under-Achievers":						
Hong Kong	22	12	–10	30,822	81.8	.88
Saudi Arabia	76	45	–31	13,825	72.0	.72
Turkey	92	70	–22	7,753	68.9	.81
Equatorial Guinea	120	30	–90	20,510	42.8	.77
South Africa	121	55	–66	11,192	47.0	.80

Source: UN Human Development Report, 2006.
* A positive score indicates better HDI ranking than GDP ranking.
† Index based on literacy rate and combined school enrolment.

because they *can* be measured. GDP underestimates the total value of work performed in the economy, and hence misjudges our productivity. It undervalues the unpaid work done within our homes and our communities. Because of sexism at home and in the workplace, most of that unpaid work is done by women; hence, GDP underestimates the economic contribution of women.

GDP and Human Well-Being

The United Nations Development Program produces an annual ranking of countries according to their "human development." The UN defines human development on the basis of three key indicators: GDP per capita, life expectancy, and educational attainment. We've already seen that GDP is a highly misleading measure, so the UN's approach is far from perfect. It attaches no value to social equity, leisure time, and other important human goals.

Nevertheless, it is interesting to compare the ranking of countries according to human development, with their ranking according to GDP. In general, countries with high human development also have high levels of GDP per capita (partly because GDP is itself one of the three variables considered, and partly because higher GDP allows a society to devote more resources to health and education). This indicates that economic growth is indeed very important to standard of living.

However, the link between GDP and human development is not perfect. Some countries (such as the Nordic countries) rank higher in the UN list than they do on the basis of GDP alone. This indicates they are more efficient at translating GDP into genuine human welfare (usually thanks to extensive public services, financed with high taxes). On the other hand, countries which rank lower on the UN list than in the GDP standings are relatively ineffective at translating GDP into well-being; these countries (like the US and the UK) have relatively low taxes and relatively weak public programs.

Table 1.1 summarizes the key human development statistics for selected countries. High-tax Norway (where government spends over 50 percent of GDP on public programs) ranks first; low-tax America ranks eighth (despite having the second-highest GDP in the world). For each country, the difference between its GDP rank and its human development rank summarizes its success at translating GDP into genuine well-being; this difference is reported in the fourth column (shaded). A positive score in this column indicates that a country makes the most of its GDP; a negative score indicates the opposite. Socialist Cuba – where average health outcomes are superior to those in the US – manages to do more, given its GDP, to improve human welfare than any other country in the world. On the other hand, oil-rich Equatorial Guinea does the worst job of any country at channelling GDP into well-being. South Africa also has a very low human development ranking, despite its relatively advanced economy (by African standards), primarily because of low life expectancy and a very unequal distribution of income.

It's especially misguided to interpret GDP as a measure of human well-being. We've seen that there are many valuable things that are not included in GDP. On the other hand, many of the goods and services that *are* counted in GDP are utterly useless, annoying, or even destructive to human well-being – like dinner-hour telephone solicitations, many pharmaceuticals, excess consumer packaging, and armaments production. Moreover, just because a society produces more GDP never ensures that most members of society will ever receive a larger slice of that growing pie.

So we must be cautious in our use of GDP statistics, and we must never equate GDP with prosperity or well-being.

Despite these caveats, GDP is still an important and relevant measure. It indicates the value of all production that occurs for money. This is an important, appropriate piece of information for many purposes. (For example, the ability of governments to collect taxes depends directly on the money value of GDP.) We need to understand the weaknesses of GDP, and supplement it with other measures. Above all, we must remember that expanding GDP is never an end in itself. At best, properly managed, it can be a means to an end (the goal of improving human well-being). Indeed, there is a positive but imperfect relationship between GDP and human welfare (see box, p. 27). This suggests that we need to be concerned with how much we produce, but equally with what we use it for.

To be meaningful, GDP figures must take several additional factors into account. If the apparent value of our work grows purely because of INFLATION (which is a general increase in the prices of *all* goods and services), then there hasn't been any real improvement in the economy. Therefore we distinguish between NOMINAL GDP (measured in dollars/ pounds) and REAL GDP (which deducts the effect of inflation). There are many other economic variables (such as wages and interest rates) for which this distinction between nominal and real values is also important. ECONOMIC GROWTH is usually measured by the expansion of real GDP.

In addition, a country's GDP could expand simply because its population was growing – but this does not imply that the country is becoming more prosperous. This is important when comparing growth rates across countries. For example, in countries with near-zero population growth (such as Europe and Japan), even a slow growth of real GDP can translate into improved living standards; this is not the case where population is growing more quickly. Therefore, economists often divide GDP by population, to get a measure called **GDP PER CAPITA**. This, too, can be expressed in both nominal and real terms. Growth in real GDP per capita over time is often used as a rough indicator of prosperity – although we must always remember that GDP excludes many valuable types of work, and says nothing about how production is distributed.

What is a good economy?

Economics tries to explain how the economy works. But economists are equally (and justifiably) concerned with trying to make it work *better*. This inherently requires the economist (and every citizen) to make value judgements about what kind of economy is more desirable. Most economists, unfortunately, are not honest about those value judgements; they like to pretend that their profession is "scientific" and hence value-free, but this is a charade.

Deciding what economic goals to pursue will reflect the priorities and interests of different individuals, communities, and classes. It is an inherently subjective choice.

Here is my list of key economic goals. In my view, the more of these goals an economy achieves, the better it is:

1. **Prosperity** An economy should produce enough goods and services to support its citizens and allow them to enjoy life to the fullest. Prosperity does not just mean having more "stuff." It means enjoying a good balance between private consumption, public services, and leisure time. (Incidentally, leisure time is another valuable thing that doesn't appear in GDP statistics.)

2. **Security** The members of an economy should be confident that their economic conditions are reasonably stable. They shouldn't have to worry about being able to support themselves (so long as they work, if they're able), to keep their home, and to pass on decent economic opportunities to their children. The economic insecurity and turmoil experienced by billions of people today imposes real costs on them. Even people who may never lose their job or home spend a great deal of time and energy worrying that they might. That fear is costly. By the same token, economic security – being able to sleep at night without worrying about your livelihood – is valuable in its own right.

3. **Innovation** Economic progress requires us to think continuously about how to make our work more productive. This innovation includes imagining new goods and services (products), and better ways of producing them (processes). An economy should be organized in a way that promotes and facilitates innovative behaviour, or else it will eventually run out of creative energy and forward momentum.

4. **Choice** Individuals have different preferences, hopes, and dreams (although those preferences are strongly shaped by social pressures). They should have reasonable ability to make economic decisions – including the sort of work they do, where they live, and what they consume – in line with those preferences. There is a gigantic, ideological myth that only free-market economies truly respect individual "choice." This is obviously wrong: the choices of billions of human beings are brutally suppressed by the economic hardship and social divisions which are a natural outcome of global capitalism. Moreover, the services offered by the public sector (schools, health care, culture, parks) substantially expand the choices available to people (especially those with lower incomes). I accept that individual choice is an important economic goal – and I argue there are better ways to enhance true choice than through free-market capitalism.

5. **Equality** Inequality is harmful if it means that large numbers of people are deprived of the ability to work and enjoy their lives. In this sense, the goal of equality is bound up with the goal of prosperity (so long as we define "prosperity" correctly, as widespread well-being, rather than equating it with the growth of GDP). But I am also convinced that inequality is inherently negative in its own right. Even if those at the bottom of the economic spectrum still enjoyed some decent minimal standard of living, a concentration of wealth at the top will nevertheless undermine social cohesion, well-being, and democracy. For example, economists have identified a phenomenon called "positional consumption," by which people's emotional well-being is negatively influenced by unfavourable self-comparisons to the lifestyles of the rich and famous. When this occurs, inequality carries distinct negative consequences, quite apart from the consequences of poverty. To this end, limiting the economic distance between rich and poor is an important

economic goal. Equality also requires decent provisions to support those members of society who cannot work.

6. **Sustainability** Humans depend on their natural environment. It directly enhances our quality of life (through the air we breathe, and the spaces we inhabit). And it provides needed inputs that are essential to the work we do in every single industry. All production involves the application of human work to "add value" to something we got from nature. Maintaining the environment is important in its own right (all the more so if we accept that humans have some responsibility to the other species which inhabit our planet). It is also important in a more narrowly economic sense, since our ability to continue producing goods and services in the future will depend on finding sustainable ways to harvest (without continuously depleting or polluting) the natural inputs we need.

7. **Democracy and accountability** We've seen that the economy is an inherently social undertaking. Different people perform different functions. Some individuals and organizations have great decision-making power, while others have very little. How do we ensure that economic decisions, and the overall evolution of the economy, reflect our collective desires and preferences? And how do we monitor and ensure that people and institutions are doing the work they are supposed to? Modern capitalism has a well-developed but narrow notion of business accountability, through which corporations are compelled to maximize the wealth of their shareholders. Competitive markets also impose another narrow form of accountability, enforced through the threat of lost sales and ultimate bankruptcy for companies which produce shoddy or unduly expensive products. Democratic elections allow citizens to exert some influence (through their governments) over economic trends – although the ability of elected governments to manage a capitalist economy is fundamentally limited by the unelected power of businesses and investors. None of these limited forms of accountability provide for thorough or consistent ways of subjecting the economy to democratic control. Yet given the overarching importance of the economy to our general social condition, we are entitled to more genuine and far-reaching forms of economic democracy and accountability.

Is our present economy a good economy? In some ways, modern capitalism has done better than any previous arrangement in advancing each of these goals. In other ways, it fails my "good economy" test miserably. The rest of this book will endeavour to explain how the capitalist economy functions, the extent to which it meets (and fails to meet) these fundamental goals – and whether or not there are any better ways to do the job.

2

Capitalism

Capitalism: one kind of economy

This book focuses mostly on describing one very particular kind of economy: capitalism.

There, I've said it: the "C-word." Just mentioning that term sounds almost subversive, these days. Even talking about capitalism makes it sound like you're a dangerous radical of some kind. But we live in a capitalist economy, and we might as well name it. More importantly, we might as well understand what we are dealing with.

Curiously, even though capitalism dominates the world economy, the term "capitalism" is not commonly used. Even more curiously, this word is almost *never* used by economists. Neoclassical economics is dedicated to the study of capitalism; in fact, other kinds of economies (that existed in the past, or that may exist in the future) are not even contemplated. Yet the term "capitalism" does not appear in neoclassical economics textbooks.

Instead, economists refer simply to "the economy" – as if there is only one kind of economy, and hence no need to name or define it. This is wrong. As we have already seen, "the economy" is simply where people work to produce the things we need and want. There are different ways to organize that work. Capitalism is just one of them.

Human beings have existed on this planet for approximately 200,000 years. They had an economy all of this time. Humans have always had to work to meet the material needs of their survival (food, clothing, and shelter) – not to mention, when possible, to enjoy the "finer things" in life. Capitalism, in contrast, has existed for fewer than 300 years. If the entire history of *Homo sapiens* was a 24-hour day, then capitalism has existed for two minutes.

What we call "the economy" went through many different stages en route to capitalism. (We'll study more of this economic history in Chapter 3.) Even today, different kinds of economies exist. Some entire countries are non-capitalist. And within capitalist economies, there are important non-capitalist parts (although most capitalist economies are becoming *more* capitalist as time goes by).

I think it's a pretty safe bet that human beings will eventually find other, better ways to organize work in the future – maybe sooner, maybe later. It's almost inconceivable that the major features of what we call "capitalism" will exist for the rest of human history (unless, of course, we drive ourselves to extinction in the near future through war, pollution, or other self-inflicted injuries).

So we shouldn't understand "the economy" and "capitalism" as identical. They are two different things. In this book we will study capitalism, as the dominant current form of economic organization. But we must always distinguish between what is *general* to all types of economy, and what is *specific* to capitalism.

What is capitalism?

There are two key features that make an economy capitalist.

1. Most production of goods and services is undertaken by privately-owned companies, which produce and sell their output in hopes of making a profit. This is called PRODUCTION FOR PROFIT.

2. Most work in the economy is performed by people who do not own their company or their output, but are hired by someone else to work in return for a money wage or salary. This is called WAGE LABOUR.

An economy in which private, profit-seeking companies undertake most production, and in which wage-earning employees do most of the work, is a capitalist economy. We will see that these twin features (profit-driven production and wage labour) create particular patterns and relationships, which in turn shape the overall functioning of capitalism as a system.

Any economy driven by these two features – production for profit and wage labour – tends to replicate the following trends and patterns, over and over again:

*   Fierce *competition* between private companies over markets and profit.

- *Innovation*, as companies constantly experiment with new technologies, new products, and new forms of organization – in order to succeed in that competition.

- An inherent tendency to *growth*, resulting from the desire of each individual company to make more profit.

- Deep *inequality* between those who own successful companies, and the rest of society who do not own companies.

- A general *conflict* of interest between those who work for wages, and the employers who hire them.

- Economic *cycles* or "rollercoasters," with periods of strong growth followed by periods of stagnation or depression; sometimes these cycles even produce dramatic economic and social crises.

Some of these patterns and outcomes are positive, and help to explain why capitalism has been so successful. But some of these patterns and outcomes are negative, and explain why capitalism tends to be economically (and sometimes politically) unstable. The rest of this book will explain why these patterns develop under capitalism, and what (if anything) can be done to make the economy work better.

Capitalism began in Europe in the mid-1700s. Until then, these twin features – production for profit and wage labour – were rare. In pre-capitalist societies, most people worked for themselves, one way or another. Where people worked for someone else, that relationship was based on something other than monetary payment (like a sense of obligation, or the power of brute force). And most production occurred to meet some direct need or desire (for an individual, a community, or a government), not to generate a money profit.

Capitalism and markets

Even when economists bother to "name" the economy they are studying, they usually use a euphemism instead of the "C-word." They don't call it capitalism. They call it a "market economy." This implies that what is unique about capitalism is its reliance on markets and market signals (like supply, demand, and prices) to organize the economy. But that is wrong, too.

Markets of various kinds do indeed play a major role in capitalism. A market is simply a "place" where various buyers and sellers meet to haggle over price and agree on sales of a good, a service, or an asset. (By "place," I do not mean that a market has to have an actual physical location – it just needs to provide a way in which buyers and sellers can communicate and strike deals. In the internet era, markets can exist in cyberspace, not just at a community hall or stock exchange.)

Markets usually (but not always) imply some kind of competition, in which different buyers and sellers compete with each other to get the best deal. We will study the particular nature of competition under capitalism in detail in Chapter 11.

But capitalism is not the only economic system which relies on markets. Pre-capitalist economies also had markets – where producers could sell excess supplies of agricultural goods or handicrafts, and where exotic commodities (like spices or fabrics) from far-off lands could be purchased. Most forms of socialism also rely heavily on markets to distribute end products and even, in some cases, to organize investment and production. So markets are not unique to capitalism, and there is nothing inherently capitalist about a market.

Just as important, there are many aspects of modern capitalism that have nothing to do with markets. Within large companies, for example, very few decisions are made through market mechanisms. Instead, relationships of command, control, and plan reign supreme. (Remember, some corporations are economically larger than many countries, so these internal non-market relationships are important.) And there are other ways in which capitalism reflects powerful *non-market* forces and motivations – like tradition, habit, politeness, reciprocity, altruism, coercion, even (sometimes) brute force.

By pretending that capitalism is a system of "markets," economists imply that it is based on relationships between essentially equal parties. Neoclassical economists study two main kinds of markets: markets for FACTORS OF PRODUCTION (things that are used in production, like labour, land, and natural resources), and markets for the final GOODS and SERVICES produced with those factors. Neoclassical economists even describe the relationship between a large company and its workers as a form of market exchange. Everyone comes to the "market" with something to sell, and in theory they're all better off (than they were in the first place) as a result of trading in that marketplace.

Imagine a bustling bazaar, to represent the whole economy. In one corner of the hall is General Electric, which brings US$500 billion worth of capital assets to the market. In the other corner are some workers, with only their brains and brawn – their intelligence and their physical strength – to sell. Will a trade between these two sides be equal or voluntary, in any meaningful sense of those words? Not at all. And neoclassical economics doesn't bother explaining the historical process by which one stall at the bazaar is stocked with US$500 billion in capital, while another is stocked with just hard-working human bodies.

By pretending that capitalism is just a system of "markets," neoclassical economics deliberately blurs the real power relationships, and the often-violent historical processes, which explain the economic system we actually live in. Yes, we must study markets when we study capitalism – their flaws, as well as their virtues. But markets are not the idealized institutions portrayed in economics textbooks. And capitalism is equally shaped by other, non-market forces and structures, too.

So capitalism is not a "market economy." Capitalism is a system in which most production occurs for private profit, and most work is performed by wage labour.

Fads in capitalism

Of course, capitalism can change its "look" a lot, while still preserving its core, underlying features. Many economists and commentators have argued that capitalism today is not at all like capitalism in its early days (back in the soot and grime of the Industrial Revolution). These are some of the ways in which modern capitalism is supposedly a "new" system:

1. **The "post-industrial" economy** As discussed in Chapter 1, every economy produces both goods and services. Over time, a growing share of total value added in advanced capitalist countries consists of services. Today, services account for about 70 percent of GDP in advanced economies – and an even larger share, if we count non-traded output, like housework. The shrinking importance of goods is partly because technology and globalization have reduced their costs compared to services, and partly because most consumers prefer to buy a greater proportion of services (especially "luxuries"

such as restaurant meals and tourism) as their incomes rise. As large-scale industry becomes less important in the big economic picture, some economists argue that capitalism has changed, and that old stereotypes about "workers and bosses" no longer apply in this post-industrial system.

2. The "information" economy   A related argument suggests that the advent of computer technology and the internet have created a fundamentally new economy – one centred on information, rather than commodities. Some pundits simply called this the "new economy." They even argued it would be immune to the traditional boom-and-bust cycles of earlier times. This theory was popular in the late 1990s, and helped to justify the ridiculous behaviour of internet-mad stock markets during this time. Beginning in 2000, however, the "dot-com" stock market boom collapsed (like all other stock market bubbles before it), and investors lost trillions of dollars. Since then, jargon about the "information economy" has become much less popular.

3. The "shareholder" economy   Some observers have focused on the role played by pension funds, mutual funds, and other so-called "institutional" investors in modern stock markets. They argue that capitalism is fairer than it used to be, since more individuals now own shares and other forms of financial wealth (either directly, or indirectly through mutual and pension funds). They claim that this new "shareholder" system has somehow "solved" the age-old conflict between workers and capitalists.

There is a grain of truth in each of these portrayals – but only a grain. And in no case is it reasonable to conclude that capitalism has *fundamentally* changed.

Yes, services are increasingly important. But many services are produced in large-scale, factory-like workplaces. Think of a long-distance call centre, with hundreds of workers sitting in small cubicles, whose work is electronically paced and constantly monitored. And the services sector of the economy is still dominated (just like goods-producing industries) by profit-seeking private companies, many of them very large – and very profitable.

Yes, information is more important and faster-flowing than ever. But people cannot "eat" information; it is economically useful mostly as an input to other, more traditional goods and services industries.

And far from ushering in a new era of decentralization and supposed "participation," computer-related industries are still dominated by huge, profit-hungry companies (like Microsoft and Google).

Yes, pension and mutual funds are important players in stock markets. But the vast majority of financial wealth is still owned the old-fashioned way: by a surprisingly small elite of very wealthy families. In fact, in most capitalist countries financial wealth has become *more* concentrated among the rich, not less (we will discuss this in more detail in Chapter 7).

So while capitalism produces more services and less goods than it used to; while companies rely on sophisticated computer technology to manage their affairs; and while a significant proportion of households in the developed countries own *some* financial wealth (but not much, in the grand scheme of things), the core features of capitalism are still very much visible. Most production is undertaken by profit-seeking private companies. And most work is performed by people who do not own those companies, but who instead must work for wages. There is still incredible inequality, and an inherent conflict of interest, between the people who own successful companies, and the rest of us.

In short, there's nothing much "new" about capitalism at all.

3

Economic History

A short history of the economy

In the early days of human civilization, the "economy" was a pretty simple affair. Our work consisted of hunting animals for meat, fur, and bones; gathering wild produce (like berries); and constructing simple shelters. These hunter-gatherer economies were often nomadic (moving in tune with the weather or animal migrations). They were cooperative, in that everyone in a family or clan grouping worked together (with some division of tasks across genders and ages). And they were mostly non-hierarchical: no-one "owned" anything or "hired" anyone. (While priests, chiefs, or other leaders had special authority, that authority did not derive from their economic position.) In general, these economies produced just enough to keep their members alive from one year to the next.

Eventually humans learned they could deliberately cultivate useful plants, and agriculture began. This caused corresponding social and economic changes. First, it allowed for permanent settlements (with the opportunity to build better homes and other structures). Second, the greater productivity of agriculture allowed society to generate an economic SURPLUS: production beyond what was required just to keep the producers alive. Third, with that surplus came the task of deciding how to use it. The existence of a surplus allowed some members of society, for the first time, not to work. This opened up a whole new can of worms. Who would avoid working on the farm? What would they do instead? And how would they keep the rest of society – those who had to continue working – in line?

With permanent settlements and a growing economic surplus, therefore, came the first CLASS divisions within society – in which different groups of people fulfilled fundamentally different economic roles, depending on their status and their relationship to work. Different economic systems handled this fundamental issue in different ways. For example, under monarchist systems, a powerful elite controlled the surplus and its allocation based on inherited birthright. The monarch needed the acceptance or at least acquiescence of his or her subjects, which generally needed to be imposed (from time to time, anyway) by brute force.

Many of these societies also relied on SLAVERY, where entire groups of people (often designated by race or caste) were simply forced to work, again through brute force. In case this sounds like ancient history, remember that the US economy (the most powerful capitalist country in the world) was based largely on slavery until fewer than 150 years ago, and human trafficking still forcibly enslaves millions of people around the world today. The resulting economic surplus was used in various ways: luxury consumption of the ruling elite; the construction of impressive buildings and monuments; the financing of exploration, war, and conquest; the work of non-agricultural artisans and scholars; and re-investment into new and improved economic techniques.

While slavery and direct authoritarian rule were certainly powerful and straightforward ways for elites to control the economy and the resulting surplus, they had their drawbacks, too. Slaves and subjects often revolted. Their work ethic was not always the best: slaves tend to be grudging and bitter (for obvious reasons), requiring "active supervision" (often with a whip!) to elicit their effort and productivity.

Eventually a more subtle and ultimately more effective economic system evolved, called FEUDALISM. In this case, a more complex web of mutual obligations and rights was used to organize work and manage the surplus. Peasants were allowed to live on land that was governed by a higher class (gentry, landlords, or royalty). They could support themselves and their families, but in return had to transfer most of their surplus production to the gentry (in the form of annual payments or tithes). The gentry used this surplus to finance their own (luxury) consumption, the construction of castles, the work of artisans and priests, maintenance of a simple state apparatus, wars, and other "fringe" activities. In return, they were supposed to protect the peasantry on their land (from attack by competing landlords), and ensure their security.

Agriculture became steadily more productive (with the invention of techniques such as crop rotation, the use of livestock, and plant breeding). The surplus became larger, allowing the development of more complex and ambitious non-agricultural activities – including the emergence of a more powerful and well-resourced central government, more ambitious non-agricultural production (including the emergence

Figure 3.1 **Economic Evolution**

of early manufacturing workshops), and farther-reaching exploration and conquest. More effective transportation (like ocean-going ships) allowed the development of long-range trade (bringing in specialty goods from far-flung colonies and trading partners). Later in the Middle Ages, this trade sparked the emergence of a whole new class: merchants, who earned an often-lucrative slice of the surplus by facilitating this growing trade. These merchants would play an important transitional role in the subsequent development of capitalism.

This is a ridiculously short review of economic history. Yet it still conveys some crucial lessons that are relevant today:

- Human beings learn by doing. As they work at something for a while, they identify and implement ways to do it better. In economic terms, this leads to improvements in technology and productivity over time – sometimes very slowly, sometimes very quickly.

- These ongoing changes in productivity and technology tend to require corresponding changes in the way work is organized, and indeed in the way society is organized. The evolution of workplaces, class structure, markets, even politics has occurred hand-in-hand with the ongoing evolution of the economy.

- Economic systems come, and economic systems go. No economic system lasts forever. Capitalism is not likely to last forever, either.

Where did capitalism come from?

Capitalism first emerged in Western Europe, especially Britain, in the mid-1700s. It evolved from relatively advanced feudal monarchies, in which non-agricultural production and long-distance trade had become important economic activities, and in which central state power was relatively strong. Historians have spent a lot of time trying to determine the causes of this incredible economic and social transformation, and arguing about why it occurred in Europe instead of elsewhere in the world. (During the Middle Ages, China and India had been about as wealthy as Europe – but for various reasons, the social and technological changes which led to capitalism did not occur there.)

There is broad agreement on at least these key factors which contributed to the rise of capitalism:

- **New technology** The invention of steam power, semi-automated spinning and weaving machines, and other early industrial technologies dramatically increased productivity. Also, these technologies needed completely new ways of organizing work: in larger-scale factories which required more complex (and expensive) equipment. And they implied new structures of ownership: the machinery (and associated costs of raw materials and other necessary inputs) was too expensive for individuals or groups of workers to finance on their own. An owner was needed to finance the large up-front investments needed to get the factories working.

- **Empire** The fact that Britain (and, to a lesser extent, other European colonial powers) possessed the organizational and military ability to conquer and dominate far-off lands contributed to the development of capitalism in many ways. It fostered the emergence of a class of merchants – which itself eventually evolved into a class of industrial capitalists. It provided raw materials and exotic goods, including the importation of cheap foodstuffs to feed the growing non-agricultural workforce. It extracted wealth from the colonies by brute force (including good old-fashioned slavery, in many instances) to support the growth of capitalism at home. It provided an inflow of precious metals to serve as money and lubricate commerce. And empire also provided captive markets for the impressive output of the new factories.

- **Government** In addition to the role of colonialism, the centralized state power that existed in Britain, France, and Holland was crucial to the emergence of capitalism. A strong government provided a reliable currency, standardization of commerce, and protection of the private property of the ambitious new capitalists. It could also help to keep peasants and workers in line, as they endured the painful shift from feudalism to capitalism. As we will discuss in Chapter 19, a strong central state was also crucial to the successful development of capitalism in subsequent countries, too (like America and Japan).

- **Resources** Conveniently, Britain had ample supplies of coal and iron needed for the new industries. Water-power in rural areas was also important in the early days of the Industrial Revolution. The availability of resources shouldn't be over-emphasized, however: many countries with abundant resources failed to develop quickly, while some countries (like Japan) successfully developed with very few resources.

The birth of capitalism was not pretty. Wages and conditions in the early factories were hellish. How did the first capitalists recruit workers? They were former peasants, driven off their former lands (which they never formally owned) by a process called the ENCLOSURES. Lands which were once held in common and worked under feudal rules were fenced in and assigned as formal private property to landlords – whose status became legal rather than traditional in nature. This also facilitated the depopulation of rural areas – necessary in light of the tremendous increases in the productivity of agriculture (far fewer farmers were needed to produce all the food the whole country needed). In this way, capitalism produced two entirely new economic classes: a group of industrial capitalists who owned the new factories, and a group of workers who possessed nothing other than their ability to work in those factories.

The evolution of capitalism

The "birth" of capitalism, amidst the smoke and soot of the Industrial Revolution, was a painful and in many ways violent process. Workers were forced off their land and driven into cities, where they suffered horrendous exploitation and conditions that would be considered intolerable today: seven-day working weeks, twelve-hour working days, child labour, frequent injury, early death. Vast profits were earned by the new class of capitalists, most of which they ploughed back into new investment, technology, and growth – but some of which they used to finance their own luxurious consumption. The early capitalist societies were not at all democratic: the right to vote was limited to property owners, and basic rights to speak out and organize (including to organize unions) were routinely (and often violently) trampled.

Needless to say, this state of affairs was not socially sustainable. Working people and others fought hard for better conditions, a fairer share of the incredible wealth they were producing, and democratic rights. Under this pressure, capitalism evolved, unevenly, toward a more balanced and democratic system. Labour laws established minimum standards; unions won higher wages; governments became more active in regulating the economy and providing public services. But this progress was not "natural" or inevitable; it reflected decades of social struggle and conflict. And progress could be reversed if and when circumstances changed – such as during times of war or recession. Indeed, the history of capitalism has been dominated by a rollercoaster pattern of boom, followed by bust.

Perhaps the greatest bust of all, the Great Depression of the 1930s, spurred more changes. New banking regulations were aimed at preventing financial chaos. Government income-support and make-work projects tried to put people back to work. To some extent, these projects were influenced by the economic ideas of John Maynard Keynes (more on this in the next chapter). The greatest (and deadliest) make-work project was World War II. The war spurred massive military spending which suddenly kicked all the major economies back into high gear, and eliminated unemployment.

After World War II, a unique set of circumstances combined to create the most vibrant and in many ways most optimistic chapter in the history of capitalism – what is now often called the "Golden Age." This postwar boom lasted for about three decades, during which wages and living standards in the developed capitalist world more than doubled. Strong business investment (motivated in part by postwar recovery and rebuilding) was reinforced by a rapid expansion of government spending in most capitalist economies. Unemployment was low, productivity grew rapidly, yet profits (initially at least) were strong. This was also the era of the "Cold War" between capitalism (led by the US) and communism (led by the former Soviet Union). In this context, business leaders and Western governments felt all the more pressure to accept demands for greater equality and security, since they were forced by global geopolitics to defend the virtues of the capitalist system.

Neoliberalism

It is now clear that beginning in the late 1970s, global capitalism entered a distinct and more aggressive phase. The previous willingness of business owners and governments to tolerate taxes, social programs, unions, and regulations petered out. Businesses and financial investors rebelled against shrinking profits, high inflation, militant workers, and international "instability" (represented most frighteningly by the success of left-wing revolutions in several countries in Asia, Africa, and Latin America in the 1970s). They began to agitate for a new, harder-line approach – and eventually they got it.

In retrospect, there were two clear "cannon shots" that signalled the beginning of this new chapter in the history of capitalism:

1. Paul Volcker became the head of the US Federal Reserve (the American CENTRAL BANK) in 1979. He implemented very strict MONETARY POLICY, heavily influenced by the ideas of Milton Friedman and the MONETARIST school (we'll discuss them more in Chapters 16 and 17). Interest rates rose dramatically, and economic growth slowed. Superficially, Volcker's high-interest-rate policy was motivated by a need to control and reduce inflation. But it quickly became clear that a deeper shift had occurred. Instead

of promoting full employment as their top priority (as during the Golden Age), central bankers would now focus on strictly controlling inflation, protecting financial assets, and keeping labour markets strictly in check.

2. Margaret Thatcher was elected as UK Prime Minister in 1979, followed by the election of Ronald Reagan as US President a year later. Both advocated an aggressive new approach to managing the economy (and all of society) in the interests of private business. They fully endorsed the hard-line taken by Volcker (and his counterparts in other countries). They were even tougher in attacking unions and undermining labour law and social policies (Reagan crushed the US air traffic controllers' union in 1981, while Thatcher defeated the strong British miners' union in 1985). Reagan and Thatcher shattered the broad Golden Age consensus, under which even conservative governments had accepted relatively generous social benefits and extensive government management of the economy. Despite forceful opposition in both countries, both leaders prevailed (supported by business interests), and became role models for hard-right conservatives in many other countries. Thatcher justified her initiatives with the now-classic (but false) slogan: "There is no alternative."

It gradually became clear that capitalism had fundamentally changed. The "kinder, gentler" improvements of the Golden Age era came under sustained attack, and would gradually (over the next quarter-century) be partially reversed – though not without a stubborn fightback by workers and communities. Some argued that capitalism could no longer afford those Golden Age programs; in my view, this is invalid, although there is no doubt that the Golden Age recipe began to encounter significant economic problems. Others argued that with the decline of communism and the weakening of left-wing parties, capitalism no longer *needed* to mollify its critics with compassionate policies (since it no longer faced a serious challenge to its continued existence).

This new era in capitalism has gone by several different names: neoconservativism, the "corporate agenda," and others. The most common term now used is NEOLIBERALISM. This term is confusing, since in some countries "liberal" refers to a centre or centre-left political ideology which still sees room for some Golden Age-style policies. In economics, however, "liberal" means something quite different: it means *an absence of government interference*. In this sense, "neoliberalism" implies going back to a more rough-and-tumble kind of capitalism, in which governments play a smaller role in regulating the economy and protecting social interests. But even this definition is not quite accurate: in fact, there are still many ways in which government and the state continue to wield real economic power under neoliberal capitalism (we will discuss these in later chapters). What has changed is *how*, and in *whose interests*, that power is now exercised.

Table 3.1   **Key Goals and Tools of Neoliberalism**

Key Goals:
- Reduce and control inflation; protect the value of financial wealth
- Restore insecurity and "discipline" to labour markets
- Eliminate "entitlements"; force families to fend for themselves
- Roll back and refocus government activities to meet business needs; cut taxes
- Generally restore the economic and social dominance of private business and wealth
- Claw back expectations; foster a sense of resignation to insecurity and hardship

Key Tools:
- Use interest rates aggressively to regulate inflation and control labour markets
- Privatize and deregulate more industries
- Scale back social security programs (especially for working-age adults)
- Deregulate labour markets (including attacks on unions)
- Use free-trade agreements to expand markets and constrain government interventions

The main goals of neoliberalism, and the tools used to achieve those goals, are listed in Table 3.1. They include controlling inflation; disciplining labour; downsizing and focusing government; and reinforcing business leadership. The broadest but perhaps most important goal is the last one listed in the first part of Table 3.1: ratcheting down popular expectations. There has been a deliberate and multidimensional effort since the early 1980s to construct a whole new cultural mindset, in which people stop demanding much from the economy, and accept insecurity and vulnerability as permanent, "natural" features of life. In the 1970s workers in most capitalist countries were uppity and feisty, ready to demand a better deal from their employers and their society. Today, after a quarter-century of neoliberalism, many are tempted to bow down in thanks that they at least have a job. Overturning this passive, defeatist mindset will be crucial for motivating people to challenge the inequality and imbalance that typify our economy today.

Kinds of capitalism

Even under neoliberalism, however, and despite the pressures for conformity that arise from globalization, there are still clear differences between capitalist economies – even those at similar levels of development. (There are even bigger differences, of course, between richer capitalist countries and poor ones.) So it would be a dangerous mistake to imply that all capitalist economies must now follow exactly the same set of policies. And those differences produce very different outcomes for the people who live and work in those economies.

Table 3.2 identifies four broad "types" of capitalism among the most developed countries in the world. They operate very differently in terms of how harshly workers are treated, how economically active government is, and the sectoral make-up of the economy. The "Anglo-Saxon" variant of capitalism is, by most indicators, the most unequal of all. It is characterized by a small role for government, an overdeveloped financial sector, and the largest inequalities in income. Other variants of capitalism – like the Nordic, the continental, or the Asian variants – offer generally better outcomes for working people.

Clearly, different societies still have considerable leeway to put their own stamp on the economy, even when the fundamental rules and structures of capitalism remain in place. Working for incremental improvements in capitalism, making it a little bit fairer and less degrading, is clearly important.

After capitalism?

At the same time as we fight for positive reforms in capitalism, we may also want to consider whether it's possible to move *beyond* the fundamental rules and structures of the system. After all, capitalism represents just one phase (and a relatively short phase, so far) in the evolution of human economic activity. That long process of evolution is not going to suddenly stop. We haven't arrived at some kind of economic "nirvana": a perfect system which can't possibly be improved. Collectively, we will continue developing new technologies, new goods and services, and new ways of organizing work. And it is

Table 3.2 Types of Capitalism (in the advanced countries)

Type of Capitalism	Role of Government: Taxes as Share GDP	Role of Government: Economic Regulation	Financial Sector (Banks, Stock Market)	Income Distribution	Managing Income Distribution	Union Coverage as % Workforce
Anglo-Saxon (US, UK, Canada, Australia)	30–35%	Weak	Very Large	Very Unequal	Market Power	10–30%
Continental (France, Germany, Italy)	35–45%	Moderate	Moderate	Somewhat Equal	Mild Corporatist[†]	20–50%
Asian (Japan, Korea, soon China)	25–35%	Strong	Relatively Small	Somewhat Equal	Paternalist Corporatist[†]	20–30%
Nordic (Sweden, Denmark, others*)	45–55%	Strong	Relatively Small	Very Equal	Strong Corporatist[†]	50–80%

* Some other European countries (like Austria and the Netherlands) have features similar to the Nordic type.
† CORPORATISM refers to a system of centralized negotiation between business, labour, and government.

almost certain that we will ultimately find new forms of ownership, and new forms of economic management, to make the most of those new tools – and, hopefully, to do a better job of meeting our human and environmental needs in the process. Sooner or later, I suspect we'll end up with something quite different from capitalism: some system in which most production is no longer undertaken by private, profit-seeking companies, and most work is no longer undertaken solely in return for a money wage.

The world has some experience with "life after capitalism," but that experience has been difficult and in most cases unsuccessful. Communist-led economies were built in Eastern Europe, China, and some developing countries in the mid-twentieth century; most of these failed in the face of economic stagnation and/or political breakdown. A few countries (like Cuba) have tried to preserve aspects of that system, and others (like Venezuela) are trying to build new forms of socialism. Successful smaller-scale experiments in non-capitalist economic development have taken place in parts of other countries – like the Basque region of Spain, or the Indian state of Kerala.

We will discuss the problems and prospects of post-capitalist society in the last part of this book. We don't know what will come after capitalism, or when or how it will happen. But it would be folly to expect capitalism to last forever.

4

The Politics of Economics

Early economics

In earlier eras, human economic activity was pretty straightforward. You worked hard to produce the things you needed to survive. Powerful people (slave owners or feudal lords) took some of what you produced. You kept what was left. End of story.

As the economy became more complex, however, the relationships between different economic players became more indirect and harder to decipher. Economics was born, as the social science which aimed to explain those increasingly complex links. The first economists were called "political economists," in recognition of the close ties between economics and politics. They began to theorize about the nature of work, production, value, and growth just as Europe's economy was evolving from feudalism toward capitalism.

The first identifiable school of economics were the Mercantilists, based mostly in Britain in the 1600s. Their theories paralleled the growing economic power of the British empire, so not surprisingly they emphasized the importance of international trade to national economic development. In particular, they believed that a country's national wealth would grow if it generated large trade surpluses: that is, if it exported more than it imported. Mercantilists were also forceful advocates of strong central government, in part to strengthen colonial power and hence boost the trade surplus. Even today, the mercantilist spirit lives on (in modified form) in modern-day theories of "export-led growth" – such as those followed in recent years by the industrializing countries of Asia.

Across the English Channel and a century later, a group of French thinkers called the Physiocrats developed a very different approach to economics – one that also lives on in modern economics. They focused on the relationship between agricultural and non-agricultural industries (such as early artisans and workshops), and traced the flow of money between those different sectors. They likened this flow to the circulation of blood through the human body; indeed, the most famous Physiocrat was François Quesnay, a physician to the French king. Their early efforts to trace the relationships between different sectors of the economy inspired modern theories of monetary circulation (which we will consider in Part Four). And they were the first school of economics to analyze the economy in terms of CLASS.

Adam Smith is often viewed as the "father" of free-market economics, but this stereotype is not quite accurate. Nevertheless, his famous *Wealth of Nations* (published in 1776, the same year as American independence) came to symbolize (like America itself) the dynamism and opportunity of capitalism. Smith identified the productivity gains from large-scale factory production and its more intensive division of labour (whereby different workers or groups of workers perform a variety of very specialized tasks). To support this new system, he advocated deregulation of markets, the expansion of trade, and policies to protect the profits and property rights of the early capitalists (who Smith celebrated as virtuous innovators and accumulators). He argued that free-market forces (which he called the "invisible hand") and the pursuit of self-interest would best stimulate innovation and growth. However, his social analysis (building on the Physiocrats) was rooted more in *class* than in individuals: he favoured policies to undermine the vested interests of rural landlords (who he thought were unproductive) in favour of the more dynamic new class of capitalists.

Defunct Economists

"The ideas of economists and political philosophers, both when they are right and when they are wrong, are more powerful than is commonly understood. Indeed the world is ruled by little else. Practical men, who believe themselves to be quite exempt from any intellectual influence, are usually the slaves of some defunct economist."

John Maynard Keynes, British economist (1936).

Smith's work founded what is now known as CLASSICAL ECONOMICS. This school of thought focused on the dynamic processes of growth and change in capitalism, and analyzed the often conflictual relationship between different classes. In general, classical economists accepted the idea that the value of a product was determined by the amount of work required to produce it (what became known as the "labour theory of value"). After Smith, the most famous classical theorists were David Ricardo and Thomas Malthus. Ricardo developed a hugely influential theory of free trade known as COMPARATIVE ADVANTAGE. It claims that every country will be better off through free trade, even if *all* its industries are inefficient. (The theory is true, but only under very restrictive assumptions; we'll discuss it further in Chapter 21.) Meanwhile, Ricardo's friend Thomas Malthus developed an infamous theory of population growth which justified keeping wages very low. He argued that if wages were raised above bare subsistence levels, workers would simply procreate until their growing population absorbed all the new income. Therefore, wages should naturally settle at subsistence levels. Malthus was dead wrong: in fact, birth rates *decline* as living standards improve. Nevertheless, the classical economists (and Karl Marx after them) did accept the broad idea that workers' wages tended to stagnate in the long term (rather than rising automatically with economic growth).

Needless to say, the oppressive working and living conditions of the Industrial Revolution, and the glaring contrast between the poverty of the new working class and the wealth of the new capitalist class, sparked abundant economic and political turmoil. Workers formed unions and political parties to fight for a better deal, often encountering violent responses from employers and governments. An economic underpinning for this fightback was provided by Karl Marx. Like the classical economists, he focused on the dynamic evolution of capitalism as a system, and the turbulent relationships between different classes. He argued that the payment of profit on private investments did not reflect any particular economic function, but was only a *social* relationship. Profit represented a new, more subtle form of EXPLOITATION: an indirect, effective way of capturing economic surplus from those (the workers) who truly do the work. Marx tried (unsuccessfully) to explain how prices in capitalism (which include the payment of profit) could still be based on the underlying labour values of different commodities. And he predicted the ultimate breakdown of capitalism, in the face of both economic instability (the ongoing boom-and-bust cycle) and political resistance. Marx's ideas were very influential in the later development of labour and socialist movements around the world.

Neoclassical economics

After Marx, the capitalist economies of Europe continued to be disrupted by regular interludes of revolutionary fervour. Gradual economic and political reforms were achieved through the nineteenth century in response to these upheavals: limited social programs and union rights were introduced to moderate the worst inequalities of industry, and democracy was gradually expanded (at first, workers were not allowed to vote since they didn't own property). And it was in this context that a whole new school of economics arose.

Following an especially strident wave of revolutionary struggles in Europe (including the first attempt to establish a socialist society in Paris in 1871), NEOCLASSICAL ECONOMICS strove to justify the economic efficiency and moral superiority of the capitalist (or "free market") system. The neoclassical pioneers included Léon Walras (in Switzerland), Carl Menger (in Austria), and Stanley Jevons (in Britain); Walras was ultimately the most influential.

These theorists seemed to start from the precepts of their market-friendly classical predecessors (in fact, "neoclassical" simply means "new classical"), but in fact they made important changes to the classical approach. First, they focused on individuals, not classes. Second, they focused on the existence of market EQUILIBRIUM at any particular point in time – like a snapshot of the economy – rather than on the evolution and development of an economy over time. Third, they began to apply mathematical techniques to economic questions. And they adopted a more abstract approach to theory: instead of explaining concrete, visible realities in the economy, neoclassical theory uses abstract logic to build complex economic theories on the basis of a few starting assumptions, or "axioms."

Neoclassical theory still dominates the teaching of economics in developed countries, although there are many cracks in its walls. The key premises of the neoclassical approach include:

- Every individual starts life with some initial "endowment" of one or more of the FACTORS OF PRODUCTION (labour power, skill, wealth, or other resources). The theory does not concern itself with explaining how that initial endowment came about.

- Every individual also has a set of PREFERENCES which determine what goods and services they like to consume. Again, the theory does not concern itself with explaining how those preferences evolve.

- Technology determines how those various factors of production can be converted into useable goods and services, through the process of production. Initially, neoclassical theory did not try to explain technology; more recent neoclassical writers have begun to study how and why technology evolves.

- Through extensive market trading (in both factors of production and produced goods and services), the economic system will ensure that all factors of production are used (including all labour being employed) in a manner which best satisfies the preferences of consumers. Important and unrealistic assumptions about the nature of markets and competition are required to reach this optimal resting point – a market-determined economic nirvana.

If supply equals demand in all markets (both factors of production and final goods and services), then the system is considered to be in GENERAL EQUILIBRIUM. Walras was the first to describe this situation, and the theory came to be known as *Walrasian general equilibrium*. Modern neoclassical thinkers have tried to prove mathematically that this general equilibrium is in fact possible; they have failed repeatedly, and today general equilibrium theory has fallen out of favour with many academic economists. Even in theory, the model depends on incredibly extreme and unrealistic assumptions (regarding perfect competition, perfect information, and perfect rationality). The theory has almost no practical applications. Nevertheless, the policy conclusions of the Walrasian view remain very influential, even though their logical underpinning is weak. Here are the key neoclassical conclusions:

- Left to its own devices, the economy will settle at a position of full employment, in which all potential economic resources (including labour) are used efficiently. For this reason, the economy is SUPPLY-CONSTRAINED: only the supply of productive factors limits what the economy can produce.

- This works best when private markets are allowed maximum leeway to operate. Attempts to regulate market outcomes (such as by imposing minimum wages or taxes) will reduce economic well-being by interfering with market forces. Governments should limit their role to providing essential infrastructure and protecting private property rights.

• Expanding trade (including international trade) will always expand the total economic pie, and this creates the *potential* for improving the economic outcomes of everyone in society.

• The profit received by investors reflects the real "productivity" of the capital that they own, and hence profit is both legitimate and economically efficient. Proving that profit is economically and morally justifiable, rather than the result of exploitation, has been a central preoccupation of neoclassical economics.

Economics after Keynes

The development of neoclassical theory reflected the debates and conflicts of industrial capitalism. The capitalist economy continued to develop through the nineteenth and twentieth centuries in fits and starts, with periods of vibrant growth interspersed with periods of sustained stagnation and recession. But with the Great Depression of the 1930s, it became very obvious that neoclassical faith in the economy's self-adjusting, full-employment equilibrium was painfully misplaced. In reality, capitalism was visibly unable to ensure that all resources (especially labour) were indeed employed.

A new era of thinkers arose to explain both the failure of capitalism to employ labour, and advise what could be done about it. The most famous was John Maynard Keynes, who worked in Britain between the two world wars. Just as important but lesser known was Michal Kalecki, who was born in Poland but also worked in Britain. Working separately, they developed (at about the same time) the theory of EFFECTIVE DEMAND. In general, they found, an economy's output and employment were not limited only by the supply of productive factors (as believed in neoclassical theory). The economy can also be DEMAND-CONSTRAINED by the strength of aggregate purchasing power. If purchasing power is weak for some reason (due to financial or banking problems, pessimism among consumers or investors, or other factors), then unemployment will exist. Worse yet, there is no natural tendency for that unemployment to resolve itself.

To deal with this problem, Keynes advocated proactive government policies to adjust taxes, government spending, and interest rates in order to attain full employment. Kalecki went further than Keynes, and showed that effective demand conditions also depend on the distribution of income (and the distribution of power) between classes; he advocated socialism as the ultimate solution to the problem of unemployment.

As it turned out, massive government military spending during World War II did indeed "solve" the Great Depression. Then, during the vibrant postwar expansion that followed, neoclassical economics uncomfortably tried to digest a watered-down version of Keynesian ideas. The leading economists of this era (such as America's Paul Samuelson and Britain's John Hicks) tried to construct a "synthesis" of neoclassical and Keynesian approaches. They concluded that unemployment and depression could only occur under very particular conditions. In most cases, however, they felt that the basic neoclassical model was still valid.

Eventually even this limited departure from key neoclassical commandments was abandoned. Global capitalism experienced growing instability and stagnation in the 1970s, as the Golden Age drew to a close. A new group of hard-nosed neoclassical thinkers – led by Milton Friedman and his colleagues at the University of Chicago – attributed this instability to misplaced government intervention. They resuscitated the core neoclassical policy framework (according to which government should provide a stable, market-friendly environment, and do nothing else), and hence provided the intellectual foundation for neoliberalism. This approach has become dominant in economics in most countries.

There is still much debate and controversy within economics today – although not nearly as much as there should be. In particular, economics instruction in English-speaking countries conforms quite narrowly to neoclassical doctrine.

Some economists, however, reject neoclassical assumptions and methodology. For example, POST-KEYNESIANS have worked to develop the more non-neoclassical aspects of Keynes' work – emphasizing the economic importance of uncertainty and the particular nature of money. (Keynes himself never fundamentally broke from neoclassical thinking, and this has caused great confusion and controversy in subsequent years about what he "really" meant.) Other economists, known as radical or STRUCTURALIST thinkers, have branched out from

Kalecki's work, emphasizing the connections between power, class, demand, and growth. Some economists continue to work within the Marxist tradition, and others in a broad stream of thought known as INSTITUTIONALIST economics (which emphasizes the evolution of economic and social institutions).

It will be essential in coming years to nurture these various "heterodox" streams within economics ("heterodox" refers here to any economist who breaks away from neoclassical orthodoxy), in order to provide some badly-needed diversity and balance within the profession.

Impure Science

"Economics has three functions – to try to understand how an economy operates, to make proposals for improving it, and to justify the criterion by which improvement is judged. The criterion of what is desirable necessarily involves moral and political judgements. Economics can never be a perfectly 'pure' science, unmixed with human values."

Joan Robinson and John Eatwell, British economists (1973).

The economy, economics, and politics

This extremely condensed history of economics reveals a couple of important lessons:

- The development of economics has paralleled the development of the economy itself. Economists have tried to keep up with real-world economic problems, challenges, and conflicts. The theories of some economists have supported those seeking to change the economy; the theories of others have justified the status quo.

- Consequently, economics is not a "pure" science; it never has been. Economists have worked to try to understand the economy and how it functions. But they have also had views – usually very strong ones, and often hidden – about how the economy *should* function. In the jargon of economics, the pure study of the economy is called "positive" economics; it is supposed

Table 4.1   Economics and Politics Through the Ages

Theory	Time	Economic Context	Political Context
Mercantilists	Seventeenth century	Expansion of European colonial empires	Support for centralized state political and military power
Physiocrats	Early eighteenth century	Expansion of non-agricultural industries	Defend agricultural surplus against undue expropriation
Classical	Late eighteenth century, early nineteenth century	Birth of industrial capitalism	Favour ascendant capitalists over landlords; promote expansion of markets
Marx	Mid-nineteenth century	Consolidation, expansion of capitalism	Explain and criticize exploitation of workers; describe socialist alternative
Neoclassical	Late nineteenth century, early twentieth century	Consolidation, expansion of capitalism; democratic and social reforms	Reaction against European revolutions; provide justification for private profit
Keynes/ Kalecki	Post-1930s	Great Depression; WWII; advent of "Golden Age"	Policies to restore full employment, expand social security
Monetarism, neoclassical resurgence	1970s to today	Breakdown of "Golden Age"	Describe failure of "Golden Age" policies; intellectual justification for neoliberalism
Modern heterodox*	Today	Consolidation of neoliberalism	Describe failures of neoliberalism; advance alternative policies

*   Includes Post-Keynesian, structuralist, institutionalist, Marxian.

to be separate from the advocacy of particular policies, called "normative" economics. But in practice, these two functions get mixed up all the time.

- The theories of economists have always been spurred by real world debates, politics, and interests (see Table 4.1). The Mercantilists celebrated the power and reach of empire. The Physiocrats tried to protect farmers against undue expropriation of their produce. The classical writers were concerned to celebrate (and hence justify) the innovative and growth-inducing behaviour of the new capitalist class. Marx's analysis of conflicts in capitalism was tied up with his vision of radical political change. Early neoclassical economics justified the payment of private profit and the dominance of markets. Keynes grappled with the destruction and lost potential of the Depression, while the subsequent resurgence of neoclassical doctrines both reflected and assisted the parallel reassertion of private-sector power under neoliberalism.

Today, economics continues to display its inherently political character. There is no economic policy debate which does not involve trade-offs and conflicting interests; discussions of economic "efficiency" and "rationalism" are therefore never neutral. When a blue-suited bank economist appears on TV to interpret the latest GDP numbers, the reporter never mentions that this "expert" is ultimately paid to enhance the wealth of the shareholders of the bank. (On the rare occasions when a *union* economist is interviewed, the bias is usually presumed, by both the reporter and the audience, to be closer to the surface.)

And when economists invoke seemingly scientific and neutral terms like "efficiency," "growth," and "productivity," we must always ask: "Efficiency for whom? What kind of growth? And who will reap the benefits of productivity?"

Part Two

The Basics of Capitalism: Work, Tools, and Profit

5

Work, Production, and Value

What is work?

As we defined it earlier, the economy is simply the amalgamation of our collective work to produce the goods and services we need and want. And once we've produced those things, we need to decide how to distribute and use them.

·By "work," we refer to any productive human activity. Most obviously, this includes work in a paid job. Indeed, in modern capitalism, wage labour is so widespread that many people wrongly equate "work" with "employment." A frustrated parent is likely to tell their lazy teenager to "Get a job!" when what they really mean is "Get up and do some work!" Under capitalism, *most* work consists of wage labour, but not all. There are other important types of work that we must also consider.

Most modern jobs and careers fall into the category of wage labour – whether they are in private companies or public agencies, blue-collar or white-collar. The stereotype of a "worker" as someone who performs menial tasks on an assembly line is badly outdated. Workers today perform a wide variety of functions, many of them requiring advanced skills. But they are still workers, so long as they perform that work for someone else, in return for a wage or salary. Scientists in a research laboratory; surgeons in a large hospital; engineers in a construction firm – these are all workers (although culturally, they may not like to define themselves as such). They perform their labour in return for a salary, and they do not own or significantly control the organization which they work for.

Some workers assume that if they are paid a monthly salary, rather than an hourly wage, then they must belong to a higher "class." This is wishful thinking. They are still paid (although usually at a higher wage rate) to perform labour. They are still utterly dependent on the decisions of their employer (including the decision to hire them in the first place). And in some ways, they may be *more* exploited than hourly wage-labourers, despite their professional incomes. Most salaried employees do not have strictly fixed hours of work, and hence must perform overtime when required (usually unpaid) to finish their assigned tasks. Their self-identification as "professionals" (and their associated willingness to tolerate unpaid overtime and hectic conditions) assists employers to extract maximum work effort for minimum compensation.

Life's Work

"Far and away the best prize that life offers
is the chance to work hard at work worth doing."

Theodore Roosevelt, former US President (1903)

Similarly, private companies need supervisors and managers to oversee production, keep the workforce in line, and make minor business decisions. But most of these so-called "management" jobs (especially lower-level supervisors and technicians) are just glorified forms of wage labour. These employees follow orders given by more senior executives, they do not meaningfully control or direct the activities of the company (despite their ability to boss around underlings), their compensation consists solely of a salary, and they are as easily dispensable as any assembly-line worker when their services are no longer needed.

So most work in capitalism consists of wage labour, in a variety of forms. There are some kinds of work, however, that add value to the economy (whether or not that value is counted in GDP) but that do not involve wage labour.

Consider, for example, the very top managers or executives of a company or agency. These senior managers do, indeed, perform work – typically very long, hard hours. Their work is essential to the performance of their companies, and to the whole economy. They enjoy a unique degree of control over the operations of their enterprises: they may be owners or partners of those companies, or they may be hired by the company's shareholders to make the most important decisions. And their income depends on the profit of the company. True, they may receive a salary (and usually an extremely high salary, at that). But their income also includes a substantial profit-related component: either a direct share of the profits (when top managers are also owners or partners of the company), or else stock options and other bonuses which depend directly on the company's financial performance. Companies have expanded their use of this type of executive compensation, because it better inspires managers to focus ruthlessly on maximizing the wealth of shareholders.

Their direct and substantial economic stake in the profits of the enterprise, and their unique control over its activity, fundamentally distinguish these top managers from other, less powerful staff (including most salaried staff). In part, their abundant compensation reflects their *work*. But it also reflects – directly or indirectly – a meaningful share in the enterprise's *profits*, which is a very different thing. (Some clever companies have taken to offering small profit-sharing bonuses to lower-level staff, too, as a way of strengthening employee loyalty and preventing unionization; but these largely token payments do not imply that the workers are actually "owners.") Nevertheless, top managers do perform useful, productive, important work, and this work must be considered in any complete description of the economy.

Based on the proportion of individuals in society who are owners or top managers of large firms, only a tiny share (perhaps 2 percent) of all work in the economy consists of this type of activity.

Another significant proportion of the population is self-employed: they work, nominally "for themselves," in a small business or on a farm. (Individuals who own a company which employs other people to do most of the work would fall into the category of "top managers" defined above.) In most capitalist countries, self-employment has declined over time as a result of agricultural depopulation and the rise of corporations. At the same time, however, there has been an expansion of self-employment in some other parts of the economy (such as smaller-scale services companies).

For example, modern corporations have often found it profitable to shift (or "outsource") many peripheral service functions to outside contractors, who may be nominally self-employed. Instead of hiring someone to make photocopies, companies may outsource this work to a small photocopy shop. The same can occur with many other functions, from cleaning to accounting. But are these contractors really any different from workers performing the same function, but on the company's payroll? They still fundamentally depend on the large company for work and income; indeed, their total compensation (considering pensions and benefits, which contractors don't usually receive) is often lower than for standard employees. Realistically, these "self-employed" people are still workers. (Technically, they may be termed "dependent contractors.")

Even for self-employed individuals who sell their services to the "market," rather than to a small number of corporate customers, the dictates of competition typically force them to accept incomes and working conditions below those attained by paid employees. Indeed, the per capita income of most proprietors of small businesses and farms in the major Anglo-Saxon economies falls below the average income of paid workers. It's safe to conclude, then, that all or most of the income received by these individuals reflects their ongoing *work*; very little of that income, if any, reflects their status as *owners* of their farms or businesses.

Finally, most individuals perform significant amounts of unpaid work in the course of operating their household, caring for family members, and supporting their communities. This work is not included in the GDP statistics, yet it is essential to our individual and collective well-being. Most of this work is performed by women. Time-use surveys in the advanced capitalist economies indicate that something less than one hour of work is devoted to these unpaid tasks for every hour spent in paid work.

To sum up, here are the main types of work that occur in a modern capitalist economy and the approximate proportion of total work time that they represent:

- Employment (wage labour): about 50 percent.

- Top management and owners: no more than 2 percent.

- Proprietors of small businesses and farms: about 10 percent.

- Unpaid work (in households or the community): about 40 percent.

Most work under capitalism, but not all, consists of wage labour, or employment. Unpaid work is the second-largest category. Moreover, as we'll discuss in Chapter 9, much of that unpaid work can be interpreted as a "cost of producing workers": that is, it's an input to the ongoing re-creation of a willing and able labour force (feeding, clothing, and caring for people, in order to send them back into paid work the next day). So the vast majority of work in our system consists either of working for someone else, or *getting ready* to work for someone else.

Only a small proportion of total work occurs outside of this central employment relationship that is a defining feature of capitalism. A small share of total work consists of people working for themselves, in a small business or farm. And a very small share of total work consists of directing the operation of larger companies, in which most work is performed by other people who work for wages or salaries.

Work and value

Just about everything we need or want in our lives requires human effort to produce it. In other words, almost nothing comes without work. The exception to this general rule is what the classical economists called "free gifts of nature": useful things that are readily and abundantly available in the natural environment, just waiting to be "picked." Plucking ripe fruit from a wild blackberry bush; fishing for trout in a clear stream; drinking fresh water from a spring. As we all know, there aren't many "free gifts of nature" left anymore (and you should never drink water from a spring unless it's been tested!). And even the previous examples required *some* work: picking, fishing, carrying. Perhaps the air we breathe is the only free gift of nature left – and even that is questionable, in many parts of the world.

Ultimately, all production involves the application of human work to various materials which we gather from the natural environment in order to make them more useful. This is obviously true of GOODS: every tangible product consists of natural materials which have been transformed or manipulated in some way to make them more useable. (Even "synthetic" products, like polyester shirts or edible petroleum coffee whitener, began life as some substance in our natural environment.) But this is also true of SERVICES. No-one produces a service solely with their bare hands – except perhaps a masseur (and even they use massage oil). So service-producing industries, too, require inputs of goods, which in turn consist of transformed natural substances. Therefore, work and the natural environment are the ultimate sources of everything produced in our economy – so in this sense, they are the source of all "value." And work is the only thing that *adds* value to the things we collect from nature.

But this term, "value," is notoriously difficult to define, and economists have been debating the nature of value, and how to measure it, for centuries. Today, economists mean various things by "value," and the term is used in many different contexts. The value of a product may refer to its price, in comparison to the prices of other products. Value can also refer to the total value created in a particular industry, or in the economy as a whole. For the purposes of GDP statistics, VALUE ADDED in the *private* sector is the sum of all goods and services produced, evaluated at their prices. In the *public* sector, in contrast, value added is defined as the cost of producing something.

An important distinction can be made here between goods and services that can be routinely produced, and those which are in some way unique and irreplaceable. Economists call these categories "producible" and "non-producible" items, respectively. In general, the value of a producible good or service will equal the cost of producing it. (In capitalism, it also includes a profit margin paid to the owners of the business.) A non-producible item, on the other hand, possesses some special characteristic which cannot be duplicated: fine art, a rare mineral, a plot of land in a very convenient location, or a very unusual and innate skill (such as possessed by sports legends and opera stars). The value of non-producible goods and services may deviate from their cost of production, depending on the extent to which purchasers are willing to pay a premium for its specific attributes.

Importantly, it is only for non-producible goods and services that these *demand* conditions (that is, what customers are willing to pay) enter directly into the determination of price (or "value"). For producible goods and services, if customers want more of something, the industry simply supplies it – and the cost of production (plus a profit margin in capitalism) determines its value. By definition, producible goods and services constitute all of what we "produce," so we will focus on them – although where scarce (and hence non-producible) land or resources are required for production, then an element of scarcity and demand does indeed enter into value calculations.

We've already seen that profit complicates the definition and measurement of value. In a capitalist economy, the owners of private capital receive a rate of profit on their investments. This does not imply, however, that capital is itself "productive," nor that profit is morally legitimate. It only implies that under capitalism, profit is a fact of life. Because of the payment of profits, the value of something in a capitalist economy – even a producible good or service – will *not* exactly reflect the amount of work that went into producing it. Two products which require an equal amount of labour to produce will generally have different prices, depending on the amount of profit that's paid out (and hence built into the price) in the production of each product. Similarly, GDP includes not just the value of all the paid work (of various sorts, including self-employment and the work of top managers) performed in an economy. GDP also includes other types of income paid out in the economy – like profits.

For simplicity, the classical economists adopted a labour theory of value. In this theory, the prices of producible commodities reflect the total amount of labour required to produce them (including both direct labour and the indirect labour required to produce machines and raw materials used in production – a complication we'll discuss in the next chapter). Marx realized this simplified theory was wrong: prices under capitalism must also reflect the payment of profit. But he was politically committed to explaining prices on the basis of their "underlying" labour values, so he undertook a complicated (and ultimately unsuccessful) attempt to explain prices on the basis of labour values. Neoclassical economists, responding to Marx, tried to provide an intellectual and moral justification for the fact that profits *are* paid on capital investments by attempting to show that capital itself is actually productive. These efforts, too, were unsuccessful.

In the end, the relevance of this long controversy is not entirely clear. Productive human effort ("work," broadly defined) is clearly the only way to transform the things we harvest from our natural environment into useful goods and services. In this sense, work is the source of all value added. For society as a whole, just as for that lazy teenager, if we don't work, we don't eat. Nothing else – not alien landings, not divine intervention, and not some mystical property of "capital" – is genuinely productive. Under capitalism, profits are paid on capital investments. These profits reflect a social institution called "private ownership," not any real productive activity or function. (In fact, as we'll see, it's not even possible to clearly *measure* capital, let alone to prove that it is productive.) Because of this institution of private ownership of capital, profits are reflected in the prices of various goods and services (and hence also in GDP).

We can accept that human work is the sole driving force of production while simultaneously recognizing that prices (and things that depend on prices, like GDP) depend on other factors, too – namely, under capitalism, profit.

Exploitation and Algebra

Here's an interesting historical note regarding the endless controversies in economics over how to measure "value." Pierro Sraffa was an Italian economist who worked in Cambridge, England in the mid-twentieth century (alongside Keynes, Kalecki, and the other famous heterodox economists based there). He developed a technique for explaining relative prices on the basis of the amount of direct labour involved in production, the indirect

labour embodied in inputs of raw materials and machinery, and (under capitalism) the payment of profit on invested capital. He showed (with a little modern algebra) that Marx didn't need to worry about "transforming" labour values into prices. In fact, without any labour theory of value, Sraffa still proved that an inverse relationship must exist between wages and profits: if one is higher, the other must be lower. This was utterly contrary to the conclusion of neoclassical economists that labour and capital have complementary interests, rather than conflicting interests. Throw in appropriate political terminology (if desired), and Sraffa's theories prove that labour is the ultimate source of production, and that the payment of profit represents the capture (or "exploitation") of a share of the surplus that workers produce.

Work and surplus

In Chapter 3 we saw that changes in economic systems over time were closely related to changes in the production and control of an economic SURPLUS. The surplus is the amount of excess production in an economy, above and beyond what is required to sustain the workers of that economy, and restart production over again the following year. Once a surplus is produced, two crucial questions must be addressed: Who will control it? And what will it be used for? Indeed, the control and use of the surplus is a central factor determining how economies evolve over time.

The size of the surplus depends on a couple of important variables. First is the PRODUCTIVITY of an economy: how much it is able to produce, relative to the amount of work that goes into producing it. Productivity is best measured as the amount of total value added per hour of labour. If workers are more productive, then it takes less time for them to produce enough to keep them and their families alive for another year. Thus the surplus will be larger.

Second, however, there is no absolute standard for what we call the "necessities" of life. A subsistence standard of living may be defined as a physiological minimum: that is, what is required to prevent people from starving. More likely, however, it will be influenced by changing social norms about what is considered a "minimum" standard of living. In general, those norms change over time to reflect the growing productivity of the economy and social norms regarding what is "decent."

What's left after paying for a necessary minimum standard of living for workers, and setting aside enough production (for tools, materials, and supplies) to ensure that production can start again next year, is the social surplus. Measuring that surplus is a tricky exercise. In most developed countries, workers only receive about half the total value of output produced in the economy. Some of that reflects a minimum necessary standard of living, but some reflects extra income above and beyond the minimum (thanks to the successes of workers and unions in demanding higher-than-subsistence wages over time). GDP also includes allowances for the depreciation (wearing out) of capital equipment; that depreciation must be paid in order to maintain the economy's ability to produce. GDP includes income received by farmers and small businesses; most of that reflects the necessary minimum standard of living for farmers and small businesses, but some reflects profit too. Corporate profit obviously reflects the collection of surplus by larger businesses. Government collects a share of GDP directly through sales taxes and other revenue tools.

Table 5.1 provides a rough breakdown of the various components of GDP in the US. After deducting an estimate of minimum consumption for people who perform productive work (including farmers, small businesses, and even capitalists), the value of essential public services, and allowances to replace used-up capital equipment, the remaining value of output (over one-half of total GDP) is the economy's surplus.

Table 5.1   The "Surplus" in the US Economy, 2006

Every economy must set aside enough output to provide for subsistence consumption for its workers (including essential public services), and wear and tear on capital equipment. These expenditures are required just for the economy to reproduce itself. In the US, those necessary expenditures use up less than half of total output. Most of the remainder – the surplus – is consumed (allowing for a higher-than-subsistence standard of living ... at least for the affluent). Smaller amounts are allocated to wasteful public programs (like the military, police, and jails) and net investment (over and above depreciation). Foreign borrowing allows the US to use more output for all these uses than it actually produces.

Category	US$ Billion
Estimating the Surplus:	
Gross domestic product	$13,195
"Subsistence" consumption*	–$2,796
Depreciation of capital	–$1,610
Necessary public services§	–$1,311
Surplus	**$7,478**
Uses of Surplus:	
"Extra" consumption	$6,429
Net investment†	$1,034
Defence, police and jails	$778
Foreign borrowing and other adjustments	–$762
Total	**$7,478**

*   Consumption sufficient to reach the relative poverty income threshold (50% of median household income) for all Americans.

§   Government services production excluding defence, police, and jails.

†   Investment after depreciation.

Source: Author's calculations from US Bureau of Economic Analysis.

The surplus can be "gathered" in various ways. In earlier societies, it was directly collected (seized from slave labour, or gathered via the tithes of feudal peasants). In modern times, it can be collected through corporate profits or taxes. And the surplus can be "spent" in various ways. It can be consumed (either through the luxury consumption of the well-off elite, or through mass consumption by working people that *exceeds* the subsistence level). It can be spent on other projects: paying for wars, building monuments or temples, or supporting the arts. (In economic terms, these are also forms of consumption.) Or the surplus can be invested, to allow the economy to expand over time.

The advent of capitalism brought important changes in the size of the surplus (which became much larger, thanks to the impressive productivity of new factories), the way it was collected (largely through business profits, rather than forcible seizure), and what it was used for. On this score, the fact that capitalists wanted to re-invest most of their profits (partly out of hunger for more profits, and partly thanks to competition from other capitalists) was crucial to the rapid growth and dynamism demonstrated by the new system.

6

Working with Tools

Learning to work with tools

Very early in human civilization, we learned that it's much more effective to use tools instead of working with our bare hands. Indeed, many animals are intelligent enough to grasp this essential economic fact: chimpanzees use blow-tubes to extract termites from a mound; crows use custom-cut twigs to root out grubs from the underbrush; bees and beavers build structures (which are also a kind of tool) to perform their busy work. Early human tools included simple stone cutters, weapons for hunting, and cooking implements. Later we learned to melt and forge metals to produce more complicated, expensive tools, which in turn allowed us to develop permanent agriculture, long-range transportation, and complex construction – functions which were all essential to our gradual economic evolution.

Today, of course, the "tools" we use to perform our work are fantastic: computers of all kinds, massive machinery, laser beams, satellite telecommunications systems, and many more. These tools are a precondition for our productivity: without them, we couldn't produce the quantity or quality of goods and services that we do. But tools also exert a critical influence on our *social* structure. The tools we use help to determine who does what work, how our workplaces are managed, and how the economic pie is divided up.

There are several key economic implications arising from our reliance on tools:

- We learned to use tools by experimenting in the course of our work. Initially that learning process took a long time: it took generations or even centuries to devise rather modest improvements. Today, thanks to our developed and more deliberate scientific capacities, learning is much faster. But we still "learn by doing": by working, we learn (in various incremental ways) how to work better. And those improvements almost always require more tools.

76

- In general, we do not "consume" our tools, and hence they do not directly contribute to our material standard of living. (A few fanatical home-handymen might derive intrinsic enjoyment from sitting around admiring their hardware – but they are hardly typical!) Instead, we use tools to produce other things (goods or services) that we *can* consume and that *are* inherently useful. For this reason, economists call tools INTERMEDIATE PRODUCTS: things that are needed to produce something else, rather than for their own sake. FINAL PRODUCTS, on the other hand, are the goods and services that we ultimately use or consume.

- In order to use tools in our work, and hence to become more productive, we must devote some initial work effort and time to the task of *producing* those tools. Then we use the tools to produce (with added efficiency) the good or service that we ultimately desire. For simplicity, think of this as a two-stage process: first we produce the tools, then we use them to produce what we need or want. In reality, a modern economy involves a complex, overlapping network of industries producing intermediate and final products simultaneously; moreover, we need tools in order to produce tools, so the whole process takes many stages, not just two. Nevertheless, all production can be deconstructed (if you go far enough back in time) into a series of dated activities involving *first* the production of tools, and *then* the production of final goods and services.

- Tools themselves are never "productive" in their own right. Rather, we use tools in order to make our *work* more productive. No tool or machine runs by itself. Even the most automated production system needs a living person to push the "Start" button – not to mention to keep the machinery working properly. At any rate, a more "automatic" production system is simply one in which most or nearly all of the work involved has been devoted to the prior task of producing the tools; only a little work is then required to use the tools to produce the desired final good or service. But the whole process still depends completely on *work*. The reason we devote time and energy to producing tools is because we've learned that they make our overall work effort (*including* the time we spent building the tools) much more productive.

Two ways to grow corn

To understand these points a bit better, let's imagine a very simple economy. It only produces one thing: corn. In pre-capitalist societies, corn was produced solely with labour, seeds left over from the previous season, and simple hand tools. Imagine that there were 100 farmers in the community, and they produced enough corn (let's say 100 bushels) to give each farmer enough corn to support them and their families at a minimal, subsistence level (one bushel per farmer).

Now suppose that the farmers discover how to make and use a tractor. A tractor (which is a sophisticated tool) allows the farmers to plough, plant, and harvest corn more quickly, with less required labour. However, they must devote some initial time and effort to producing the tractor. Let's say that ten farmers can build the tractor with one year of work. Then the same ten farmers can use that tractor to grow corn in the second year, and subsequent years. Thanks to the tractor, those ten farmers can till just as much land as 100 farmers used to work by hand. Better yet, the tractor improves the quality of seeding and harvesting, so that total corn output (from the same land) increases: it now produces 180 bushels, up from 100. Finally, suppose that a tractor lasts for five seasons; each year of farming therefore "uses up" one-fifth of the tractor. (This gradual wearing out of the tractors, and other tools, is called DEPRECIATION.)

Table 6.1   A Corn Economy: Manual and Mechanized

	Manual	*Mechanized*
Direct labour: farming (person-years)	100	10
Indirect labour: tractor-making (person-years)	0	2*
Total labour (person-years)	100	12
Output (bushels)	100	180
Productivity (bushels per person-year)	1	15

* It takes ten person-years to make the tractor, and the tractor lasts for five seasons, so two person-years of indirect labour are used up per season.

Table 6.1 summarizes the key economic facts of this simple corn economy – both before and after the discovery of tractors. Manual farming produced 100 bushels of corn, from 100 person-years of work. The productivity of this economy, therefore, was one bushel per person-year of farming. Mechanized farming, however, dramatically improves productivity. The community now produces 180 bushels of corn per year, with just ten farmers doing the direct work. However, we must also count the indirect work of farming – a share of the time that the farmers spent building the tractor (two person-years of work, reflecting that one-fifth of the tractor's useful life is consumed each season). That implies a total of twelve person-years of work for each year: ten for the direct work of farming, and two for a proportionate share of producing the tractor. Productivity therefore equals the total output of corn (180 bushels) divided by the total input of labour (twelve person-years, including both direct and indirect work). Productivity is thus 15 bushels per person-year of labour – 15 times higher than in manual farming.

There are many amazing economic and social implications from the discovery of mechanized farming, and the incredible expansion of productivity which it brought about. The preceding example, of course, is highly simplified and, in many ways, unrealistic. For example, it would be unusual to have the same group of workers both producing tractors and then using the tractors for farming (more likely, a community would assign some workers to specialize in building tractors, and others to specialize in farming – rather than expecting the same people to do both jobs). And the production of tractors itself requires the use of many types of tools and equipment; it could not simply be undertaken directly by ten workers with their bare hands.

But even this simple example highlights some crucial and complicated questions:

- Where does the extra productivity come from? Clearly, not from the tractor itself. The tractor is not magic; it cannot produce corn by itself. Work is still essential: both to build the tractor, and to use it. The great improvement in productivity is attained because the farmers learned it was more efficient to first build a tractor, and then use it in farming – rather than trying to farm with their bare hands. In other words, the productivity improved because of the *technique of production* (first build a tractor, then grow corn), not from the tractor itself. Strictly speaking, the term TECHNOLOGY refers to a technique of production, not to a particular piece of equipment or machinery. The term is often misused to refer to equipment itself ("Wow, you have some awesome technology in here!"). In its correct use, though, "technology" refers to the *way* we produce something – not the *tools* we use to produce it. A new technology can be highly productive; but a tool or machine, in and of itself, is not.

- Who owns the tractor? Right now, nobody does. The members of this economy have simply discovered that it's smarter to first build a tractor, then grow the corn – rather than growing the corn manually. So they invest some of their own time to make the tractor, and then capture the benefit of improved productivity down the road. If someone did own the tractor, then they would probably charge a price (like a rental rate) for its use. They would receive income in return for their ownership rights – but that ownership is not productive in and of itself. The tractor is still useful, even if nobody owns it. Moreover, in this simplified example, it's not at all clear why the workers would *allow* anyone to charge them for the tractor, because they could simply build themselves another one. (In practice, various barriers prevent workers from "building" their own equipment – such as technical know-how, start-up costs, or patents. These barriers are essential to the ability of capitalists to charge for the use of their tools.)

- Whether or not anyone owns the tractor, it takes time to build it – and the tractor workers need to eat while they are building it. If the economy actually followed the two-year process implied above, it would have to set aside enough corn one year to keep the ten tractor workers alive while they were building the tractor (until the tractor could be used in the second year to produce corn). In practice, a real economy would produce both tractors and corn simultaneously, supplying just enough tractors to replace each farm's equipment once every five years. Nevertheless, *time* is an essential element of working with tools, by virtue of the fact that we need to build our tools, and then use them. And because more productive technologies use more complex tools, they take more time (from start to finish).

- What happens to the extra workers? The manual corn economy required 100 workers. The mechanized corn economy requires only ten (along with the equivalent of two workers per year in factory production). The community must decide what the surplus workers should do. They could be transferred into other industries: consuming corn to stay alive, but producing non-agricultural goods and services for the whole community (or for certain members of the community). All 100 workers could divide up the existing work amongst themselves (each working a small part of the year, and taking the rest of the year off as vacation). They would thus capture the benefits of higher productivity as extra leisure time. Alternatively, excess workers could just be relocated to other regions (like far-off cities) to fend for themselves, or simply left to starve. In historical practice, each of these "solutions" has been used, to differing extents, in different times and places, when dramatically productive new technology resulted in a sharp decrease in the amount of required labour.

- What should be done with the surplus? The economy now produces far more corn than is needed to support the ten workers involved in corn production (and the two tractor workers). This opens up dramatic new possibilities for re-investment (including the expansion of non-agricultural industries); for luxurious or wasteful consumption by a small elite (including pet projects like building monuments or waging wars); or for modest improvements in consumption for the whole population. Economies which re-invested more of the surplus grew faster. And economies which allocated a hefty share of the fruits of mechanization to support increased mass consumption tended to be more socially and politically stable.

What is capital?

Without yet naming it, this discussion has introduced the concept of CAPITAL. "Capital" can mean many different things in economics, depending on the context. Very broadly, it refers to the various "tools" we use in our work, often called PHYSICAL CAPITAL. It includes any tangible product used to produce something else (rather than being consumed in its own right). This includes buildings (factories, mines, offices, or stores) and other structures (pipelines, electricity towers) used by private businesses or other productive enterprises. It includes all forms of machinery and equipment, including tools, computers, machinery, robots, and transportation equipment – again, so long as they are dedicated to the production of something else. Sometimes, whether something is a "capital" good or not depends solely on what it is being used for: a motor vehicle used to deliver packages is a capital good, but the same vehicle used for personal purposes is a consumption good. (The arbitrariness of this distinction inspires all sorts of shenanigans on business tax returns!) Capital goods which last for some time and are installed in a certain place are called FIXED CAPITAL. But a portion of physical capital also consists, at any point in time, of inventories of partly-processed or even finished goods en route to their final productive destination.

Not surprisingly, capital plays a particularly important economic role under capitalism – which is, after all, an economic system in which private profit is paid to the people who own capital. In this context, capital takes on a particular *social relationship* (based on private property), not just a physical form. In modern times, "capital" has also come to mean a sum of money which is invested in a business, in hopes of generating profit. I prefer to call this FINANCE, rather than capital, in order to distinguish the physical and the monetary forms of investment.

The development of new technologies, and the accumulation of the physical capital (that is, tools) needed to use those technologies, have been the dominant forces behind the stunning economic changes which have occurred in the last two centuries of human civilization. And the accumulation of physical capital is crucial to our continuing economic progress.

Theories of capital and profit

In capitalist economies, tractors and most other kinds of physical capital are owned by private investors, who receive profit for their use. Neoclassical economists have attempted to justify the payment of profit on invested capital using two different, but related, arguments:

1. Capital is inherently productive, so someone who owns capital should be paid for its use just like any other factor of production. We have already seen that a tool is simply the physical embodiment

of the work required to produce it; no tool is useful separate from the work that went into making it, and the work required to operate it. But there's an even deeper, logical problem with the "capital is productive" argument. Unlike labour, land, or natural resources, capital cannot be measured in physical units. A modern economy uses thousands of different kinds of tools, and it makes no sense at all to speak broadly of capital in "tons" or "machines" or "tractors" (as we can speak of labour in hours, or land in hectares). Capital, in aggregate, is always measured in money terms – and, indeed, that's how profit is paid (as a percentage of invested money). But the prices of tools (like other prices in capitalism) themselves depend on the profit rate. We need to know the profit rate before we can even know the value of the physical capital (that is, tools) that's been invested. So how can profit reflect the amount of invested "capital" (measured in aggregate), when the amount of invested "capital" itself depends on the profit rate? This neoclassical argument collapses in circular reasoning.

2. Production with tools takes time, and profit should be paid to the owners of those tools to reflect their patience and thriftiness while they wait for production to occur. It is certainly true that when someone owns something, they will usually demand to be paid for lending it and waiting to get it back. This payment reflects the social reality of their ownership right. But "waiting" is not, in itself, a productive activity. Indeed, poor and working people spend billions of hours waiting every week without ever receiving a cent for it – waiting for the bus, waiting for service in public institutions, waiting to work. It is only because someone *owns* the capital that they get paid for "waiting." In this manner, the payment of profit is inevitably tied up with the social institution of ownership, not any inherent characteristic of production itself. Moreover, the "compensation for waiting" argument gets caught in the same circular reasoning as the "capital is productive" argument. Whether one particular technology requires more "waiting" than another is seldom self-evident, independently of the rate of profit that is being paid out. This is because the "waiting" typically occurs in different patterns over different periods of time. A technology that involves relatively more "waiting" (and hence more paid profit) at one rate of profit could involve relatively less "waiting" (and hence less profit) at another, because the different

bits of waiting must be evaluated and compared to each other (using the profit rate). The measurement of "waiting" (like the measurement of aggregate capital) cannot occur without knowing the profit being paid, and hence it cannot in turn determine the payment of profit.

By the 1960s, it was clear that both neoclassical approaches were invalid. At that point, pure neoclassical economists began to pursue other directions in their thinking. Some developed a very strange concept called "intertemporal equilibrium," which sidesteps the problems noted above by avoiding any measurement of aggregate capital. Instead, it calculates separate rates of profit for each specific tool, calculated at each particular point in time. The theory is internally consistent but useless for practical applications. Other economists effectively abandoned the notion of general equilibrium altogether (including its effort to explain and justify profit), and began to pursue other interests. Despite this high-level intellectual retreat, however, the broad belief that profit is a legitimate and efficient payment that reflects the real productivity of capital still rules the roost in economics instruction and economic policy-making.

The other major approach to understanding capital views the payment of profit as a way of collecting and controlling some of the economic surplus. As we saw in Chapter 4, this view originated with the classical economists, was modified by Marx, and lives on in the theories of modern heterodox thinkers (inspired by the work of Sraffa, Kalecki, and others). Profit is a residual, what's left after a company pays its bills (including the cost of keeping its workers alive). Understanding profit in this way does not imply that profit is somehow equivalent to "theft," nor that profit should be eliminated (so that workers would get the full value of everything they produce). Indeed, if workers actually received (and consumed) everything they produced, any economy (not just capitalist ones) would soon collapse for lack of investment. Until we find a better way to organize the economy, profit is a fact of life under capitalism, and investors' demands for profit will always constrain (to varying degrees) our economic and social actions.

However, this is very different from accepting that profit is a natural and legitimate payment to the real economic "productivity" of private capital. One can certainly recognize and even tolerate the power of private owners to collect profit on their investments, without celebrating it. And understanding capital and profit in this way allows us to better explain what is actually occurring in the modern economy.

For example, profit rates have increased substantially in most countries in the wake of the often-painful, pro-business policies associated with neoliberalism. Does this rise in profits really reflect the market's valuation of some improvement in the real productivity of capital, and is hence an outcome that's both natural and fair? Not likely. More convincing is to recognize that higher profits reflect pro-business changes in economic policies and structures; these have enhanced business power, and reduced what companies have to pay out in wages, taxes, and other costs. In this understanding, higher profit rates reflect a social and political shift, not an automatic and somehow "natural" reward for capital's supposed productivity.

7

Companies, Owners, and Profit

The private company

One defining feature of capitalism is that most production is undertaken to generate private profit. (The other defining feature of capitalism is that most of the work required for production occurs via wage labour.) In order to generate and collect that profit, a specialized institutional form has emerged: the private company. Today private firms dominate the economy: their decisions about investment, production, and employment are the most important factors determining whether and how the economy grows, and how people work. The actions of those private companies are far more important on a day-to-day basis than things that governments do. This makes it incredibly ironic to hear government officials claim credit for "good economic management," or opposition leaders berate the party in power for "bad economic management." These political debates are mostly beside the point since in reality businesses, not government, sit in the economic driver's seat.

Companies come in all shapes and sizes. A few thousand very large corporations exercise decisive influence over global economic development; the largest are as big (in value added, employment, and assets) as a medium-sized country (see Table 7.1). Tens of thousands of medium-sized businesses, and millions of very small firms and partnerships, also play critical economic roles. Together, the few

Table 7.1 The Biggest of the Big, 2006 (US dollars)

Category	Large Corporation	Equivalent Country
Value added	ExxonMobil ($195 billion)	Finland ($195 billion)
Employment	Wal-Mart ($1.9 million)	Ireland ($1.9 million)
Assets	General Electric ($675 billion)	Austria ($650 billion)

thousand huge companies produce as much as all the others put together. And since many smaller companies depend directly and indirectly on bigger companies for their business, these megacorps are all the more important to the overall economy.

All companies have two crucial features in common:

- Somebody owns them (usually one or more private investors – but some companies are owned by governments, public agencies, or cooperatives), and hence any profits produced by the company become the property of those owners.

- The owners must ensure their company is governed and managed in accordance with their wishes. Usually the owners' goal is simply to maximize the company's profits.

The structure of the private firm has changed over time, as have the methods by which firms are managed and governed. In the early days of capitalism, most private companies were owned outright by well-off individuals, who also managed them on a day-to-day basis. In this case, it was easy to ensure that a company acted in the best interests of its owner, since the owner *was* the manager. Today, many private companies still conform to this model – mostly very small businesses, called proprietorships. In some cases a group of proprietors will cooperate on joint business endeavours, called partnerships, in order to share the costs, risks, and rewards.

The most common business form in modern times, however, is the CORPORATION. A corporation is a private firm which has been granted the legal rights and responsibilities of a person, but in a manner which keeps the corporation itself separate from the (real) people who own it. The main benefit of this approach is that it limits the extent to which individual owners are liable for losses or damages resulting from a corporation's activities. This is called the principle of limited liability. It allows well-off investors to protect their total wealth: the amount put at risk in any particular business venture is limited to the assets they directly invest in that business. Even if the corporation then goes bankrupt, or incurs large legal damages, the owners' *other* wealth is protected.

As a separate, artificial entity, corporations are well-suited to the joint-stock system, whereby a company is owned by a number (possibly a large number) of different individual investors. These corporations issue SHARES reflecting the up-front investments made by different owners; usually, these shares can then be bought and sold on a STOCK MARKET. Corporations which publicly issue shares in this manner are called publicly-traded corporations (not to be confused with publicly-owned corporations, which are owned by governments or other public agencies).

Corporations are governed according to a skewed kind of democracy: one share, one vote. Shareholders get direct input to management at annual general meetings (which elect corporate boards of directors), and through occasional special ballots when companies face unique decisions. But company directors are elected to represent shareholders, and they keep a close watch over the day-to-day actions of the corporation's top executives.

We will discuss the workings of stock markets in detail in Chapter 18. For now, keep in mind simply that the trading value of a company's shares depends on the expectations of investors regarding that company's future profits. If profits are high and expected to stay high, then a company's share price will also be high. Shareholders can thus capture the profits of the companies they own in two ways: via direct payouts from those companies (such as interest or dividend payments – see box opposite), or via increases in the price of their shares (which can be readily sold on the stock market).

The distinction between the investors who own the company and the top managers who control it on a day-to-day basis is a constant challenge facing corporations. In the 1950s and 1960s, many economists believed that corporations had become powers unto themselves. Insulated, self-interested executives ran them without real supervision from the shareholders.

More recently, however, legal and organizational changes now ensure that even very large companies operate with a strict focus on maximizing the wealth of their shareholders. The so-called "shareholder rights" movement has campaigned for many changes (such as linking executive compensation to share prices, stricter oversight on management, and a ruthless business focus on maximizing profits and share prices) that have erased any doubt about who is in charge. As much as at any time in the history of capitalism, the fundamental purpose of private companies – including the largest corporations – is clearly to generate profits for the individuals who own them.

The Centrally Planned Corporation

The largest corporations are larger than many countries. They operate thousands of facilities around the world, employ millions of workers, and deal with thousands of different suppliers. And the success of these giant, complex firms is not really a testimony to the virtues of the free market. A more important factor in corporate success has been the astounding ability of corporate managers to deliberately *plan*.

Wal-Mart   Wal-Mart operates a fantastically complicated logistics and delivery system, distributing merchandise to its far-flung stores in the most cost-efficient manner. It also maintains an immense database on sales patterns, which it uses to centrally determine the precise layout of every Wal-Mart store – right down to which socks are displayed next to which pantyhose, all in order to maximize sales, reduce inventory turnover times, and enhance profits. The immense productivity of this central planning has been the key force behind Wal-Mart's success – far more important than the poverty-level wages it pays its workers.

Toyota   The world's most successful automaker has a legendary reputation for effective central planning, right down to the tiniest nut and bolt. Toyota produces over 60 models of vehicles (8 million units a year), in at least 65 major assembly plants (and dozens of smaller factories), in 28 different countries. Yet all this manufacturing activity is centrally planned and coordinated through a complex manufacturing and logistics strategy called the Toyota Production System. Corporate planners standardize engineering and design (to allow parts to be transferred across vehicles). Relations with suppliers are minutely planned, so that specific parts are produced and delivered to assembly plants "just in time" for installation on a Toyota car.

ExxonMobil   This global behemoth recorded a $40 billion annual profit in 2006 – the largest in world history. Its profitability is carefully monitored and managed through an incredibly detailed and centralized system of financial control, through which core directors oversee over 100 business divisions and subsidiaries, operating in almost every country in the world. Divisional leaders present regular business plans, including proposals for new investment spending, which are reviewed and ranked by the company's central financial authorities. New capital is then carefully allocated to what are deemed to be the most promising initiatives from across this worldwide menu of options.

▶

These and other successful corporations have raised the art of deliberate economic planning to heights that former Soviet planners could never have imagined – utilizing both their dictatorial control over the internal activities of the company, and new technological tools for collecting and managing information. To be sure, even megacorps operate within an unplanned, competitive market environment. They must sell their output; market conditions affect what they must pay for their inputs; and they must generate a competitive profit for their investors. However, their fantastic ability to plan and coordinate is the crucial reason why corporations have emerged as the most effective institutional tool for generating private profit.

And private firms continue to evolve, always seeking new and more effective ways to generate profits for their owners. For example, in recent years a new form of ownership called PRIVATE EQUITY has emerged. A private equity firm (typically financed by a small group of very wealthy investors) takes large direct ownership stakes in other companies. Its goal is often to dramatically restructure those other businesses to boost their profits; sometimes private equity owners even break up these companies and sell off the remaining "parts." This type of company has proven itself ruthlessly willing and able to boost profits, often by sacrificing the workers and communities which depend on the former operations. And because private equity firms do not issue shares publicly, they are spared the trouble and expense of publicly reporting on their operations.

Who owns companies?

During the Industrial Revolution, it was easy to tell who was the capitalist and who were the workers. The capitalist wore a black suit and a top hat, lived in a mansion, and ran the company. The workers were the ones risking their lives in the factory, making barely enough wages to keep them and their families alive.

Capitalism has changed a lot since then, of course, and so have the dividing lines between social classes. Workers have fought for and (in developed countries, at least) won better wages and working conditions. The capitalist is harder to spot; they may not even work in the factory. But they still own the company. The distinctions between classes still very much exist. They are just a little trickier to define.

Most large corporations are owned by many different shareholders. With joint-stock corporations, investors can place bets on the success of many different companies, without having to play a central management role in any one of them. This allows investors to diversify their financial holdings. It also allows them to capture profits on their investments, without having to get involved in the dirty, troublesome business of actually running a company. (Well-paid top executives do that for them.)

And since the wealth of joint-stock companies is parcelled up into bite-size chunks, anyone with a bit of spare money can get into the action – even buying one share makes you, technically, a "part-owner" of the company. (An exception is Berkshire Hathaway, the investment company run by American billionaire Warren Buffet; its shares cost over US$100,000 each!) This seems to make it possible for anyone to become a "capitalist," in the sense of owning a little bit of a private company. Clever companies play up this seemingly "participatory" aspect of modern capitalism. Some might give a few token shares to their workers, to make them "feel" like owners and promote closer identification with management. Financial vehicles called MUTUAL FUNDS (where investors buy shares in a pooled fund, which in turn invests in many different companies) allow investors to further share the risks, and the administrative costs, associated with owning shares. On this basis, defenders of capitalism imply that anyone who owns even a single share in a company is now themselves a "capitalist."

It's easy to cut through this self-serving hype. Hard statistics on wealth ownership indicate clearly that the ownership of financial wealth (including corporate shares) is shockingly concentrated among a surprisingly small elite. Moreover, it is becoming *more* concentrated over time – not less. Table 7.2 provides some summary measures of financial wealth concentration for the largest Anglo-Saxon economies, and the whole world. In every case, the clear majority of financial wealth is owned by a group representing well under one-tenth of the population. In every case, the financial holdings of the median household – the household exactly in the middle of the income ladder – is tiny in any meaningful economic sense. Most typical households have no significant wealth outside of the equity in their own homes. And in every case, the collective financial holdings of the entire bottom half of the population are trivial.

Table 7.2   Concentration of Wealth in Selected Capitalist Economies

National statistical agencies collect data on the distribution of financial wealth through surveys of randomly selected households. This data indicates that wealth is distributed extremely unevenly: in every major economy included on this table, the richest 1% of the population owns many times more wealth than the bottom 50% of the population, and well over half of all wealth is owned by the richest 5–10% of society. However, this official data badly underestimates the inequality of wealth, since random sampling almost always misses the incredible sums of wealth owned by ultra-rich households (who make up a tiny share of the total population). Published lists of wealthy individuals indicate that billionaires alone own 5–10% of all household wealth – more than the entire bottom half of society.

Country	Year	Wealth Measure	Total Wealth:			
			Share of Top 1%	Share of Top 5%	Share of Top 10%	Share of Bottom 50%
US	2004	Net worth	34%	59%	71%	2%
UK	2003	Marketable wealth excl. own dwelling	34%	58%	71%	1%
Canada	2005	Household net worth	n.a.	n.a.	58%	3%
Australia	2002–03	Household net worth	n.a.	39%	53%	6%
World	2000	Net household wealth	32%	57%	71%	4%

Country	Published Source	The Wealth of Billionaires:				
		No. of Billionaires*	% National Population	Combined Wealth	Aggregate Household Wealth Concept	Billionaires' Share
US	Forbes 400, 2007	Approx. 500	.00017%	Approx. $1.7 trillion	Financial net worth	6%
UK	Sunday Times Rich List, 2007	169	.00028%	£233 billion	Net financial wealth	10%
Canada	Canadian Business Rich 100, 2007	54	.00017%	$145 billion	Net financial assets	5%
Australia	BRW Rich 200, 2007	37	.00018%	$81.6 billion	Net financial wealth excl. mortgages	7%

* Billionaires defined as having net worth over $1 billion in national currency for US, Canada, and Australia; and over £500 million for UK (equivalent roughly to US$1 billion).

Source: Author's calculations from data in US Federal Reserve Board of Governors; UK Office of National Statistics; Statistics Canada; Australian Bureau of Statistics; Forbes; Sunday Times; Canadian Business; BRW; Lawrence Mishel et al., State of Working America 2006–07 (Washington: Economic Policy Institute, 2006); James B. Davies et al., "Estimating the Level and Distribution of Global Household Wealth," UNU-WIDER Research Paper #2007/77, United Nations University, 2007.

Most business wealth is owned (and increasingly tightly controlled) by a surprisingly small minority of society. It is still meaningful, therefore, to speak of a class of "capitalists," defined as those individuals who control, and own a dominant stake in, the private businesses which undertake most production in modern capitalist economies.

I would include in that group of capitalists both major owners and top managers. By "top managers," I refer to those individuals who control the day-to-day actions of businesses through their positions as top managers and executives. (We can exclude very small businesses, in which the owner and family members perform most of the required work.) As we discussed in Chapter 5, those top managers account for no more than 2 percent of all the work done in the economy; moreover, they almost universally have significant ownership stakes in the companies they work for.

There is another group of individuals who may not work for any particular company, but who own enough business wealth to support themselves comfortably without having to work at all. The wealth of these "major owners" may be held directly through ownership of particular companies, or indirectly through large amounts of corporate shares. Let's conservatively assume an ongoing average profit rate of 5 percent (most businesses earn much more than this). Then an individual owning $2 million in business and financial wealth (not counting the value of their own home) can receive an income of $100,000 per year purely from their wealth. That's enough to rank well within the top 5 percent of the income distribution, without having to do any work at all (other than go to the bank to deposit dividend cheques!). Many of these rich individuals work; but the key distinction here is that they don't *have* to work, since they own enough business wealth to support themselves very comfortably *without* working. Statistical surveys indicate that less than 2 percent of individuals in Anglo-Saxon economies own business and financial wealth on this scale; and there is considerable overlap between this category and the top managers.

Either way, these top managers and major owners have a substantial, direct personal stake in the profits of business. They tend both to identify closely with those businesses and to exert their (disproportionate) political, social, and personal influence on behalf of those businesses. Put together, this class of top managers and wealthy investors accounts for less than 5 percent of the population of developed capitalist economies. They are the modern capitalists:

less visible, more sophisticated, possibly even more compassionate than the capitalists of the 1700s. But they are richer than ever, and they are still capitalists. And their actions and decisions are dominant in determining how the economy develops.

Roughly another 10–15 percent of individuals in developed capitalist economies are owners of much smaller businesses (including farms), for which they and their family members perform most of the required work. But these owner-managers are not really "capitalists," for two reasons: they must actively work (since their ownership of wealth is not sufficient to provide a comfortable living on the basis of ownership income alone), and their companies do not primarily function on the basis of the wage labour of others.

The vast majority of households in capitalist societies – the remaining 85 percent or so of the population – depend almost exclusively on the wage labour they supply to employers for their lifetime income. At any given point in time, not all the workers in these households are employed: some are unemployed, sick or disabled, or retired (in which case, in modern capitalism, they rely on government social programs to supplement their incomes). But over their lives, their ability to sell their labour is their only source of independent income. They do not own significant financial wealth. They are the modern working class.

Of course, there are many differences between different groups of workers: their skills and training, the nature of their work, their

Table 7.3   Useless and Destructive Activities that Also Happen to be Profitable

Activities Performed by Profit-Seeking Companies that are Socially Useless:

- Advertising
- Spending to develop copycat products (such as imitation pharmaceuticals) that have no real additional value
- Excess packaging added by producers to attract buyer interest
- Maintaining more capacity than required, in order to "catch" new sales or supplies before a competitor does
- Producing things designed to break down or become obsolescent, forcing customers to buy new ones

Activities Performed by Profit-Seeking Companies that are Socially Destructive:

- Selling products that are harmful, unsafe or dangerous
- Tricking consumers into thinking they are buying something they're not
- Spending to directly undermine competitors (by spying or sabotage)
- Spending to prevent others from duplicating your work (such as patents or anti-copying protections)
- Limiting production of a useful product in order to boost profits
- Shifting costs (including hidden costs like pollution) to consumers, suppliers, or the public at large
- Advertising that makes people feel inferior or inadequate if they don't purchase a product

Please Hold

How often have you called a large company, only to be placed on hold or transferred into an automated answering system? Several minutes later (if you're lucky!) you are finally connected with the person you wanted to speak to.

Are these modern telephone systems "efficient"? Not exactly. They clearly reduce the company's *private* costs, since a computer is cheaper than a live receptionist. Yet the total expenditure of human time increases, because each caller now spends longer reaching their desired party. Since the company doesn't pay for your wasted time, it seems "free" – but it isn't free for you. Technology enhances profit by shifting costs from the private company onto others. But true efficiency and productivity suffers.

The pursuit of private profit often leads to waste and inefficiency, because of the conflict between private costs and social costs.

incomes, and their relative security. But they all have one fundamental thing in common: they all support themselves by offering their labour to someone else in return for a wage or salary. And together they constitute the vast majority of society.

The logic of profit

The hunt for profit is the dominant driving force of a capitalist economy. And there are important consequences arising from the fact that most production is undertaken with the explicit goal of generating maximum profits for the people who own the company.

Since Adam Smith's time, many economists have emphasized the broader social benefits of "greed." They argue that the pursuit of profit will encourage people to work harder, and be more creative in developing new products and new ways of producing them. In reality, however, we've seen that at least 85 percent of people in capitalism don't actually work for profit – they work for wages and salaries. So the importance of the profit motive in eliciting work, at the level of *individual* psychology, is vastly overstated.

At the corporate level, however, profits are indeed very important. In fact, for private businesses, they are the meaning of life. Corporate managers and directors act powerfully and quickly to ensure their businesses generate as much profit as possible. They closely supervise the work of their paid employees (and in this way, profits can be an *indirect* motivation for individual workers – not because they'll earn profits if they work hard, but because they'll be fired by their profit-seeking boss if they don't!). And they adjust their companies' activities in line with that never-ending hunt for profit. Some of these adjustments are beneficial to the overall economy, but many are not. It is utterly unjustified to assume that profit-seeking activity leads to efficiency and productivity – especially if we define "efficiency," appropriately, as the extent to which economic activity translates into human well-being.

Creative companies can devise all sorts of different ways of earning profits. Some of these are useful: developing higher-quality new products, and developing better, more efficient ways of producing them. But competitive markets can also reward companies with profits for doing things that are utterly useless, from the perspective of human welfare (see Table 7.3). And if lax laws and regulations allow them to, profit-seeking companies will do things that are downright destructive to workers, communities, customers, and innocent bystanders.

The problem arises from the distinction between the *private* costs of an economic activity, and its *social* costs. A private company aims to maximize its own private profits. It does this by maximizing its private revenues, and minimizing its private costs. One way to minimize costs is to shift them to someone else. For example, pollution is a way for a company to avoid a cost of production (namely, the waste it produces) by simply dumping it into the broader environment. Alternatively, a company may do something that is socially destructive but privately profitable. Selling harmful products like cigarettes is an example of this activity. By the same token, there are things that would benefit society hugely, but which are *not* undertaken because the private benefits to companies are insufficient. The failure of pharmaceutical companies to distribute drugs to combat malaria, AIDS, measles, and other diseases to low-income populations in Africa and elsewhere is a sickening example of this failure.

Private companies are efficient and creative at maximizing their private profits and minimizing their private costs. But there's no reason to assume that those actions will maximize the social benefits and minimize the social costs of economic activity. To attain a closer match between private cost-benefit and social cost-benefit calculations requires forcing companies to respect goals other than just maximizing their private profits. In turn, this requires that government regulators, unions, and other broader actors be empowered to intrude into the realm of company decision-making – pushing companies to reduce their social costs and increase the social benefits of their actions.

Measuring (and Paying) Profit

Profits result when a company sells what it produces for more than it cost to produce it. A company collects revenues from its sales, out of which it must pay wages to its workers and the cost of any raw materials, parts, and services used in the course of production. The company must also account for the cost of wear and tear on capital equipment (called **DEPRECIATION**). If some of the company's finance was borrowed from banks or other lenders (rather than being provided directly by the company's owners), interest costs on those loans must

▶

also be deducted. Whatever residual is left at the bottom line, after paying all these bills, is the company's profit.

In addition to measuring the mass of profit (in dollars), it is also useful to measure the *rate* of profit. This indicates how profitable a company is, relative to the amount of capital that was invested in it. This is important for comparing profitability over time, and between different companies. There are various ways to measure the profit rate. For the ultimate owners of a company, the RETURN ON EQUITY is the best measure of profits. It is the ratio of bottom-line profits to the amount of shareholder's equity invested in the company. Most companies are expected to produce an annual return on equity of at least 10 percent, much more in some countries.

A company's financial performance is described in its financial statements. If the company is publicly-traded (with its shares bought and sold on the stock market), it is required to disclose those statements to the public. Quarterly statements (every three months) provide quick updates; annual reports provide more detail; supplementary reports filed with financial regulators (such as the large "10-K" forms required in the US, or prospectus statements issued whenever a company sells new shares) provide a detailed portrait of the company's overall business.

There are various ways for investors to get their hands on the profits of the companies they own. If they have loaned capital to a company, they receive INTEREST on those loans, at a certain percentage per year. Shareholders (and some types of lenders) receive DIVIDENDS, which are fixed cash payments paid (typically every quarter or every year) to the owner of each share. Most companies store away a portion of their profits to fund future investments; these are called RETAINED EARNINGS. Another way for shareholders to realize their profits is by selling some of their shares. If a company is profitable and growing, its share price will rise. Shareholders can convert this gain into cold hard cash by selling a few shares (this is called a CAPITAL GAIN).

The tax systems of most capitalist countries are heavily biased toward investors (not surprising, given their political and economic influence). As a result, tax rates on dividend and capital gains income are usually much lower than tax rates on labour income. This is especially ironic since the people who receive most of that investment income are very rich.

8

Workers and Bosses

Why labour is different

A COMMODITY is anything that is bought and sold for money. With the advent of capitalism and widespread wage labour, labour itself became a commodity. And neoclassical economics analyzes labour essentially like any other commodity: there are suppliers (workers), demanders (employers), and a price (the wage rate). In theory, if governments and unions stay out of the way, fluctuations in the price of labour will supposedly ensure that everyone finds a job, in which case labour supply equals labour demand and there is no UNEMPLOYMENT. If unemployment exists, just let the wage fall low enough so that employers hire enough workers to absorb all the slack in the labour market.

This neoclassical story is simplistic and very inaccurate. It is true that labour is bought and sold for money (and hence is a commodity). But lurking under the surface are several crucial differences that make labour totally unique among commodities, and explain why the labour market is different from all others. They also explain why the standard neoclassical advice – cut wages to eliminate unemployment – does not often work.

Here are the most important factors that make labour unique. They probably seem obvious to an untrained onlooker, yet they have been curiously difficult for many economists to grasp:

- Labour is alive. Labourers are living, thinking beings, who can influence their surroundings and circumstances. One important consequence of this is that they always find ways – individual or collective – to resist work arrangements or practices they believe are unfair.

- Labour itself is not produced as a commodity, for someone's profit. It is produced (or, more specifically, *reproduced*) within families, as part of the normal lifecycle of human existence.

99

- Labour is "produced" by households, which are economic *consumers*. Yet labour is "consumed" by private companies (and other employers), which are economic *producers*. Therefore, the production (or supply) of labour depends on consumption, while the consumption of (or demand for) labour depends on production.

- Unlike other commodities, the labour market seldom "clears." When labour supply equals labour demand, then everyone who wants to work can find a job (economists call this FULL EMPLOYMENT), and unemployment is zero. In practice, however, unemployment almost *always* exists under capitalism. (Bizarrely, despite observed reality, some neoclassical economists still claim that unemployment either does not exist or is a rare special case.)

- Every market exchange reflects a balance of power (economic power, and other kinds of power) between the buyer and seller, not just "pure" supply and demand. But the balance – or *imbalance* – of power is especially obvious and important in the case of labour. By definition, wage labourers must sell their labour to survive. Employers, on the other hand, are less desperate to consummate the deal. While they *need* labour to produce (and hence make profit), this need is never as immediate as a worker's need to put food on the table. And the asymmetry in size between employers (especially larger ones) and individual workers adds further to the imbalance. A large employer hardly notices the departure of any particular worker – but each worker surely notices the disappearance of their job. For all these reasons, a clear asymmetry in power between employers and employees is a fundamental feature of the labour market. Employment is indeed an exchange (trading labour for money), but it is a very unequal exchange.

- When labour is bought, there is an important distinction between what the buyer purchases, and what they actually desire. Employers need someone to perform *work* (human effort or activity). But what they purchase, usually, is labour *time*: that is, a certain number of hours a worker agrees to be on the job. Converting time into work is a central and complicated problem of employment. Moreover, it happens *inside* the firm, in a context of hierarchical control and management authority, not through a "market."

- There is not one labour market, but many different labour markets. Different groups of workers tend to work in very different types of jobs: men and women, different racial and cultural groups, different skills and occupations, and different regions. These large differences in jobs and wages are a normal, ongoing feature of the labour market; and various institutional, cultural, economic, and even legal barriers keep these various parts of the labour market separate. Economists call this phenomenon LABOUR MARKET SEGEMENTATION; it differs from other markets where competition promotes more uniform outcomes.

Labour extraction and labour discipline

The distinction between labour time and labour effort (or actual work) gives rise to a central and fundamental challenge facing employers under capitalism, which we call the LABOUR EXTRACTION problem. It is not enough for an employer to hire a worker. They must also direct the worker to perform the desired quantity and quality of work. LABOUR INTENSITY is the degree to which a worker performs the desired work effort during the hours they are employed.

Employees are paid for their time. They do not own the company, nor have any direct or meaningful stake in its profits. At the individual level, their personal work efforts seldom have any measurable impact on whether the company succeeds or not. Therefore, once they have a job, why should they work hard? To some extent, most individuals genuinely prefer to use their time productively: it helps the time pass, and adds to one's sense of self-worth. But left on their own, most workers would not work as hard or as fast as employers want, nor follow the employer's instructions precisely – especially given the unpleasant, tiring, boring, and often unsafe nature of many jobs. Employers therefore invest vast effort and resources in a system of labour extraction, to enhance labour intensity and extract maximum effort from each hour of paid labour time.

Like a farmer trying to motivate a donkey, effective labour discipline typically needs both carrots (or incentives) and sticks (or punishments). Why should a paid employee work hard? Perhaps they

will make more money if they do. And perhaps they'll get fired if they don't. Management labour extraction strategies use both carrots and sticks.

Some jobs link compensation directly to work effort. Piece-work systems, which pay workers for each bit of work they perform, are one example of this approach; so are contract workers (who are hired to perform a specific task, and are only paid when that task is completed). This strategy has limited application, however: usually employers want their workers to be more flexible, performing a range of hard-to-specify functions (rather than simply producing a certain number of widgets each hour). Even in straightforward jobs, piece-work systems produce notoriously bad quality, teamwork, and employee morale. Other attempts to link compensation to work effort are even less reliable – like profit-sharing bonuses, or tips paid to restaurant waiters. Here the link between an individual's work effort and their personal compensation is very indirect (since the total output of a factory, or the quality of a restaurant meal, depends on the performance of the entire organization – not just one particular worker's effort). Of course, if you are recognized as a "good worker" you might get a promotion or a raise, but at best this is still an indirect, long-term incentive.

That's why the stick, not just the carrot, must always be present, and the biggest stick of all is the threat of dismissal. Employers crave the power to fire workers whose performance is judged inferior – not just to be rid of those particular workers, but more importantly to motivate and discipline the rest of the workforce. Indeed, union provisions limiting the power of employers to fire indiscriminately are among the most hated (by bosses) features of union contracts; by the same token, winning protection against arbitrary dismissal is one of the greatest individual benefits of union membership. To make the job loss threat meaningful, several conditions must be met:

- Employers must have the legal and contractual right to fire staff. Even if they don't use that power often, it has to be there (to motivate frightened workers).

- Employers have to be able to distinguish well-performing workers from undesirable workers. So employers spend heavily on supervision and monitoring systems – everything from shop-floor supervisors looking over workers' shoulders, to sophisticated electronic monitoring technologies (which can measure the speed of cashiers and typists, spy on telephone and e-mail conversations, and track the precise location of truck drivers and couriers).

- Losing one's job must impose a major cost on fired workers, so that the fear of being fired elicits the desired discipline and compliance. The out-of-pocket loss that a fired worker incurs is called the COST OF JOB LOSS. It depends on several variables: how long they can expect to be unemployed (before finding another job), what (if anything) they receive in unemployment insurance benefits while they are jobless, and how the wages and benefits on their new job compare to what they earned in their old job.

Curiously, if the labour market actually worked like neoclassical economists imagine (with labour supply equal to labour demand, and competition ensuring that all equivalent workers are paid the same wage), then the cost of job loss would be *zero*. There's no unemployment, and everyone makes the same wage. So if someone gets fired, they simply go out the next day and find another job paying the same wage. This set of affairs would make it impossible for bosses to enforce any workplace discipline whatsoever (something that heterodox economists, such as Michal Kalecki, have always understood well – see box below).

Capitalism's Full-Employment Sickness

Along with John Maynard Keynes, the Polish economist Michal Kalecki discovered that government spending policies could eliminate unemployment. But would capitalism even want to achieve this seemingly fabulous wonderful result? Kalecki thought not. With remarkable foresight, he explained in 1943 why full employment, while technically possible, would eventually encounter fierce resistance from employers:

> "Lasting full employment is not at all to [business leaders'] liking. The workers would get 'out of hand' and the 'captains of industry' would be anxious to 'teach them a lesson.' Moreover, the price increase in the upswing is to the disadvantage of small and big rentiers [financial investors] and makes them 'boom tired.' In this situation a powerful bloc is likely to be formed between big business and the rentier interests, and they would probably find more than one economist to declare that the situation was manifestly unsound. The pressure of all of these forces, and in particular of big business, would most probably induce the government to return to the orthodox policy."

Kalecki thus precisely predicted the economic and political U-turn that occurred with the advent of neoliberalism. Kalecki also argued that fundamental institutional changes, especially regarding wage-setting and other aspects of the employment relationship, would be essential if full employment was to be sustained.

The implications of the labour extraction problem are many. First, workers and employers experience directly conflicting interests – not just over wage levels, but also over the organization and intensity of work. Second, employers' desire to enforce labour discipline will affect everything from the way compensation is paid, to the nature of workplace technology. In fact, sometimes companies will invest in particular technologies not because they are inherently more efficient, but simply because they facilitate "better" labour discipline (hence boosting *profitability*, which is quite separate from boosting *efficiency*).

Finally, it is clear that a central goal of neoliberal economic and social policy has been to reimpose labour discipline. After the heady, prosperous years of the Golden Age, when workers felt economically secure and more confident in the workplace, employers longed for a more insecure, fearful workforce. One way to reimpose labour discipline is through legal changes making it easier for employers to fire undesired workers.

Another way is to substantially increase the cost of job loss, once a worker is fired. Initially, this involved re-creating mass unemployment. Beginning in the late 1970s, interest rates were raised to deliberately create and maintain a "cushion" of unemployment. The disciplining power of unemployment was reinforced by reductions in unemployment benefits (in many countries, workers who quit or are fired are cut off from unemployment insurance altogether). The effect on labour discipline is obvious: now, if a worker is fired, they have nothing to fall back on. Moreover, these changes have undermined the bargaining power of all workers, even those who never needed unemployment benefits. The higher cost of job loss casts a pall over wage determination – even for workers whose jobs are relatively secure.

The widening gaps between different groups of workers, and a more intense segmentation of labour markets, have also enhanced the cost of job loss and hence labour discipline. Workers in "core" jobs (those requiring especially important skills, or in highly productive industries) receive premium wages and benefits, and enjoy some long-term job security (though never fully guaranteed). Workers in "marginal" jobs (like low-wage service sector positions) receive much lower wages, with much less security. Even if the official unemployment rate is relatively low, the threat of being "exiled" from a high-wage core job to a low-wage precarious job still constitutes a powerful disciplining threat for workers in the higher-wage positions. (The more that wages fall in marginal jobs, however, the harder it becomes for employers in *those* industries to impose meaningful labour discipline – something that is obvious from the poor quality of service that is often delivered in those low-wage industries.)

Workers and bosses: sites of conflict

Private employers do not hire workers as a public service. They employ people to produce something and sell it for profit. Companies constantly try to cut production costs to maximize the profit margin that's left over at the bottom line. In fact, as we will see in Chapter 11, competition from other capitalists *forces* companies to ruthlessly minimize costs, on pain of being driven out of business.

Employers thus aim to produce the maximum possible output, for the lowest possible labour cost. They are therefore interested both in minimizing wages and in maximizing the output of hired labour. How much workers produce in a given period of work time is their PRODUCTIVITY. Productivity depends both on labour intensity and on genuine efficiency (that is, how effectively work effort is converted into output, which in turn depends on technology, work organization, and the nature of the product being made). The ratio of labour costs to productivity is called UNIT LABOUR COST. It represents the amount that employers pay labour for each unit of output they produce.

Employers want to minimize unit labour cost, and they do this by addressing both parts of the equation: reducing wages and boosting productivity. The following simple formula is a convenient way to symbolize the various ways in which the interests of workers and employers interact – sometimes conflicting, and sometimes coinciding.

$$\text{Unit labour cost} = \frac{\text{Compensation}}{\text{Productivity}} = \frac{\text{Compensation}}{\text{Intensity} * \text{Efficiency}}$$

To reduce unit labour costs, employers can cut compensation (wages and benefits) on the top of the equation, or increase productivity on the bottom of the equation. Remember, a 10 percent improvement in productivity is just as good for employers as a 10 percent reduction in compensation. And there are two distinct ways to boost productivity: by increasing labour intensity, or by increasing true efficiency. Table 8.1 lists some of the specific ways in which unit labour costs can thus be reduced.

The more employers cut wages and benefits, the worse off workers are, so this is an obvious source of conflict between workers and their bosses. Increasing the intensity of work will also harm the quality (and sometimes the safety) of work life, so this is another obvious source

Table 8.1 Strategies to Reduce Unit Labour Costs

$$\text{Unit labour cost} \quad = \quad \frac{\text{Compensation}}{\text{Intensity * Efficiency}}$$

Strategy	Impact on Workers
Reduce Compensation:	
• Cut wages or salaries	
• Cut fringe benefits (pensions, health benefits)	
• For "core" workers: reduce the hourly cost of benefits by lengthening the working day, utilize more overtime	Negative
• For "marginal" workers: pay no benefits, utilize part-time labour	
• Outsource work to lower-cost suppliers or contractors	
Increase Labour Intensity:	
• Speed up pace of work (e.g. faster assembly line)	
• Enhance supervision and monitoring to require faster work	
• Reduce paid lunch breaks and rest breaks	Negative
• Reduce paid vacations and holidays	
• Require unpaid overtime from salaried workers	
• "Lean production": eliminate any idle time in the working day	
Increase True Efficiency:	
• Introduce labour-saving equipment	Positive,
• Use new machinery to reduce lifting or reaching	Negative, or
• Produce higher-value, more innovative products	Neutral

Increases in efficiency (and even in intensity) can indirectly facilitate higher compensation, if workers have sufficient bargaining power to win a share of the higher productivity that results.

of conflict. Improvements in the genuine efficiency of work are more complicated. Efficiency improvements can be attained in ways that are harmful, neutral, or even beneficial for workers. One example of a beneficial efficiency improvement is the use of new machinery that enhances output but also reduces workplace injuries (such as strain injuries from reaching or lifting).

Moreover, higher productivity can translate indirectly into higher compensation for workers. There's nothing automatic about the link, but when productivity grows, workers (and their unions) can demand higher compensation without threatening the profit margins of their employers. (On the other hand, any increase in productivity can also translate into layoffs and unemployment, depending on what is happening in the broader economy.)

For this reason, workers and unions sometimes cooperate with employer efforts to enhance efficiency, especially around initiatives that are deemed neutral or beneficial for workers. Even unpleasant increases in the intensity of work can be (at least partially) offset by higher compensation; this can be a way for employers to "buy off" workers into accepting (or at least tolerating) a more intense and disciplined workplace. Indeed, employers always use a carrot as well as a stick to maintain effective labour discipline; for this reason, they may not wish to drive down wages to the lowest level possible, but rather may prefer to keep them relatively "generous" as a way of eliciting more intensity and loyalty. In many ways, then, compensation and productivity can influence each other.

Let's sum up the different ways that employers and workers relate to each other. Employers want to pay less, and make jobs more intense. Workers want the opposite. That's why most of the unit labour cost-reducing initiatives in Table 8.1 are clearly negative for workers. But sometimes the interests of these two opposing sides can coincide (when productivity opens up room for higher compensation). When we study the impacts of competition in Chapter 11, we'll see other ways in which the interests of workers and their *specific* employer might further coincide: workers may feel a need to help their particular employer succeed in competition with other firms. (This strategy might help some groups of workers, but it cannot help *all* workers.) Clever employers try to emphasize this common interest, using gimmicks like free turkeys at Christmas and token profit-sharing bonuses to promote a sense of togetherness. But these efforts can only paper over the fundamental schisms between the two sides that result from the logic of private profit and wage labour.

The relationships between capitalists and workers, therefore, are complex and troubled. Like two spouses who squabble continuously but can't seem to break up, the two great classes of capitalism seem to need each other – yet they still haven't yet found a way to truly get along.

Unions and collective bargaining

We saw earlier that the employment relationship reflects an inherent asymmetry between workers and employers. Individual workers need a job to support themselves and their families. Their work choices may be limited by unemployment, labour market segmentation, or a shortage of alternative employers (especially in smaller communities). An employer, on the other hand, can easily replace any individual worker (unless they possess some very special skill). So at the individual level, workers need their employer a lot more than their employer needs them.

Collectively, however, employers depend on their workforce to perform all or most of the work required for a private company to operate and generate profits. Workers realized very early in the history of capitalism that they could make gains by combining forces to take advantage of this bargaining power, and negotiate collectively for better wages and working conditions. It is difficult (although not impossible) for an employer to replace their whole workforce at once. Therefore, workers have much more clout dealing with their employer collectively rather than one at a time.

Early efforts to organize unions encountered ruthless, often violent opposition from employers, backed up in many cases by government and police efforts to crush organizing campaigns or outlaw unions altogether. In the twentieth century, unions won more acceptance, for both economic and political reasons. Labour-friendly political parties gained influence, and sometimes power. And after World War II, business leaders felt more pressure to accommodate workers' demands (for better pay and labour rights). Initially, rapid productivity growth allowed companies to pay union-level wages while still generating strong profits. With neoliberalism, however, business has returned to a more confrontational attitude, and has been working hard to undermine the power of unions ever since. The legal, economic, and cultural environment facing unions has become hostile in most capitalist countries. The experience has been worst in the US, where unionization has been slipping steadily; unions there now represent barely one-tenth of the workforce, largely explaining why America's economy has become the most lopsided toward business of all the developed countries.

The ability of unions to organize and bargain effectively depends on several factors:

- **The legal climate** Specific laws regulating union organizing, bargaining rights, the right to strike, and other aspects of bargaining can alter union success in subtle but powerful ways.

- **The attitudes of workers** Do workers demand better treatment from their employers, or have they been conditioned to accept their lot in life? Can they stick together in order to win things collectively? (Trade unionists call this *solidarity*.)

- **The cost of job loss**   The same factors that enforce higher labour discipline in the workplace also make it harder to organize unions. Higher unemployment, reduced social programs, and sharper labour market segmentation all undermine union activity – not least because union activists may fear being fired for their activities.

- **Productivity**   If total productivity is growing rapidly, then workers can win higher compensation without harming profits or threatening their company's future. On the other hand, if higher productivity comes about mostly through greater labour intensity, then union activity may be undermined in highly-disciplined workplaces.

- **Competition**   If competition between companies is very intense, then it is difficult for a union to make gains with one employer – since it may then experience higher costs, lower profits, and lower sales than its competitors. Competitive pressures have definitely become more intense in recent decades in most industries, and this has undermined union power. The alternative for unions is to organize and bargain for all workers in an industry at once (using sectoral or pattern bargaining techniques); this is more effective, but harder to attain.

Market forces will never guarantee workers a decent share of the wealth they produce – even under vibrant economic and productivity conditions. As we have seen, employers pay wages just high enough to elicit desired labour discipline from their workers. This level depends on factors such as workers' legal and union rights, labour market conditions (including unemployment and segmentation), and broader social policies (which influence how desperate workers are to keep their jobs).

No society without strong and effective unions has ever achieved truly mass prosperity. The degree of unionization is one of the most important factors determining wage levels, the incidence of poverty, and hours of work. In my view, the ability of workers to protect and strengthen their unions will be essential if they are to limit and eventually reverse the negative economic and social consequences of neoliberalism.

9

Reproduction (for Economists!)

Where do people come from?

Economics is called the "dismal science," and that reputation is often well-deserved. Economists, it seems, can make anything dry and boring – even sex!

Whereas the rest of the world associates reproduction with love, commitment, fulfilment, and (of course) sex, economists view reproduction as a rather more dull undertaking. For them, reproduction is the *economic* re-creation of the human race. This includes the biological process of reproduction. But it also includes the sustenance, care, and training of people, so that they can lead fully productive economic lives. REPRODUCTION, therefore, is much more than making babies: it also means raising them, caring for them, and educating them. And it includes caring for the grown-ups, too: feeding them, providing them with rest and recreation, keeping them healthy and strong – and then sending them back to work, lunchbox packed, on Monday morning.

Most of the work that goes into reproduction occurs inside the home, away from the prying eyes of supply and demand. No money changes hands, no profits are made, and the value of output is not even counted in the GDP statistics. For this reason, most economists tend to ignore reproduction as a private, non-economic matter.

But this is a terrible mistake. The economics (and politics) of reproduction (broadly defined) have huge consequences for how the rest of the economy functions – everything from consumer spending to labour supply to education to pensions. The economics of reproduction are also essential to understanding economic inequality between men and women, and between different cultural and racial groups – not to mention understanding how to reduce that inequality.

Recall from earlier chapters that about 85 percent of households in developed capitalist economies depend on wage labour. They own no economically meaningful property, and must sell their labour in a paid job to support themselves and their families. This means that most households in society are worker households. And for the

most part, when households reproduce themselves, they reproduce *workers*. In this sense, households form a crucial link in the overall economic chain of capitalism. Production is where private businesses hire workers to produce goods and services for profit. Reproduction is where families buy back some of what they produce in order to reproduce the workers who produced it in the first place.

Indeed, when the classical economists were first studying wage determination in the new capitalist system, they thought of the household much like a worker-producing factory. For them, the "cost" of labour (its wage) should equal its cost of "production" – that is, the direct cost of feeding, clothing, and caring for workers, not to mention producing brand new little workers to eventually take their place on the assembly line. That's why the classical economists concluded that wages would settle at a level just high enough to pay for workers' physical subsistence. Marx had a similar view, although he accepted that social and political factors would also influence wage levels.

Today, of course, most workers (in the developed economies, at any rate) make much more than what's required simply to stay alive. This can be understood in two alternative, equivalent ways: either the (social and cultural) definition of "subsistence" has expanded over time to reflect new standards of what is considered minimal, or else workers have fought to win themselves a share of the economic surplus (allowing a better standard of living than mere subsistence).

Either way, the economic reality is that most households still spend all their income on the goods and services which they and their families need to survive and enjoy life. While they don't live solely to reproduce themselves (and many people are not interested in having children, for various reasons), giving their children a good start in life is nevertheless a central, life-defining goal for most families. In this way, understanding the household as a "factory" which produces workers may seem rather unromantic – but is probably not too far off the mark.

The economics of households

The work performed in households directly accounts for over one-third of all economic output (and even more in less developed economies). Since household output is not sold in a market, it is hard to value. Most household work involves caring for family members, cooking, cleaning, and other household tasks. Women do much more than half of it, yet they have little control over it. Reproductive work is a pivotal way that unequal economic roles for women and men are perpetuated.

Household work has changed dramatically over time, reflecting economic, technological, and cultural trends. Moreover, the boundaries which distinguish the household from the rest of the economy are fuzzy. For example, just like any workplace, capital equipment (tools) is used to perform household work faster and better. As income levels rise, families purchase more tools (dishwashers, vacuum cleaners, ovens, small appliances) to reduce their household labour. In this way, the purchase of manufactured goods (which are counted in GDP statistics) gradually replaces some unpaid labour (which is not counted in GDP).

Another way households (especially higher-income families) reduce their domestic labour is by hiring someone else to do it. This includes eating prepared meals from restaurants; hiring maids, gardeners, and other household labour; and hiring nannies to care for children. Thus some unpaid household labour is replaced with marketed, paid labour (which, like dishwashers and vacuum cleaners, is included in GDP). Usually that paid reproductive work is also performed by women, often from lower-income racial and cultural groups.

Finally, governments have assumed some of the duties of reproduction through the expansion of public services like schools, child care centres, old age homes, and hospitals. These facilities perform services that were once delivered inside the home. Their public provision (also counted in GDP) generally leads to higher-quality services, more access to the services by lower-income people, relatively well-paid jobs for women, and less burden on family members. Under neoliberalism, however, there has been some effort to shift some caring work (such as child care and elder care) back to private households.

For all of these reasons – household industrialization, purchases of commercial household services, and the growth of public services – the importance of unpaid household labour to the overall economy has declined steadily in recent decades. Meanwhile, women have transferred more of their own work effort from the home to the paid labour market, even though they're still saddled with an unfair share of household duties when they get home from their paying jobs. Nevertheless, the unpaid work that goes on inside households is still very important to our overall work and output.

Apart from their work and production, households perform other important economic functions. Most CONSUMPTION occurs within the household, through the many different goods and services which families buy and use. In developed capitalist economies, private consumption spending accounts for half or more of GDP. ▦ * Most households spend essentially all their income on consumption, and hence their SAVINGS are non-existent. (In fact, more and more households go into debt to finance consumption.) This is why (as indicated in Chapter 7) most families own little or no financial wealth.

Households are also in charge of LABOUR SUPPLY: deciding how many workers to provide to the formal labour market, for how many hours, and at what periods in their lives. Of course, labour supply decisions are always shaped by the essential, coercive challenge facing working-class households: they have to work to survive. Moreover, labour

---

* See the Economics for Everyone website for statistics, www.economicsforeveryone.com.

supply decisions are not independent from labour demand. Usually, jobs must be available before individuals bother seeking one (that's why labour supply tends to rise in good economic times, and fall during recessions). But household attitudes toward work and income can also have some independent influence over labour supply. If for cultural or other reasons households prefer to reduce their labour supply (by retiring earlier, staying home to raise children, or staying longer in college), then there will be fewer workers available, and the labour market pressures facing employers will be more binding. On the other hand, if households maximize labour supply in order to afford the latest consumer goods (working overtime or multiple jobs, or working later in life), then employers benefit from a more abundant and available workforce.

Finally, most households also directly undertake one economically important type of investment: in their homes. If the household is viewed as a site of production, then the building where that production occurs is the household's most important (and expensive) capital asset. In the developed Anglo-Saxon economies, over two-thirds of households own their own home, and this proportion has grown over time. Apart from providing shelter, home-ownership also constitutes the major wealth owned by most families, and is thus an important feature of household finances. Unlike most consumer spending (which tends to be quite stable in relation to income levels), home purchases are less predictable. In response to changes in unemployment, interest rates, and other economic trends, home purchases can fluctuate rapidly. The resulting ups and downs of the home construction and renovation industry can play a leading role in determining overall economic growth.

Women, men, and work

The economic activities of the household are fundamentally tied up with different economic roles played by women and men. For starters, the division of unpaid labour within the home is very unequal: women do more of this work than men, they perform different types of unpaid work from men (more caring, cleaning, and cooking), and the work they do generally has lower "status" and recognition than the work performed by men. This division of labour reflects sexist attitudes that women are "naturally" better-suited to caring work (based, in part, on the fact that they give birth to babies), and that men shouldn't have to do so much around the home since they work outside of the home. This sexism is reinforced by a complex mixture of tradition, religion, economic pressures, and sometimes even violence.

The inequality of men's and women's labour market experience reinforces, and is reinforced by, the inequality of their economic position within the home. Women usually earn less than men, and so some families make a supposedly "rational" choice that the woman should stay home to care for children (since her foregone wages are less than the man's). The lack of affordable and quality child care services in most countries plays a negative role in these decisions, too. Then, because men work hard in their paid jobs, many refuse to do their share of work at home. (This argument doesn't seem to work for women: women with paid jobs still have to work their "double shift.") The fact that women's career paths are often interrupted by childbirth, child rearing, or other domestic duties (like caring for sick or elderly family members) further undermines their ability to advance their careers and earn higher wages, reinforcing all of the above trends.

There has been incremental progress toward greater economic equality for women in most developed economies, but it hasn't come easily. Most women now participate in paid work, and PARTICIPATION RATES (which measure the proportion of working-age persons in the paid labour market) for men and women are converging. As shown in Figure 9.1, this is partly because men's labour market participation declined somewhat under neoliberalism (due to deteriorating job conditions).

The Nordic countries, which support women's paid work with extensive public services and labour rights, have achieved the highest levels of female labour force participation – as high as 80 percent of working-age women. Liberal social attitudes in most Anglo-Saxon economies have promoted relatively high female participation there, too. Continental European countries have lower female participation, reflecting a combination of outdated attitudes and unsupportive public programs. Women's growing paid work expands their personal incomes and enhances their power within the family. But since they are still required to do most household labour, this progress has come at a considerable cost of stress and exhaustion. In some countries (like the Netherlands), women are concentrated in part-time work; this undermines earnings equality, but may make it easier to juggle paid work and home responsibilities.

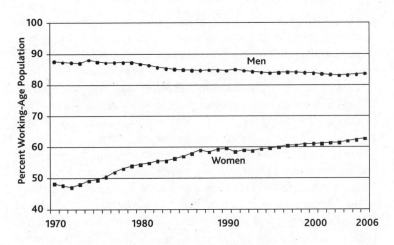

Figure 9.1   Men and Women's Labour Force Participation
OECD Average

Source: Organization for Economic Cooperation and Development.

There are three different reasons why women continue to earn much less than men in paid work, despite the gradual narrowing of the economic gender gap:

- Women still earn less than equally qualified men working in comparable jobs; this reflects both pure DISCRIMINATION, and the constraints placed on women's paid work opportunities by their domestic responsibilities (such as interrupted career paths, or the impossibility of working overtime).

- Women's employment is concentrated in jobs which tend to pay less; this reflects an intense LABOUR MARKET SEGMENTATION, sometimes called women's "job ghettos." Women are disproportionately represented in lower-paying jobs in service industries (such as retail work and personal services) and caring professions.

- Due to career interruptions and a greater reliance on part-time work, women work fewer hours in paid jobs than men (especially measured on a lifetime basis).

Putting all these factors together, employed women in the developed economies earn only about half as much as men over their paid working lives (and this doesn't consider women who do not perform paid work). As a result, women are much more likely to experience poverty than men. Poverty rates are especially high for two groups of single women: single mothers and single pensioners.

Further reducing the economic gaps between men and women will require several strategies to transfer more reproductive work to men and to public programs. Men must be challenged to pick up a larger share of unpaid domestic work, including child care. There is some evidence that this is starting to occur, but unevenly and inadequately. One interesting example was provided in France following the introduction of that country's 35-hour working week in the 1990s; surveys indicated that men's contribution to unpaid domestic labour grew significantly in subsequent years. Indeed, changes in paid employment practices will be important to assist both women and men to balance paid work with domestic responsibilities. It will take sustained pressure on private employers (from individual workers, unions, and governments) to force them to pay more than lip service to the challenge of work–family balance. Finally, public services must be expanded, to take up more of the reproductive responsibilities that still fall on women's shoulders. The sorely inadequate child and elder care systems which exist in most economies (with the exception of Nordic countries) are only the most glaring example of this need.

It is possible (though not inevitable) that labour markets in developed countries will become "tighter" in coming years, leading to lower unemployment rates and more labour recruitment headaches for employers. If so, this will be a great opportunity for working women, and working households more generally, to demand more support from both employers and governments for the challenging task of combining production and reproduction.

10

Closing the Little Circle

Meet the players

The previous chapters of Part Two introduced the major actors in the economy and their assigned tasks. This chapter now summarizes how they all fit together in a circular loop that reflects the repeating cycle of the economy: work, production (with tools), distribution, consumption, and reproduction. These are the core functions and relationships that make up capitalism. We'll even draw a simple map of this circular system. We'll call this map the "little circle." In later chapters, our map will get bigger as we consider more of capitalism's real-world complexity (including the roles of competition, the environment, banks, government, and globalization).

You can't tell the players without a program, so here's a handy listing of the key actors, what they do, and where they work and live:

- **Workers** These people (and their families) make up roughly 85 percent of the population of advanced capitalist economies. They own no economically meaningful property (other than, for many, their own homes). To survive, they must sell their labour for wages and salaries to private companies, which they do not meaningfully own or control. At any point in time some workers are unemployed, supported by their families or by government income security programs; even though these people are not currently employed, they are still workers.

- **Capitalists** These people (and their families) make up less than 5 percent of the population of advanced capitalist economies. They own the clear majority of financial wealth (including most business wealth – via either direct ownership of companies, or large holdings of corporate shares). They also control the operation of large businesses, either directly as owner-managers or indirectly through their appointment of professional executives (who themselves own important portions of the businesses they run). Hired employees do most of the work in these businesses. Capitalists do not need to work to survive, since their ownership of financial wealth can generate enough income to live very comfortably. However, many do work (including as managers of their own firms), and that work is productive (unlike their status as owners – which is not, in and of itself, productive).

- **Small business owners**   These people (and their families) make up roughly 10 percent of the population of advanced capitalist economies (more in less developed countries). They work, nominally for themselves, in small companies or farms, in which they (and often their family members) perform most of the work required for production. Those businesses may sell goods and services to consumers (like a neighbourhood corner store) or to other, larger businesses (like a photocopy shop). Either way, they are always dependent on the more important, central "loop" of capitalism: namely, the decisions by larger businesses to invest, hire labour, and produce. The profits received by small business owners reflect a combination of hard work and their status as owners. But most can be safely ascribed to their work effort, since the total incomes of most small business owners are no higher than the wages and salaries of paid workers, even though they generally work longer hours. (To keep our map nice and simple, we don't draw small businesses directly, reflecting their small share of the population and their subsidiary economic status.)

- **Worker households**   This is where wage-labourers live and reproduce themselves. They raise and educate children; feed, clothe, and care for each other (including sick and elderly family members); and spend essentially all of their wages and salaries to buy the consumer goods and services that they need to survive and enjoy life. A great deal of unpaid, unmarketed work occurs inside the household, most of it performed by women.

- **Capitalist households**   The capitalists live here, and in fine style. Like workers, they also buy goods and services for consumption: in greater quantities than workers, and higher quality. Some of their income (most of which comes from profits or their financial wealth) is saved – presumably to be re-invested back into their companies.

• **Private companies**   Workers go here to perform their labour in return for wages and salaries. The capitalist (or a hired executive) also works here, to organize production and supervise and discipline the workers. The output of this work is a good or service which the company then sells. Hopefully, the resulting sales revenue is sufficient to cover wages and salaries, the wear and tear of machinery, and any raw materials or inputs used in production. What's left is a bottom-line profit for the owner. The output from these companies is sold into three distinct markets. Worker households buy run-of-the-mill consumer goods. Capitalist households buy luxury consumption goods. And other companies buy things (like machinery, equipment, and supplies) needed for production. If for some reason the company can't sell its output, the capitalist will never see the hoped-for profits, and production will slow or stop altogether. (We will discuss how and why this actually happens in Chapter 24.)

Follow the money

We've introduced the main players. Now let's sit back and watch the show. Figure 10.1 overleaf illustrates how these players interact with each other, in a normal day (or year) of work.

In addition to the players and places introduced above, our map also illustrates the major flows of money resulting from their productive activity. We label these money flows with shorthand symbols commonly used in economics. Like a forensic accountant trying to solve a corporate fraud, following the trail of money around the circle is a good way to understand what actually happens as capitalism unfolds. In fact, there's a whole branch of economics – called *circuit theory* – based on "following the money" in this manner.

Let's discuss each flow of money, in the order in which it appears on the economic stage:

Step 1: **Investment (I)**   Before anything else happens in capitalism, the capitalist must decide to make an initial investment: establishing their company and starting production. This requires an initial expenditure on FIXED CAPITAL (including the workplace itself, and all the machinery and tools inside). The capitalist must also invest in WORKING CAPITAL, to pay the initial wages of the company's employees and meet other day-to-day expenses. Workers must be paid every week or two; they

Figure 10.1   Economic Road Map: Little Circle

can't wait for production to finish and the product to be sold before getting their wages, and hence the capitalist needs a certain revolving fund of cash to get production started. (After a full cycle of production has occurred, the company can use some of its revenues to pay for wages and other expenses in the next production cycle.)

This initial investment creates new jobs in its own right (both inside the company itself, and in the companies which produce capital equipment, raw materials, and other inputs). Even more crucially, this initial investment pushes the "Start" button on the whole process of production. Investment is the most important form of spending required for the successful functioning of capitalism. When investment is strong, capitalism is vibrant and growing. When investment is weak, capitalism stagnates.

Where did the capitalist get the money to make this initial investment? We'll discuss this in Chapters 16–18, when we discuss money, banking, finance, and stock markets. For now, all we need to know is that the capitalist just needs a credible business plan and a bit of start-up equity; they can then borrow all the additional funds they need, in one way or another, from the financial system. Importantly, the capitalist doesn't need to first *save* the money in order to *invest* it. This is how neoclassical economists assume investment works, but (thankfully) it doesn't happen this way in practice: in fact, if investors actually needed real savings on hand before making any investments, capitalism would grind to a halt.

Step 2: **Wages (W)**   Once workers start their new jobs and perform their work, they begin to earn wages and salaries.

Step 3: **Consumption (C)**   The take-home pay earned by workers doesn't gather dust. As soon as they get their first paycheques, workers start spending. (In fact, thanks to credit cards, workers – like capitalists – can start spending long before that first paycheque arrives!) In aggregate, workers spend all their income on consumer goods and services, which are consumed inside the home to reproduce themselves and their families (and, hopefully, enjoy life a bit in the process). Most of what is spent on consumption goes back to the private companies who produced those goods and services in the first place. A smaller portion is directed to small businesses for the services they provide; small businesses in turn spend the money they receive to purchase inputs for their own businesses, and consumer goods for their own families.

Workers' consumption is the largest single expenditure that occurs in the economy. But it is also the most predictable. In effect, "workers spend what they get," and hence worker consumption spending closely tracks employment and wage levels.

Step 4: **Profit** (Π) Assuming the private company successfully sells its output and generates enough revenue to cover its costs, it then pays a profit back to its owner (the capitalist). Indeed, the hunger for profit was the motive that got the whole ball rolling in the first place. (Capitalists certainly don't invest their own money as a public service.) The capitalist eventually expects to get back their initial investment, plus some profit margin on top of that (otherwise why would they bother?). The Greek letter *pi*, or Π, is commonly used in economics to symbolize profit – perhaps because it resembles the ostentatious faux pillars which some modern capitalists erect at the entrances to their mansions! If the capitalist borrowed some of the money for the initial investment, then some of the resulting profit must be paid back to the lender (like a bank) as interest.

What do capitalists do with their profit? Generally, it doesn't gather dust either. (If it does, then the economy will experience a recession.) Some of it is spent on the luxury consumption of capitalist households (we call that $C_\Diamond$ on the map, with the luxurious diamond distinguishing it from workers' more humble consumption). The rest is set aside to be re-invested (in the next cycle) in the capitalist's business: both to replace the wear and tear of the company's capital assets, and to eventually expand the company's total output.

For completeness, we could also draw smaller flows of profits going to small business owners, and smaller flows for their own consumer spending and investment. This would make our diagram very complicated. For now, just keep in mind that small businesses play a subsidiary role in capitalism: they depend on the larger flows of corporate investment and worker consumption that are shown in the map.

Reading the map

This map is a vast simplification of how capitalism actually works. But we can already learn some very important lessons by studying it. First, there are two broad categories of arrows (or money flows) on the map: those which flow from companies to households (both worker households and capitalist households), and those which flow from households back to companies. The arrows flowing from companies to households represent flows of *income* (wages and profits). The arrows flowing back to companies represent forms of *expenditure* (mass consumption, luxury consumption, and investment).

Ultimately, the total flow of income will equal the total flow of expenditure. We summarize this in Table 10.1.

Table 10.1   Income and Expenditure: Little Circle

Class	Income	Expenditure
Workers	Wages (W)	Worker Consumption (C)
Capitalists	+ Profits (Π)	+ Luxury Consumption (C_0)
		+ Investment (I)
	= Total Income	= Total Expenditure

The centre column of this table shows the total income of the economy. The right column shows total expenditure. These are in fact the two methods that statistical agencies use to add up the total value of GDP (which excludes, remember, the value of unpaid work inside the home). The "GDP by income" tables report labour income, profits (broken down into corporate profits, depreciation, investment income, and small business profits), and some other, smaller categories of income. The "GDP by expenditure" tables report consumption, investment, and other forms of spending (such as government consumption and exports) that we haven't considered yet. (Visit the Economics for Everyone website for a how-to guide on reading and interpreting GDP statistics.)

Recall that we identified two broad kinds of consumption: workers' mass consumption (C) and capitalists' luxury consumption (C_0). Mass consumption (C) in the right column of Table 10.1 tends to equal workers' wages (W) in the centre. Unlike workers, however, capitalists have a meaningful choice regarding how to spend their income: on luxury consumption, or reinvesting in their businesses. How much they consume, and how much they invest, will influence how strong the economy is today, and how fast it grows in the future. In earlier times, frugal capitalists tended to reinvest most of their profits, and hence capitalism developed quickly.

Today, however, capitalists consume much of their profit (or find other unproductive uses for some of it, like financial speculation), and this has been associated with a visible slowing of business investment during the years of neoliberalism. Indeed, if the goal of neoliberalism was to strengthen investment and growth, then it has clearly failed: despite new powers and freedom, the world's capitalists invest less of their profit than in previous epochs.

Where's the work?

Our map locates the main players in the basic economic loop that is capitalism, and the major flows of money that link them. Don't forget, though, that it is ultimately work that explains production, not money. What actual work is performed in this system, and where?

We discussed the main forms of work that occur in capitalism in Chapter 5. The biggest share of work is performed by workers in private firms in return for wages and salaries. Their work is supplemented there by the work of their owners and top managers. Another large share of work is performed, without pay, inside households. Smaller amounts of work are performed in small businesses.

Part Three

Capitalism as a System

11

Competition

Kill or be killed

Part Two of this book outlined the basic functions and relationships that define capitalism: between the owners of private companies (who invest in hopes of generating a profit), and the workers who perform most of the productive labour in those companies (in return for wages and salaries). The "little circle" we drew in Chapter 10 illustrated the cycle of production, income, and spending linking one particular firm, its owner, and its workers.

In the real world, however, there isn't just one private company. There are many thousands of them. And they cannot focus only on keeping their own workers in line, extracting maximum work effort for minimum cost, and making sure their businesses operate efficiently and profitably. They also have to worry about the economic threat posed by competing firms, who are also trying to maximize their own profits.

Competition – ruthless, unforgiving, to-the-death competition – is a crucial feature of capitalism. It opens up new opportunities for individual firms: they can expand revenues and profits by winning a larger share of sales from competitors. But competition also poses new challenges, since other companies are trying to do the same thing – capture more market share at the expense of competitors. It's not just *greed* that motivates company efforts to minimize costs and maximize profits; with competition, it's also *fear*. If a company can't stand up to the competition, it's not just that they won't make quite as much profit as other companies. Far worse, eventually they will be destroyed by these competing firms producing better products at lower cost.

For most people, fear is usually a more powerful motivator than greed, and this is true for companies, too. Most of the behaviours exhibited by companies in the modern economy – the good, the bad, and the ugly – are motivated, and indeed *enforced*, by competitive pressures from other companies. This pressure leads companies to do dramatic, innovative, often painful and even destructive things – not solely because their owners and executives are greedy, but because they desperately want to stay in business. Competition is thus the disciplining force that compels companies to act in particular ways. And in so doing, competition ensures that the whole system behaves in particular ways.

Locating competition: Y vs Z

Figure 11.1 reproduces our "little circle" map from the last chapter. But this time, there are two companies operating side by side in the middle of the circle, not one. Company Y and Company Z produce similar products – let's say they manufacture televisions – and they sell into the same general market (households who want a new TV). Both firms also hire their workers from the same general community of worker households. Each firm has its respective capitalist owner, who wants to see their own firm succeed and the other firm fail. But each owner also measures the profit they earn from their company

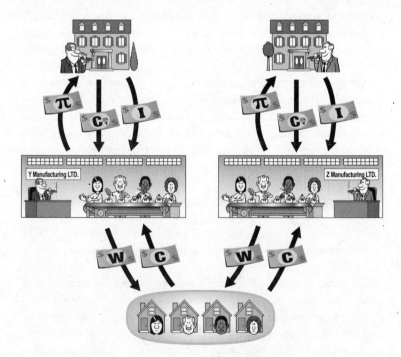

Figure 11.1   Economic Road Map: Competition

against the general rate of profit earned by other companies (including the competing television manufacturer).

Figure 11.1 therefore highlights the three distinct places where the two companies confront each other. The most important is in the market for new TVs – or what economists call the PRODUCT MARKET. Here each company must convince customers that its TV offers superior quality for a lower price. If they can't do this, then they won't sell the televisions they have carefully produced, and the owner will never earn a profit.

Companies Y and Z also compete in the labour market. In practice, the labour market rarely "runs out" of workers – that is, there usually exists a comfortable cushion of unemployment, from which companies can hire new workers when needed. Nevertheless, a company's ability to recruit, hire, and discipline new workers affects its overall performance. When companies must compete with other employers for labour, their power over their workers is somewhat reduced. (This is why large companies often locate major facilities in rural or semi-rural areas, where they will be the dominant employer; or concentrate their hiring among particular neighbourhoods, demographic groups, or cultural communities where they can carve out a similar slice of the labour market for their own use.)

Finally, companies must also compete for capital. Again, as with labour, this is not to imply that there is a fixed amount of capital which will get allocated to one company or the other. Rather, capital is actually *created* (through the financial system) whenever a capitalist decides to invest (we'll discuss this process in more detail in Part Four). But a company must still generate a competitive rate of profit for its owners, or else they will stop investing. And through incremental investment decisions, capital can eventually "move" from less profitable countries, industries, or companies toward more profitable ones. Indeed, one crucial outcome of competition is that it tends to *equalize* the rates of profit paid out across different firms or industries.

"Perfect competition" and real-world competition

Neoclassical economists rely heavily on an idealized notion of competition, which they call PERFECT COMPETITION. Perfect competition is one of the most bizarre ideas in the whole of economics. It was not designed to explain reality: competition in capitalism has *never* resembled perfect competition. Instead, it was designed to provide intellectual justification for a theory: the Walrasian theory of general equilibrium, which claims that free-market exchange is the best way to maximize human well-being. Without perfect competition, the Walrasian model cannot sustain this claim. (And as we saw in earlier chapters, there are other reasons why the Walrasian theory fails, too.)

In perfect competition, individual firms are tiny. They cannot grow bigger, because neoclassical theory assumes that their average production costs rise as they grow (due to a process called "diminishing marginal returns"). This assumption is quite wrong. In reality, larger companies have clear cost advantages in producing most goods and services. They must pay for overhead costs (like factories, equipment, engineering, and marketing) before they produce their first unit of output. After that, average costs fall dramatically as the volume of output grows (since overhead expenses get spread over a larger volume of output), and this is a powerful stimulus for companies to grow.

Table 11.1   **Economies of Scale: Hypothetical Television Manufacturer**

Overhead Cost (Fixed Cost): $100 million
(capital equipment, engineering, marketing)

Extra Costs per Unit (Variable Cost): $200
(materials, parts, labour)

Output	Fixed Cost	Variable Cost (output * $200)	Average Cost (per TV)
1	$100 million	$200	$100,000,200
1,000	$100 million	$200,000	$100,200
100,000	$100 million	$20 million	$1,200
1,000,000	$100 million	$200 million	$300
10,000,000	$100 million	$2 billion	$210

An example of this is provided in Table 11.1. To get into the television business in the first place, Company Z has to spend $100 million on capital equipment, engineering, and marketing. The very first TV set to come off the assembly line therefore costs over $100 million: the total overhead cost, plus the roughly $200 in materials and labour that are built into the TV set itself. But average costs then decline quickly, as output grows. If the "going" price for a new TV is about \$300, Company Z has to be able to produce (and sell) over a million units before it will hope to earn any profit at all. This example is quite realistic, and explains why there is only room, even in the global economy, for just a few television manufacturers. This powerful arithmetic also explains why small companies cannot compete in most industries, and why companies always try to boost sales and make better use of fixed capacity (something neoclassical theories don't allow for). Growing sales generate a double benefit for firms: higher revenues, along with lower average costs. An industry is said to demonstrate ECONOMIES OF SCALE when average production costs tend to decline as the volume of output grows.

In addition to the false assumption that all firms are tiny, there are several other equally unrealistic aspects to the theory of perfect competition. Firms are assumed to produce completely identical products (so that consumers can't tell the difference between one variety of a product and another). They cannot influence market trends through advertising or other efforts. And they cannot try to anticipate or respond to the behaviour of their competitors. In this theory, competition is so intense and anonymous that it actually *eliminates* profits altogether: prices are driven to such a low level that companies can only just cover the costs of the inputs they hired (such as labour and borrowed capital), leaving no bottom-line profit whatsoever. Why any capitalist would bother investing in a private company in this environment is one of the great unanswered questions of neoclassical economics.

Real-world competition is very different from this strange notion – but it is still real, powerful, and unforgiving. Importantly, the fact that companies can be very large in no way implies that competition has become less intense. The incredible resources, technology, and managerial abilities that modern large corporations have at their disposal allow them to compete in ways, and in places, that were never before feasible.

Table 11.2 summarizes the key ways in which the reality of competition differs from the idealized neoclassical theory. The larger a company becomes, in general, the lower its production costs become (thanks to economies of scale). What prevents a single company from then taking over the whole market, on the basis of scale efficiencies? Consumers generally want some choice in their purchases (and hence will buy competing brands for the sake of variety). Financial investors will recoil at the increasing investment risks they would face if all their

Table 11.2   Contrasting Theories of Competition

Issue	Neoclassical "Perfect Competition"	Real-World Competition
Firm size	Firms are tiny, and there is an infinite number of them	Firms can be very large; a few thousand dominate the world economy
Impact of firm size on costs	Average production costs increase for bigger firms due to diminishing returns	Average production costs decrease for bigger firms due to economies of scale
Limit on size of firm	Diminishing returns, rising costs	Consumers' desire for variety, increasing risk to investors, threat of entry by new firms
Relationship to other firms	Firms cannot guess what other firms will do; competition is anonymous	Firms observe and react to the actions of competing firms; competition is strategic
Ability to influence market	Firms cannot influence prices or sales volumes	Firms strive to influence prices and sales volumes
Product differentiation	Consumers cannot tell the output of one firm from another; products are homogeneous	Firms invest in research and advertising to distinguish their products; products are differentiated
Competition and profits	Firms do not make *any* "pure" profits, over and above market payments to hired inputs (wages, interest)	Firms strive to earn "pure" profits with differentiated products, unique production methods, or unique cost advantages

eggs, in any particular industry, had to be placed in one company's basket. And if one company becomes too large (especially if it gets lazy, enjoying its dominant position), other companies will try to challenge (or "contest") the market with new products, technologies, or production methods. Even the *threat* of this occurring can be a powerful disciplining force on large companies.

Meanwhile, companies keep working to create unique or novel features in their particular products. Sometimes this is done in genuine ways (with real technical innovations), sometimes in utterly phony ways (such as the billions of dollars spent on ads claiming that one brand of jeans is sexier than the others). Unique technologies, production methods, and cost savings can also give a firm a unique ability to earn profits (over and above the "normal" returns to employed inputs). Those profits are what lure the corporate leaders; the threat of economic extinction motivates the followers.

Today enormous global companies can be driven from business if, for whatever reason, they lose the competitive battle. Think of General Motors, which for decades was the largest company in the world – and more recently has teetered on the brink of bankruptcy thanks to competitive gains by other enormous corporations (like Toyota, which recently surpassed GM in total vehicle sales). And bankruptcy for smaller and medium-sized businesses is a frequent event. Meanwhile, footloose investors (utilizing new financial tactics, such as PRIVATE EQUITY) can meaningfully threaten to enter any industry, in any country, to challenge market leaders.

The largest companies are bigger than ever, they have unprecedented resources at their disposal, and incredible ability to reach into markets around the world. In large part *because* of this size, not *in spite* of it, there's no doubt that competition in capitalism is fiercer than ever. But is that a good thing?

The consequences of competition

Clearly there's nowhere to run, nowhere to hide, in the brave new world of uber-competition. If even the world's largest corporations aren't safe, who is? Neoclassical economists celebrate competition as an efficiency-enhancing force. Governments, more often than not, agree, and this had led them to enact laws promoting and enforcing competition. But is competition always a useful, beneficial force? Certainly not.

To be sure, the competitive struggle to survive elicits some forms of business behaviour that are genuinely efficient. These can translate into broad social benefits (assuming that new efficiency is shared, one way or another, with workers and consumers). Spurred by competition, managers will work hard to imagine ways of producing better products, and better processes (that is, ways of producing goods and services more efficiently). This leads to more investment in both capital equipment and technology. Competition also allows consumers some degree of choice in their purchases. It thus imposes a particular form of accountability on companies to deliver high-quality, competitively-priced output. (Of course, all too often the range of "choice" provided by capitalist competition is rather monotonous. Competition in the fast food industry ensures that consumers can clog their arteries in several different, but equally unappetizing, ways!) Table 11.3 lists some of the positive responses to competitive pressure.

Table 11.3 Competition: the Good, the Bad, and the Ugly

Positive Effects of Competition:

Innovation	Companies try to develop new products, and more efficient production systems.
Choice, accountability	Consumers can go to a competing firm if they are not satisfied with the price of quality of output.
Quality	Firms must try to improve the quality of their output or service, or else lose customers.
Investment	To earn more profit, some firms will invest in capital equipment and research & development.

Negative Effects of Competition:

Unacceptable cost-cutting	Firms will try to cut wages and benefits, and increase the intensity of work, imposing costs on their workers.
Externalize costs	Firms will shift their costs onto others if it improves their competitive position (example: pollution).
Wasteful differentiation	Firms spend vast amounts on advertising to differentiate their products; often they "trick" consumers (example: excess packaging).
Wasteful duplication	If competition is too intense then all companies in an industry may operate below efficient scale, resulting in wasteful duplication.
Inadequate profits	If competition is too intense, struggling companies will have inadequate profits to invest in high-quality output or innovation.
Poaching	Firms will be unwilling to invest in (non-patentable) innovation, or in higher-skilled workers, for fear that competitors will copy or poach.
Battle costs	Firms invest in activities which are not efficient or productive, but which undermine the position of competitors (example: aggressive marketing, sabotage).
Dislocation costs	When companies fail, owners lose vast sums of capital, workers lose their jobs, and communities suffer spin-off losses.

System-Wide Effects of Competition:

Profit equalization	Rates of profit tend to equalize across companies and industries (assuming there is freedom of entry).
Herd mentality	Many companies follow each other's strategies, entering or exiting particular activities at the same time.
Cycles	The herd mentality of competing firms creates unplanned booms and busts in overall activity.
Uneven development	Competition has winners and losers, and they are distributed in "clumps" (not evenly); as a result, some companies, sectors, regions, and even entire countries grow and prosper, while others decline.

At the same time, however, competition imposes many economic and social costs, as well. We can't ignore these costs. Competition can also lead to irrational or destructive outcomes for the whole system. The downside of competition is summarized in Table 11.3. Some of the downsides are exactly opposite to the upsides, indicating the complex and often contradictory character of real-world competition.

Companies will respond to competition by cutting costs in any ways imaginable – including by reducing wages or intensifying work in socially damaging ways. They may even try to shift their costs onto others, through a phenomenon called EXTERNALITIES: if they can find ways (often underhanded or even illegal) to impose costs of their operations on innocent parties, then their own bottom line is strengthened. Ways of doing this include pollution, the sale of unsafe products, and forcing consumers of their products to bear hidden or unexpected costs. Remember that having a product that's differentiated in the minds of consumers is a key source of competitive profit. Companies try to create this differentiation in ways that are wasteful, useless, or even destructive: massive (and often misleading) advertising, excess packaging (to make products look "bigger"), and artificial obsolescence (where products are deliberately designed to wear out or become useless prematurely). Companies will not invest in innovations which they can't patent, for fear that competitors will simply copy them. For similar reasons, private firms consistently underinvest in on-the-job training and skills development for their workers, since they worry those trained workers may subsequently be hired away (or "poached") by competitors. Yet ironically, companies *will* spend money on attempts to frustrate or undermine their competitors' strategies (for example, by spying, sabotaging, or needlessly duplicating their competitors' projects). This spending is utterly unproductive in economic terms.

Competition can clearly be too intense. It may result in all companies in an industry operating below their normal efficient scale of production, imposing a wasteful duplication of excess capacity. It can drive profits too low, undermining the ability of firms to invest in new capital or research & development (R&D). Companies which are utterly challenged just to survive will produce inferior products, simply because they cannot invest in higher quality. If all companies in an industry suffer from the same over-competition, then the whole industry will be marked by shoddy, stagnant, even unsafe products. And when companies fail, both their owners and workers suffer massive economic losses. Competition is not, therefore, "free." It constantly imposes real and substantial costs on the economy, which must always be evaluated against its much-heralded benefits.

The politics of competition

In Chapter 8 we discussed the complicated economic relationships between owners and workers. The interests of these two great sides often conflict, but sometimes they can converge. A private company's interest in maximizing profits gives it a powerful, ongoing incentive to minimize wages and maximize work intensity, at the expense of its workers. On the other hand, when productivity is growing then companies can "buy" the loyalty of workers (if they feel pressured to do so) by sharing that productivity dividend through higher incomes, without undermining profits.

Competition between firms adds another layer of complexity to these relationships. Now the workers at one particular company will be tempted to identify even further with their own employer, in the competitive battle against other companies. This commonality of interest doesn't go very deep. Workers as a whole still want better wages and safer, more enjoyable jobs; and employers as a whole still want lower wages and higher intensity. But when the choice seems to be between working harder for less money for your specific employer, or losing your job when that employer goes out of business altogether, then many workers will indeed start to identify with the employer.

It is the task of unions and political activists to try to convey a broader perspective on these trade-offs. Worker restraint or concessions at one company may be copied at others, in which case they've had no impact at all on the balance of competition (all they've done is reduce wages at *both* companies). And workers have a general interest in shifting the balance of economic power in their favour (through government policy changes as well as organizing efforts at particular workplaces), regardless of the competitive strengths and weaknesses of any particular company.

The seemingly impersonal logic of competition has been "internalized" by many people, including many workers. It seems they will often accept painful changes – even the loss of their job – if those changes seem to be the anonymous result of "market forces." Individual workers rarely have any meaningful influence over the fate of the company they work for, so they shouldn't take its failures (or its successes, for that matter) personally. Nevertheless, the anonymous and seemingly neutral pressures of competition are invoked to justify incredible pain and dislocation: if a company folds and all its workers lose their jobs, it's somehow fair because "they just couldn't compete." But we shouldn't forget that "competition" is nothing more than the way we experience the efforts of different companies (and their owners) to boost their profits at the expense of others. It is not a natural or inevitable force, it does not (in and of itself) justify anything, and people who are negatively affected should still complain about it.

12
Investment and Growth

Investment, and why it matters

We learned in Part Two of this book that the initial decision by a capitalist to invest in a private profit-making business is the first and most important step in the cyclical process of production, income, and consumption. Without it, nothing else happens.

When we speak of investment in this context, we are thinking of a real expenditure on buildings, machinery and equipment, or any other tangible tools used in production. We are not thinking of a *financial* investment (like stocks, bonds, or other financial assets). We will discuss the (weak) relationship between financial investments and real investments in Chapters 16–18. In theory, financial investments are supposed to translate into real capital investments, but in practice it doesn't work that way.

Investment comes in several different forms. The most important is private business investment in FIXED CAPITAL. The two major types of fixed capital are STRUCTURES (buildings, factories, offices, pipelines) and MACHINERY AND EQUIPMENT (machines and tools of all kinds, computers and software, telecommunications equipment, transportation equipment). Businesses also invest smaller amounts in WORKING CAPITAL to pay for day-to-day operating costs. Governments invest in public infrastructure and in the capital assets used by public enterprises (like utilities or schools). Individuals invest in their own homes. Of all these investment flows, business fixed investment is the largest; it is also the most important to the rise and fall of the overall economy.

Capitalists have a two-sided relationship to investment. They experience a range of motivations for making an investment. On the positive side is the hunger for additional profits that comes with a larger operation. Reinforcing this is the threat of competition, which pushes companies to invest in new products or new equipment as a way of creating or maintaining a competitive edge.

At the same time, however, capitalists are very cautious about making new investments. They think carefully about the risk that they might not make a profit, or might even lose their up-front investment altogether. Modern financial institutions (including pension funds and other "institutional" investors) strictly monitor new corporate investments. If they don't think the expected profits are high enough, they will demand that companies reduce their investment spending. So there's never any guarantee that capitalists actually *want* to invest, even though it is their profit motive that drives the whole system. If they don't reinvest their profits, they can always spend them on other things (like luxury consumption or financial speculation), or just store them away in the bank.

For the overall economy, however, there is no doubt that investment is a positive and hugely important economic force. Some of the broader economic benefits of strong investment include:

- **Growth**   Investment spending is the most important source of economic growth under capitalism. (It can be supplemented, at times, by new spending power in the form of exports and government spending.) When investment is strong, economies grow more quickly, and so do incomes. Table 12.1 lists some of the greatest episodes of economic growth and rising living standards in modern economic history. In every case, the expansion was led by very strong investment. Of course, we don't want growth for its own sake: we need the right kinds of growth, and we need active measures to make sure that growth translates into improved living standards for all.

Table 12.1   **Golden Ages of Investment and Labour**

	Investment as Share of GDP	Annual Growth in Real Wages
Europe (1960s)	25%	4%
Japan (1960s and 1970s)	32%	5%
Korea (1990s)	35%	5%
Canada (1960s and 1970s)	23%	3%
Australia (1960–75)	22%	3.5%
China (1995–2005)	38%	5–10%?

Source: Author's calculations from national sources, Organization for Economic Cooperation and Development.

- **Job creation**   In our current simplified economy (illustrated by the map we drew in Chapter 10), almost all paid jobs depend on private investment. In reality, some jobs are also created by government. Nevertheless, the strength of business investment is crucial to employment levels. The relationship between investment and jobs is complex, because sometimes new capital equipment can *replace* workers, resulting in a decrease in employment at a particular firm. The level of *overall* growth and employment, however, still depends very positively on the overall level of business investment.

- **Transformation**   Economies don't just *expand*, they also *evolve* over time: adapting to new technology, new consumer preferences, new social and environmental challenges. Structural and technological changes don't occur seamlessly, however. New technologies, products, and ways of working almost always have to be embodied in new capital (like equipment, buildings, and infrastructure). We need investment, therefore, to allow the economy to incorporate these structural changes.

- **Productivity and competitiveness**   Employers can boost apparent productivity simply by intensifying work – forcing workers to work harder and faster. But that can only go so far. To improve true *efficiency* requires genuine enhancements in products and processes, and this requires investment. Statistical studies have proven that investment in new machinery and equipment is especially important to productivity growth.

- **Environment**   We'll discuss environment concerns in detail in Chapter 15. However, one way to reduce the environmental damage caused by the economy is through major investments in energy-efficient technologies and pollution abatement: high-tech heating and cooling systems, fuel-efficient vehicles, cleaner power generation equipment. Building a more sustainable economy will require massive investments in these green technologies.

In general, because of all these positive "spin-offs" from investment spending, the broader economy has more of a stake in strong business investment than business itself does. In economic language, the *social benefits* of investment spending are greater than the *private benefits* (that is, the benefits pocketed by the private companies which do the investing).

This is why governments regularly implement measures aimed at stimulating more business investment. Some of these measures have been more effective than others. Policies which reward financial investments in the hope that these incentives will boost real investment are generally very ineffective. On the other hand, policies which directly reward real investment expenditure (such as investment tax credits and targeted investment incentives) can be more effective. Eventually, if efforts to entice more business spending are unsuccessful, governments and communities must learn to supplement profit-driven business investment with other forms of public or non-profit investment.

Excessive Influence

"Economic prosperity is excessively dependent on the political and social atmosphere which is congenial to the average business man."

John Maynard Keynes, British economist (1936).

What determines investment?

At a basic level, investment is motivated by the expectation that a capitalist will earn back their money, plus a sufficient profit margin. Investment is therefore a *forward-looking* decision – and this is incredibly important to understanding its behaviour. Capitalists review current business conditions to judge whether an investment will be profitable in the future. But they always temper those judgements with additional information about how the business environment may change. Most investments, after all, are irreversible: once an investment is made in fixed capital, it is impossible to "take it back" for a refund. At best, purchased buildings and equipment can be sold for scrap or salvage (usually for a tiny fraction of the purchase price). So the fact that investment involves long-term, irreversible commitments makes capitalists inherently cautious, and this makes business investment especially hard to predict.

Table 12.2 (overleaf) lists several of the factors influencing the expected profitability of a new investment, and hence influencing investment spending. Current profits are important, as an indication

Table 12.2   Understanding Investment

Determinants of Amount of Investment:

Current profits	Affects expectations of future profits; provides cash to finance new investments.
Capacity utilization	If current capacity is tight, firms are more likely to invest; but if they have spare capacity, then they won't invest even if profits are high.
Current and expected growth	Firms must be confident that they can sell their output.
Interest rates	Low interest rates (and other finance costs) reduce the cost of borrowing, and reduce the appeal of non-productive "paper" investments.
Political, legal environment	Investors want certainty that their property is secure, and that policies will remain business-friendly.

Determinants of Location of Investment:

Unit labour costs	Companies seek places they can extract more labour effort and productivity, for less compensation.
Infrastructure	Companies need reliable infrastructure (such as electricity, transportation, and communications).
Taxes	Firms will be attracted to jurisdictions with lower taxes on profits, and/or which offer investment subsidies.
Transportation costs	A location must be near major suppliers and to major markets; transportation must be reliable and affordable.
Supply chain	Companies must be able to purchase parts, raw materials, and other inputs reliably and affordably.
Local market	Firms often locate their investments near to the major markets where they sell their output.
Trade policy	Tariffs and other trade policies can make it more or less profitable to produce and sell in a particular market.
Political, legal environment	Concerns over legal and political risks can easily overwhelm the appeal of low production costs.

of future profits. Current profits also provide most of the funds for new business investment. Whether a company's existing facilities are being used to the utmost is another crucial factor; this is called CAPACITY UTILIZATION. Even if current profits are high, a company will not invest in new facilities if its existing capacity is still partly idle.

We know that investment causes growth. But it is also true that growth causes investment. If an economy is growing quickly, then companies are likely to expand their investment: they are more confident that they'll be able to sell their output, and it's less likely that they'll have any excess capacity. Investment and growth thus reinforce each other: more investment leads to more growth, which in turn leads to more investment (but only up to a point). Economists call this positive feedback the investment ACCELERATOR effect.

Because of this relationship between investment and growth, investors' collective attitudes can actually become self-fulfilling. If investors are optimistic about the future, they increase their investments. This stimulates growth, strong demand conditions, and healthy profits, thus validating their original optimism. When investors are pessimistic, they cut back their spending. But this undermines growth, sales, and profits – and ironically can actually leave companies worse off than they were *before* they cut their own spending.

At the same time, strong investment can sometimes *undermine* future profits if it generates too much competition (especially from new companies entering an industry) or too much supply. So it's clear that the links between investment, growth, and profits are complex and uncertain, making capitalists extremely cautious before committing to an expensive new investment.

Interest rates (and financing costs more generally) also affect investment spending. When companies borrow external funds to pay for a new investment (in cases where internal cashflow is insufficient), interest costs are a necessary deduction from revenues. Interest rates also indicate how much investors could earn by buying a purely financial asset (like a bond). If investors can earn high profits on paper assets (say, 8–10 percent), they are much less likely to take on the extra risk and trouble of investing in a real business. On the other hand, if purely financial returns are low (say, 4–5 percent), then more will be willing to put their money into motion in the real economy.

Finally, private investors will also take account of the broad political, economic, and legal climate before they commit funds for a new investment. They worry about regulatory, tax, or policy changes that might undermine future profits. They worry about their ability to extract desired labour effort from paid workers, while minimizing their compensation costs. More deeply, they may worry (at times) about the stability of the whole arrangement called capitalism that affords them such unique economic power and prosperity in the first place.

The dependence of investment on broader socio-political factors has caused longer-run fluctuations in investment – like the 25-year postwar boom in private investment that was the engine behind the Golden Age expansion, and the subsequent downturn in investment spending that accompanied the turmoil and retrenchment of the 1970s and 1980s. It also poses a major hurdle for efforts aiming to challenge the dominance of private business in our societies. If it appears that such efforts are likely to be successful in a particular country, private investment spending will decline quickly. The economy then deteriorates before the challengers have even implemented their own policies. This is why many left-wing movements go out of their way to try to "reassure" investors of their intentions long before ever getting elected. (Unfortunately, this catering to business creates its own political problems, because it undermines the movement's subsequent ability to implement change.)

Investment location

The preceding factors are all important in determining *whether* a company chooses to invest in a new project, or not. In many cases, the investing company then faces a second and largely separate decision: *where* should it make that investment? Some types of business (especially many service industries) must locate very near to their customers; these industries are called NON-TRADEABLE industries, because their product cannot be shipped long distances. These include retail, hospitality, and many business and personal services, as well as some kinds of perishable agriculture and manufacturing. Most goods-producing industries, however, and many service industries (including telecommunication, banking, and even some education and medical services) can trade their output over long distances. In these cases companies can freely choose an investment location that maximizes their profit (depending, of course, on any legal or trade barriers affecting their businesses). Table 12.2 also lists several of the factors that influence the location decision.

Obviously, production costs will be a crucial influence on investment location. Labour costs are important here. Low wages will be appealing, but must be considered relative to the level of productivity (since, as discussed in Chapter 8, companies aim to minimize unit labour costs, not wages). Indeed, most low-wage countries are not at all attractive to investors, because their ultra-low wages are associated with very poor productivity, poverty, and instability. Other cost factors which enter the equation include the availability of reliable infrastructure (such as good electricity and telecommunications services), the costs of transporting supplies and finished goods, the level of taxes levied on company profits, and the availability of reliable, cost-competitive supplies of raw materials, parts, and supplies.

Major firms will often establish facilities in countries or regions where they also sell significant volumes of their output. This reduces transportation costs for their finished output, avoids tariffs and other trade barriers, and keeps companies in touch with local consumer tastes. Trade policy (the use of tariffs and other levers to enhance local investment and production) can reinforce this "local market effect" by making it more attractive to produce locally rather than importing.

Socio-political stability is a crucial determinant of investment location, too. Companies will not make expensive, long-term commitments in jurisdictions – even in low-cost jurisdictions – where they fear for the long-run security of their businesses. Competing efforts by countries around the world to make themselves more "investor-friendly" during the neoliberal era, assuring investors of their stability and business-friendly attitudes, have been a crucial factor behind changing patterns of foreign investment in recent decades. Nationalization and even expropriation were real threats to investors in many parts of the world in the 1970s. Today this risk is rare; even left-wing governments are desperate to lay out the welcome mat to investors, in light of the importance of investment to overall growth and productivity.

Concerns and conflicts about investment location are under-standably intense in a world that is desperate for investment and the benefits it brings. In higher-wage developed countries, workers fear a flight of investment to lower-cost jurisdictions. Developing countries, meanwhile, face an uphill challenge to win a larger share of investment – most of which is still concentrated in the advanced capitalist world. The simplistic fear that under globalization all investment will flow to low-wage countries is wrong. But the opposite claim that low wages are always offset by low productivity, and hence pose no threat to higher-wage workers, is just as wrong. Modern factories in China demonstrate productivity levels quite comparable to those in Europe or North America, yet pay wages 90 percent lower.

No wonder manufacturing companies are pouring new investment into China at a rate of over US$100 billion per year.

The reality of investment mobility, then, is nuanced and complex. If a country can combine low wages, a disciplined and productive workforce, a decent infrastructure and supply network, and political stability, then investors will line up at the door. The long-term migration of investment to lower-cost, pro-business jurisdictions (like China and Mexico) proves that pro-business policies can have a dramatic impact on investment location. Incoming investment generates some benefits for working people in those jurisdictions (although their ability to win a healthy share of resulting GDP growth is constrained by the same pro-business policies which attracted the investment in the first place). At the same time, economic pain is experienced in those jurisdictions which lose investment. Finding ways to manage this competition for investment, and to expand the total global amount of investment (thus making it easier for all jurisdictions to capture a healthy share), is an essential challenge for those hoping to develop a more humane and progressive global economy.

Investment under neoliberalism

If investment depends on current and expected profits, and on the existence of a stable, business-friendly political and legal climate, then capitalists should be supercharging their investment effort under neoliberalism. Right? Wrong. Curiously, despite the dramatic pro-business shifts in laws and policies which have occurred in the last quarter-century, and the consequent rise in profits in most jurisdictions, business investment has actually remained quite sluggish.

Figure 12.1 illustrates that net investment spending (after depreciation) has markedly deteriorated under neoliberalism. Global investment slowed in the 1980s, as the system adjusted to the initial shock of neoliberal medicine: much higher interest rates, cutbacks in government spending, and other tough-love measures. Even as the system adapted to new rules of the game, however, investors did not respond to the more favourable climate with a more vigorous economic effort. Investment is still weaker, despite bullish business attitudes and supposedly strong economic "fundamentals," than in the crisis-ridden 1970s. Largely because of this failure of the world's capitalists to reinvest their booming profits, average world growth in productivity and incomes has been similarly unspectacular. So while neoliberalism has been successful in restoring business profitability and, more generally, business power, it has not led to stronger world growth.

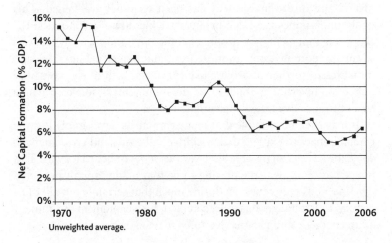

Figure 12.1   The Investment Slowdown
G-7 Economies, 1970–2006

Source: Author's calculations from Organization for Economic Cooperation and Development data.

Why has the big U-turn of the past quarter-century not elicited a more energetic response from the world's capitalists? This is an unanswered puzzle. Even the International Monetary Fund and other global institutions have admitted that global business investment is weak, compared to the high level of business profits.

New investment spending has fallen far behind the growth of profits; as a result, companies are accumulating large hoards of inactive cash (which may be paid out to shareholders, invested in financial assets, or allocated to other unproductive outlets). ▤ * Perhaps investors understand the strict limits that have been placed on global growth by CENTRAL BANK policies. Growth in modern capitalism is deliberately curtailed, in order to prevent labour markets from "overheating" and to keep workers perpetually insecure (as we'll discuss more in Chapter 17). Understanding this new regime, businesses may decide there's little point accelerating investment (although the competitive urge for individual companies to grow at the expense of their competitors still

* See the Economics for Everyone website for statistics, www.economicsforeveryone.com.

exists). The intense but pointless hyperactivity of financial markets has probably also diverted attention from real business investment.

Whatever the reason, it is clear that the link between current profits and future investment has been seriously weakened. This badly undermines the logic behind "trickle-down" economics: the claim that enhancing the profits of companies and their owners will stimulate more investment, more jobs, and higher incomes. In fact, measures to further improve business profits will likely have little impact on investment at all, given the mountains of idle cash which corporations have already accumulated.

It may even be possible that many capitalists have simply lost the primal hunger to expand their wealth at all costs, and are content to consume a larger share of it (in luxurious style) or hoard it away. This hunger, after all, was the driving force that made capitalism such a dynamic and creative system during much (but certainly not all) of its history. If that hunger has indeed abated, then capitalism's legitimacy as an energetic and progressive force may be in question.

13

Employment and Unemployment

Supply and demand?

Based on the economic picture we have drawn so far, it is clear that the total level of employment depends very much on the decisions of employers and investors. Capitalists invest money in private businesses in search of profit. They hire workers to produce. Other jobs are created in companies which supply those businesses (with capital equipment, raw materials, and other inputs). More jobs are created in the companies which then supply consumer goods and services to newly-employed workers (who quickly begin to spend their wages). The ultimate level of employment therefore depends on the initial amount of business investment, and on the extent to which it generates spin-off activities through both supply industries and consumer industries. In other words, total employment depends on the *demand* for labour from investing and producing businesses.

So far there is no reference at all in this story to the issue of labour *supply*: that is, how many workers are willing to offer their services in return for a wage or salary. We have only considered the demand side of the equation: that is, how many workers employers need, given their investment and production plans. Indeed, there is no particular reason why employment (which depends on business output) should equal the number of people who wish to work. In other words, there is no reason to expect FULL EMPLOYMENT (see box, p. 152). If there is not enough investment and production to usefully employ all willing workers, then unemployment will exist – and capitalism has no sure-fire internal mechanism to eliminate it.

Having large numbers of desperate people sitting around without work is a recipe for trouble, however – both economic and political. So there are various ways in which capitalism has generally managed to avoid long-term, mass unemployment. One is through conscious efforts by governments to influence employment levels (using government spending, interest rates, and other tools to stimulate job creation when needed). But adjustments in labour supply are also important.

Measuring the Labour Market

Labour market statistics are among the most important economic data reported by statistical agencies. Their release (usually each month) is eagerly anticipated by economists, government officials, and financial traders, and they offer the most immediate and direct glimpse into broader economic trends. The key numbers reported include:

- **Working-age population** How many people are considered to be of "normal" working age (say, between the ages of 16 and 65)? The specific ages used in this definition vary from country to country.

- **Labour force** How many working-age people are employed, or want to be employed? These people are considered to be "in" the labour market.

- **Employment** How many people in the labour force are employed? This number can be subdivided into full-time and part-time employment; temporary and permanent; private sector and public sector; and self-employment and paid employment.

- **Unemployment** How many people want to work (and hence are in the labour force), but cannot find work? To count as officially "unemployed," a person must be actively seeking work. (Each country has its own definition of what qualifies as "actively" looking.) Ironically, unemployment can decline simply because unemployed people give up looking, and hence drop out of the labour market (these people are known as discouraged workers).

From these data, several key ratios are calculated. The PARTICIPATION RATE is the proportion of working-age population that "participates" in the labour market (by working or looking for work). The UNEMPLOYMENT RATE is the proportion of the labour force that can't find a job, despite looking for one. The EMPLOYMENT RATE is the proportion of the working-age population that is employed. The unemployment rate depends on whether non-employed individuals are counted in the labour force or not, but the employment rate does not. For that reason, the employment rate can be a more accurate indicator of the true health of the labour market.

In practical history, labour supply has clearly tended to *follow* labour demand. This has helped maintain a rough balance between the two sides of the market, but with a more-or-less permanent "cushion" of unemployment. As capitalism was first established, employers (helped by governments) consciously developed new supplies of landless workers to sweat and strain in the early factories. As capitalism expanded, a growing share of the population was gradually recruited to wage labour (leaving their former, non-wage activities behind). It's important to remember that the demand for their labour came first. This pattern of labour demand stimulating new sources of labour supply as an economy develops can still be seen in developing countries.

Even in modern times, it is clear that labour supply follows labour demand. When employment conditions are strong, more workers enter the labour market to search for a job – including women, older and younger workers, immigrants, and other "incremental" sources of labour supply. When demand is weak, many of these people are simply pushed back out of the market. Immigration can be reduced; women can be encouraged to give up their paying jobs (as they were in the years following World War II); early retirement options can be introduced.

It is certainly possible (although rare) that business can actually "run out" of workers. Capitalists feel this constraint via the pressure that labour shortages place on their profit margins. If unemployment is very low, workers (individually and collectively) feel confident to demand higher wages. Employers must pay them, in order to retain staff and maintain labour discipline. But they will also work hard (supported by governments) to develop new sources of labour supply. Unemployment never disappears.

Unemployment: "natural," and otherwise

Unemployment is thus a normal feature of the capitalist labour market. Neoclassical economists, who believe in full employment, try to downplay the importance of the unemployment we see all around us. They claim it represents only "frictional" effects (determined by how long job-seekers spend looking for work), or even "voluntary" decisions (a view that assumes unemployed people don't really *want* to work).

In reality, however, unemployment plays an ongoing and important role in the whole system of wage labour (as we discussed in Chapter 8).

Employers need a believable threat of job loss to enforce labour discipline in their workplaces. If unemployment falls too low for the good of employers, central banks will intervene: raising interest rates to re-establish enough unemployment to restrain wages and reinforce labour discipline. Even if they didn't, investment and job creation would eventually falter as a result of diminishing profitability until sufficient unemployment exists again.

Conventional economists have given a name to this ongoing unemployment. Monetarists like Milton Friedman misleadingly called it the NATURAL RATE OF UNEMPLOYMENT (revealing their obvious bias that there's no need to worry about something that's only "natural"). More neutrally, other economists call it the NON-ACCELERATING INFLATION RATE OF UNEMPLOYMENT (or NAIRU, for short). The theory suggests that if unemployment falls too low, wage pressures will be passed on by companies in the form of inflation. (In fact, while inflation is one possible outcome of the tension between workers and employers in a low-unemployment environment, it is not the only possible outcome. And while wages that grow faster than productivity can be one source of inflation, they are not the only source of inflation, nor even the most important source.)

Many neoclassical economists have tried to identify the precise level of the NAIRU, using sophisticated statistical techniques. These efforts have failed, and it is now clear that the NAIRU is neither constant nor measurable; its usefulness as a guide for interest rate policy is thus highly doubtful. Today, modern central banks tend not to target a specific NAIRU in their efforts to regulate labour markets. But they still explicitly believe that the system needs a certain degree of unemployment to restrain wages, and they act forcefully (with higher interest rates) to maintain that cushion.

How much unemployment is needed to discipline labour will depend on various factors – most of which we introduced in Chapter 8, in the context of the problem of labour extraction. If social benefits are generous, then unemployment is less painful (and hence less "effective" in disciplining workers). If workers enjoy extensive legal protections against arbitrary dismissal, then they will be less fearful of job loss. If unions are stronger, then workers can demand higher wages, even when unemployment is significant.

NAIRU advocates interpret all of these factors as sources of "inflexibility" in labour markets. They argue that weaker unions, workplace protections, and social benefits will allow labour markets to function more "efficiently" (that is, profitably) with a lower long-run level of unemployment. They have thus pushed strongly for policies to enhance what they call labour market "flexibility." This term is another deliberate, highly ideological misnomer. In fact, there are many ways in which a highly disciplined labour market is quite *inflexible*: for example, insecure workers are less likely to quit jobs they aren't well-suited for. The real issue is not flexibility (in the common-sense meaning of being able to adapt to change); the real issues are power and discipline.

There is statistical evidence that central banks permit lower interest rates in countries where workers are structurally disempowered (with weak unions, poor social benefits, and weak workplace protections). In this sense, the belief of central bankers that a "flexible" (that is, business-friendly) labour market can safely attain a lower long-run unemployment rate without threatening profits, becomes self-fulfilling. They allow interest rates to fall, stimulating more investment (and other kinds of spending), and reducing unemployment. However, this is not the result of an automatic, market mechanism. It is, rather, the result of central banks' deliberate and biased economic *management*.

Wages and employment

The argument is regularly made (by neoclassical economists, employers, and business-friendly politicians) that unemployed workers could find work if they simply cut their wage demands and agreed to work for less. Following the same logic, these same powerful voices oppose minimum wages or any other attempts to deliberately increase wage levels (to reduce poverty or attain other social goals). Higher minimum wages encourage more people to look for work, but discourage companies from offering employment. For both reasons, they argue, minimum wages (and other attempts to boost wages, like collective bargaining) backfire, producing unemployment instead of higher living standards.

Many statistical studies, however, have indicated that modest changes in minimum wages have little if any impact on employment levels. More broadly, there is no demonstrated statistical relationship between high wages and lower employment. This is because employment levels are not determined, primarily, in the labour market. As we have seen, employment mostly depends on how much private businesses want to *produce*, which in turn determines the level of labour demand. Wages can affect output levels (and hence employment), but the links are indirect, unpredictable, and relatively weak.

Table 13.1 lists several ways in which lower wages might stimulate higher employment (and higher wages might result in lower employment). But it also lists some ways in which lower wages might lead to *lower* employment – so that wage cuts would be self-defeating.

Let's start with the ways lower wages could stimulate more jobs. Once companies decide how much they want to produce, they have a certain amount of leeway to choose *how* to produce it. In particular, there is limited flexibility in how they combine labour, capital, and other inputs to produce the desired output. In most industries, the use of capital and labour is determined quite rigidly by technology. To

Table 13.1 Will Cutting Wages Save Your Job?

Effect	How it Works	Strength
Ways that Lower Wages Lead to MORE Jobs:		
Capital substitution	If wages fall, employers use more labour and less machinery.	Weak
Profit-investment link	Lower wages mean higher profit margins, encouraging capitalists to invest more.	Weak
Competition for jobs	Cutting your wages may attract jobs from other companies or jurisdictions.	Zero (net)
Central bank behaviour	Structural weakness in wage demands may "permit" lower interest rates.	Modest
Ways that Lower Wages Lead to FEWER Jobs:		
Consumer spending	Lower wages mean less worker consumption spending, hence less demand and less production.	Modest
Labour discipline	Reducing wages too low undermines labour effort, productivity, and hence profits.	Weak

competitively produce any modern, high-technology product, firms cannot utilize old-fashioned labour-intensive production methods (even if labour were cheap). They must use up-to-date technology and equipment. Occasionally, low wages might allow an employer to use a few extra workers instead of using machinery: imagine a landscaping company using ten low-paid workers to dig a ditch, instead of one bulldozer. These situations are rare, however, and the resulting "substitutability" between workers and machinery is never sufficient to automatically establish full employment. And for many other reasons, it is seldom desirable for economies to use backward, labour-intensive technologies (even if wages are low). So this link between wages and employment levels is very weak.

As discussed above, lower wages might stimulate higher investment and hence more job creation if they resulted in stronger business profits. This result depends on there being enough purchasing power in the economy, despite falling wages, to purchase all output and hence generate strong profits. Even then, however, as we noted in Chapter 12, the relationship between profits and investment is uncertain anyway.

From the perspective of an individual company, which competes against other firms, growth may be enhanced if its own *particular* labour costs are reduced. Its products can then be sold more competitively, and its market share will grow. Remember, however, that the growth of one company's market share produces offsetting contractions in output (and hence employment) for other firms – which lose sales as a result of their higher wages. On a net basis, cutting wages at one company cannot expand overall employment; at best it merely transfers employment from one company to another. It is likely, moreover, that *other* companies will respond by cutting their wages, too – in which case there is no impact on employment at all (or even a negative impact, if consumer spending falls as a result). The same logic applies to trying to "steal" jobs from another region or country by cutting wages; total global employment is unchanged, and other regions are likely to eventually respond by cutting their own wages.

Perhaps the most important economic link between lower wages and higher employment is the indirect, policy-driven relationship between wage trends and central bank behaviour discussed above. Central banks tightly control the growth of the whole economy to keep a lid on wages and protect profit margins. If wage demands are weak, for whatever reason, then bankers may allow the economy to expand a bit further. This whole relationship is rooted in the belief of central bankers that wage pressures are the dominant source of inflation, as well as their assumption that there are no other possible ways of attaining low inflation and low unemployment at the same time.

We must also consider the ways in which lower wages could perversely translate into *less* employment. The most important of these is through the impact of lower wages on workers' consumption spending – which, remember, accounts for about half of GDP in the advanced countries. Workers tend to spend their whole income on household consumption (both goods and services). Lower wages mean less spending, and hence less demand for output. Unless this is more than offset by new investment or exports, total output will contract as a result of the wage cut, and employment will fall.

This relationship is the foundation for the argument, made by some trade unionists and labour advocates, that high wages can actually be "good for business." The precedent set by Henry Ford in 1914, who offered his workers $5 per day (a very high wage at the time) so they could afford to buy the same cars they made, is often invoked. There are indeed some situations in which the positive

Buy My Cars

"The commonest laborer who sweeps the floor shall receive his $5 per day. We believe in making 20,000 men prosperous and contented rather than follow the plan of making a few slave drivers in our establishment millionaires."

Henry Ford, US industrialist (1914).

boost to spending power (and hence output) resulting from higher wages can outweigh the negative impacts of higher wages on profits, exports, and other sources of spending. Economists call this situation a "wage-led" economy. Its practical relevance, however, should not be overestimated. It generally requires several conditions to be valid: a very low level of capacity utilization, relatively weak globalization (so that workers' higher wages stimulate domestic production, not a flood of imports), a coordinated rise in all workers' wages (so that no companies suffer a disadvantage by raising wages first), and investment levels that are relatively insensitive to profitability.

Statistical evidence suggests that most advanced capitalist economies are not wage-led. In other words, merely increasing wages is no guarantee that output and employment will grow. Therefore, efforts to boost wages (in the interests of alleviating poverty, for example) need to be supplemented by other measures to stimulate investment (and other forms of spending), to ensure that higher wages do not undermine employment. The proposal outlined in Chapter 26 for a *high-investment, sustainable economy* provides one example of this sort of double-barrelled strategy.

Another factor to keep in mind is the necessity for employers to pay sufficiently high wages to elicit desired work effort from their workers. This is why many companies (especially larger, high-tech firms) will not cut wages even when high unemployment might allow them to. It is more important to their profitability to continue paying relatively high wages, as part of their effort to retain and discipline workers. If they did cut wages, productivity and hence profitability could suffer, with negative long-run effects on the company's employment.

On the whole, in summary, fluctuations in wages have very little impact on employment. Wages cannot be so high that they unduly undermine profits and prevent adequate investment spending. They cannot be too low, either: they must provide for the reproduction of workers and their families, they must allow employers to elicit desired work effort and labour discipline, and they must support enough consumption spending by workers to absorb much of the nation's output. Between these two extremes is a range of possible wage levels. Where precisely wages settle will depend on a mix of structural, institutional, and political factors (such as the strength of trade unions), and broader economic conditions (most importantly, the level of output and hence the level of employment). Wage levels themselves play at most a weak, secondary role in determining the level of employment.

Demographics and labour supply

Most countries in the world are experiencing significant demographic shifts. Higher living standards have led to growing life expectancy and falling birth rates in most parts of the world, and hence to an increase in the proportion of the population that is elderly. This "problem" (most people would not consider living longer to be a problem at all!) is most acute in developed countries. But some developing countries (notably China) are also ageing rapidly.

This has sparked considerable concern among employers and some governments, who warn of an impending era of labour shortages. Employers worry about higher wages and difficulties in recruitment. Governments worry about paying for retirement benefits and health costs. Both concerns are exaggerated. And the main proposed "solution" – namely, encouraging or even requiring people to work longer in life – could be worse than the "problem."

We know from history that employers are very adept at identifying and recruiting new sources of labour supply whenever tight labour markets impinge on their profitability. There are plenty of potential new labour sources still available, without forcing older people to stay in the workforce – so long as employers are required to make those opportunities sufficiently appealing. For example, women's labour force participation is still lower than men's, and hence (with appropriate supports, such as child care services and family-friendly work schedules) more women could be encouraged to accept paid work.

Immigration is another tried-and-true source of "flexible" labour supply. Immigrant workers (especially workers on temporary visas, and "illegal" migrants) are an especially vulnerable workforce, and are exploited accordingly. More humane immigration programs (featuring good legal protections, training, and settlement supports) could expand labour supply in a manner that enhances, rather than undermines, labour standards.

Employers could also respond to a genuine labour shortage by investing in new capital and new skills. Labour would thus be transferred from menial, degrading, and unproductive work toward higher-value, better-paid occupations. But it is only when labour shortages really begin to "bite," impinging on profit margins, that employers will be forced to treat labour as a valuable and scarce commodity – and hence upgrade the quality and productivity of work. If central bankers clamp down on growth to ensure that labour remains "cheap," then this positive transformation of work will never occur.

It is always structural factors, more than "supply and demand" forces, that ultimately determine the economic position of labour. Nevertheless, the coming demographic shifts may provide workers with some opportunity to enhance their economic and political position in society. But this will not happen if employers are permitted to re-create abundant supplies of cheap, desperate labour by exploiting vulnerable immigrants or compelling older workers to keep working.

14

Dividing the Pie

Distribution across factors

Economics is the study of work: what we produce. But it is also the study of distribution: who gets what, from what we produce. Production and distribution are closely linked, since what we produce, how much of it, and how we produce it all depend on who gets what, and what they do with it.

There are two broad ways to think about the distribution of income: across the major FACTORS OF PRODUCTION (that is, labour, capital, and other inputs), and across different individuals or groups of individuals. These two approaches are related, of course, since what we call "factors" are actually economic resources that belong to quite distinct groups of *people*.

Distribution across factors depends on the economic, political and social power of the owners of each factor. Under capitalism, as we have seen, employers pay wages and salaries on the basis of their need to attract and retain employees, and extract necessary labour effort and discipline from them. How much they have to pay depends on broad social and institutional factors like trade unionism, minimum wages and other labour regulations, the level of unemployment, and the generosity of social policies.

Profits are then determined as the residual remaining after wages and other input costs have been paid out. (Remember, the costs of purchased inputs such as capital equipment, parts, and raw materials all reflect a similar split between wages and profits. By decomposing the factor income generated within each company, eventually a wage-profit split for the whole economy can be obtained.) The incomes of small business owners and farmers, meanwhile, mostly reflect their hard work; a portion also reflects their status as owners of their businesses.

These determinants of factor incomes clearly evolve over time. Economists used to assume that the distribution of factor incomes was more-or-less fixed. But this assumption was clearly wrong. As indicated in Figure 14.1, labour increased its share of total income in

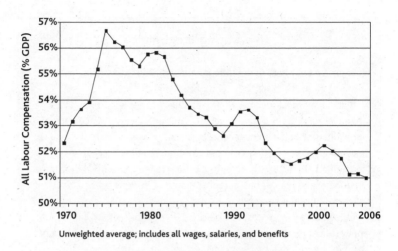

Unweighted average; includes all wages, salaries, and benefits

Figure 14.1 Labour's Shrinking Share
G-7 Economies, 1970–2006

Source: Author's calculations from Organization for Economic Cooperation and Development data.

the OECD economies significantly during the Golden Age expansion – not because of "supply and demand," but because of steady improvements in labour's economic and political bargaining position. Since the early 1980s, however, the shoe has been on capitalism's other foot, and labour's share of output has fallen steadily. Capital income has increased in the wake of neoliberal economic and social policies which undermined labour and reinforced the power of businesses and their owners. Small business income, meanwhile, has stagnated or declined over time, reflecting agricultural depopulation and the marginalization of most non-farm small businesses.

Distribution across individuals

The other way to understand distribution is to measure differences in income across different individuals or households. Most individuals receive income from more than one source: from their own work, from government programs (like unemployment insurance, public pensions, or child support benefits), and perhaps from investments. After totalling income from all these sources, how large are the income differences between individuals and households? (See box, p. 164.)

Measuring Inequality

It is not an easy task to describe inequality. Here is a brief introduction to the various methods that economists use.

First, we must decide what variable we are measuring. Income inequality measures differences in the amount of current income which individuals or households receive in a year. Income is more unequal for individuals than it is for household groups or families. Some low-income individuals are fortunate enough to belong to families with high-income members, and hence their actual standard of living is higher than their own income would allow.

Income can be measured before tax, or after tax. It can include **TRANSFER PAYMENTS** from governments (such as unemployment benefits or public pensions), or it can include only "market" incomes (such as wages, salaries, investment income, and small business income). *After*-tax income *including* transfer payments is much more equal than *before*-tax income *excluding* transfers. This is because high-income individuals in most countries pay more income tax, but low-income individuals receive proportionately more transfer payments.

Wealth inequality can also be measured. This compares the accumulated wealth of different households – including home-ownership, direct business wealth, and financial assets (such as stocks, bonds, and savings accounts). Wealth is distributed far more unequally than income. And financial wealth is distributed the most unequally of all (since the only significant form of wealth for most working people is the equity they own in their homes). As discussed in Chapter 7, business and financial wealth in advanced capitalist countries is owned by a surprisingly small and wealthy elite; in most countries, less than 10 percent of society owns a clear majority of financial and business wealth.

Once the variable of interest has been chosen, a convenient way must be selected to summarize inequality in that variable. One way is to compare the income or wealth of the top fifth (or tenth) of the population, to the bottom fifth (or tenth). Another way is to calculate a statistic called a **GINI COEFFICIENT**. This figure varies between 0 (a situation of perfect equality, where everyone has an equal share) and 1 (a situation of perfect inequality, where the richest person gets everything). A rise in the Gini coefficient indicates an increase in inequality. Needless to say, Gini coefficients have been rising steadily in most capitalist countries under neoliberalism.

Of course, investment income is concentrated among the wealthy households who own most financial wealth. Working households, on the other hand, receive most of their income from employment (supplemented, to varying degrees, by government programs).

Thus, there is a clear overlap between the distribution of income across factors, and the distribution of income across households – for the simple reason that particular households have particular types of factor income. After all, capitalism is a class society precisely because certain groups of people play such different economic roles. As the overall income of capital has grown under neoliberalism, so too has the share of personal income captured by the very richest segment of society (the ones who own most capital).

Indeed, there is no better way to measure the reasons for, and success of, neoliberalism than by analyzing the evolving share of income received by the richest 1 percent of society. This share declined steadily in the postwar Golden Age, and has recovered dramatically since 1980. This rebound has been particularly successful in the US, where the richest 1 percent of society now receive as large a share of total income as they did in the 1920s.

It's Better

"I've been rich and I've been poor. Believe me, honey, rich is better."

Sophie Tucker (1884–1996), American vaudeville singer (c. 1930s).

Inequality and labour market segmentation

Even among workers, however, there are large and important differences in income. The overall share of wages in GDP depends on the broad economic and political power of working people. Wages in particular industries or occupations will also depend on the specific bargaining position of workers in different jobs. Job-specific wage levels depend on factors such as:

- Productivity in each industry (which affects an employer's ability to pay higher wages without pinching profit margins).

- Profitability in each industry (employers in some hyper-competitive, low-profit industries genuinely can't afford higher wages without going out of business).

- Unionization and other industry-specific institutions and practices.

- The specific skills of particular workers. Workers with unique or hard-to-replace skills enjoy a strong bargaining position with their employers, since they are harder to replace. (This is quite different from the neoclassical explanation of the relationship between skills and wages, which falsely assumes each worker is paid according to their productivity and hence their skills.)

Even otherwise identical workers earn very different wages, depending on the balance of bargaining power they experience in their specific job. This is the economic basis for the persistence of clear divisions, or segmentation, between different groups of workers (discussed in Chapter 8). Some workers have access to relatively better and more secure positions, with higher wages. Others tend to be channelled into occupations or industries with lower wages, few if any benefits, and precarious employment prospects.

With such persistently unequal outcomes in labour markets, it is not at all surprising that society has found various ways to "organize" the resulting inequality. Rather than randomly assigning individuals to better or worse jobs, practices develop over time to ensure that certain groups have systematically better chances of capturing the better jobs. Individuals with better jobs are understandably anxious to pass on their relatively lucky situation to their offspring, relatives, friends, and neighbours. Hence clear patterns in segmentation emerge over time. In particular, gender, race, and ethnicity come to be associated with labour market divisions. Racist and sexist attitudes about the supposed "suitability" of different types of people for different jobs emerge to reinforce and "justify" those divisions in jobs and incomes.

Employers actually appreciate these systematic cleavages in the labour market, for various reasons. Economically, the existence of more desperate and hence "flexible" pools of labour (such as workers of colour and immigrants) allows employers to recruit willing workers when they are needed – and easily "dispose" of them (by pushing them back into unemployment) when they aren't. Workers of colour thus tend to be the last hired in an upswing, and the first fired in a downturn. Politically, the existence of large divisions between workers allows employers to play one group against another, undermining worker solidarity (which is essential for winning better wages and conditions), and preventing the emergence of a more united workers' consciousness. In these ways, racial and gender divisions among working people are reinforced by capitalism, and simultaneously help to reinforce capitalism.

For those lucky workers who benefit from better jobs and incomes, preserving and reinforcing their relatively privileged positions might seem logical. Professional and salaried workers might buy into the idea that they "deserve" better incomes and working conditions, and hence try to suppress competition from more desperate groups of workers. For example, professional associations have been among the most successful trade unions in society, by limiting entry to their high-income occupations through strict licensing and regulation. Similarly, the mainly white, male workers who hold higher-income positions in core industries (like heavy manufacturing and construction) might be tempted to view marginalized groups of workers as a threat, rather than a potential ally.

Deserving

"Clearly the most unfortunate people are those who must do the same thing over and over again, every minute, or perhaps twenty to the minute. They deserve the shortest hours and the highest pay."

John Kenneth Galbraith, Canadian-American economist (1964).

Thoughtful trade unionists will recognize, however, that even relatively well-off workers are undermined by the systematic creation of pools of more desperate and exploited workers. And all workers suffer from the loss of bargaining power that comes from division and segmentation. That's why fighting to reduce inequality between workers and build solidarity across gender and racial divisions (through initiatives such as anti-racism and anti-harassment campaigns, and affirmative action hiring) is crucial for unions – just as important as fighting for a better overall deal between labour and capital as a whole.

Poverty

One of the most glaring failures of capitalism is the continuing widespread existence of poverty – often extreme poverty. Even in the advanced economies, many millions of people endure terrible economic and social deprivation, despite the incredible wealth all around them.

Even worse is the oppressive and grinding poverty that is so widespread in less developed countries: most of Africa, large parts of Asia and Latin America, and some former Communist countries in Eastern Europe. Indeed, the widest gaps in income distribution in the world are the ones between richer and poorer countries. We will discuss these international dimensions of poverty and income distribution further in Chapter 22.

The extent of poverty varies greatly across the advanced economies, as summarized in Table 14.1. The Anglo-Saxon countries (especially the US) generally experience the worst poverty. They have the weakest unions and labour market protections, and hence produce more low-wage jobs. These countries also, not coincidentally, have the weakest social programs (to supplement wage incomes, and support those who do not earn wages). In most of these countries, poverty has grown notably during the neoliberal era.

Table 14.1   **Poverty Rates in Advanced Economies**

Country	Poverty* Rate 2005 (%)
US	17.0
Ireland	16.2
Italy	12.7
UK	12.5
Australia	12.2
Japan	11.8
Canada	11.4
Germany	8.4
France	7.3
Netherlands	7.3
Sweden	6.5
Denmark	5.6
Finland	5.4

* Poverty defined as individual receiving less than 50% of median income (relative measure).

Source: United Nations Development Program.

Measuring Poverty

Statisticians have long argued about the best way to measure poverty. The main debate is over whether to use absolute or relative indicators.

ABSOLUTE POVERTY measures whether an individual's concrete material standard of living is lower than some arbitrary, fixed level. That level is determined at a certain point in time, based on a level of income sufficient (at that time) to pay for the "necessities" of life (basic shelter, food, clothing, and other essentials). The cost of buying that bundle of basic goods usually grows over time (due to the effects of inflation), and the poverty line is adjusted accordingly.

The problem with this approach, however, is that it ignores the evolution of social standards regarding a "minimum" acceptable standard of living. One hundred years ago, it was a luxury to have an indoor flush toilet. Today it is considered essential for decency and good health. An absolute poverty line established a century ago would therefore assume that people can still survive quite acceptably with outdoor facilities. The same goes for television sets, access to education and health care, transportation, and other amenities once considered "luxuries" – but which are now clearly essential to an individual's full participation in modern life.

For these reasons, most poverty experts prefer measures of **RELATIVE POVERTY**. These determine whether someone is poor, based on the level of income enjoyed by the rest of society. If a person or household's income falls below some threshold relative to average incomes in broader society, then they are considered to be poor – even if their income may be sufficient to meet the basic needs of survival. This recognizes that whether or not a person "feels" poor (and this deeply affects their overall status in society) depends on the distribution of income in society, not just on their absolute standard of living. Relative poverty measures thus consider the degree of inequality, not just absolute poverty.

Different poverty measures produce very different estimates of poverty. The US government uses an absolute definition of poverty – one that has not been updated since 1964. By this measure, poverty in the US declined slightly over the last quarter-century. Using a relative poverty measure (the proportion of population receiving less than 50 percent of the median income), however, it is clear that poverty

▶

has been growing steadily in the US. The relative poverty rate in 2004 (18.5 percent) was one and a half times higher than the official, absolute rate (12.5 percent).*

Poverty measures also must be adjusted for other factors, including the number of individuals living in a household, and whether a household lives in a rural region or a (more expensive) urban location.

* Lawrence Mishel, Jared Bernstein, and Sylvia Allegretto, *The State of Working America* (Washington: Economic Policy Institute, 2006), Figure 6-G.

In contrast, the Nordic and some continental European economies demonstrate very low levels of poverty. This indicates that there is nothing inevitable about poverty, despite the seeming universality of neoliberalism. Countries which invest in social programs, labour market supports, and other proactive measures can generate higher-wage jobs and achieve very low rates of poverty.

Many economists blame poverty on the characteristics of poor people, rather than on the functioning of the labour market. Poor people are urged to upgrade their skills, or improve their work ethic, or refine their job search strategies – often with very trite advice (such as preparing a more attractive resumé). Obviously, learning new skills or improving one's job search can enhance the job chances for any particular *individual* – even someone from a relatively disadvantaged segment of the labour market. But this will never eliminate poverty in an economy with weak social programs and labour market supports, where concentrations of low-wage jobs (and low-wage workers to fill those jobs) are naturally *re-created* over time.

Suppose that every low-wage worker in the US (or any other highly unequal economy) graduated from college and prepared a sophisticated, modern resumé. Some would find better jobs. Yet the US economy would still need poor, desperate workers to fulfil the nastiest, worst-paid jobs in the system: washing dishes in restaurants, cleaning office towers at night, stocking cheap made-in-China products at Wal-Mart. Moreover, the whole low-wage strategy of employers depends on the (highly visible) existence of poverty. It provides a constant reminder to employed low-wage workers of why they should follow the rules and work hard, despite their lousy jobs. So other groups of workers would eventually be channelled into marginal labour market segments, and poverty and inequality would be reproduced.

Challenging poverty will ultimately require challenging these basic mechanisms of the capitalist labour market – rather than blaming or hectoring its most desperate victims.

15

Capitalism and the Environment

Nature and the economy

From the outset of this book, we have identified "work" (human effort) as the driving force behind economic activity. Work is required to transform the materials we obtain from nature, into useful goods and services. All those goods and services, therefore, require two things: human work, and essential resources and supplies from nature. The environment also directly provides us with things that are essential to a high quality of life: fresh air and water, environmental quality, and recreation opportunities. Therefore, no production is possible without the supplies and resources we harvest from nature, and without a liveable environment in which to live and work.

Figure 15.1 presents, once again, our map of capitalism. (For simplicity, we once again portray capitalists collectively as one big company, rather than showing competition between firms.) Now the map adds the natural environment as an explicit part of the economic system. Three broad links between nature and the economy are indicated:

- **Ecological benefits** Human beings need, and directly "consume," certain goods from the natural environment: the air we breathe, the water we drink (hopefully after it's been purified!), the general quality of the environment in which we work and live, and the parks and other natural places where we enjoy some of our free time. Our map indicates this direct use of ecological benefits with an arrow running from nature to worker households (which is where most people live – but capitalist and small business households, of course, also need and enjoy nature). The loss or degradation of those ecological benefits can seriously undermine the quality of life; it can also disrupt the other functions that occur in the economy.

- **Natural resources** Nature also provides many different material inputs to the for-profit production activities of private firms:

Figure 15.1   Economic Road Map: Environment

agricultural output, minerals and resources, energy, timber, and land (for both agricultural and non-agricultural purposes). These inputs are illustrated on the map by an arrow running from nature to productive companies. The availability and quality of natural inputs affect the productivity and profitability of business production. If natural resources become more costly to extract, decline in quality, or even "run out" altogether (this seldom occurs), then the productive capacity of private firms will suffer accordingly.

- **Pollution** Unfortunately, most economic activities produce byproducts and waste that are eventually dumped back into the natural environment. (Some byproducts, like compost, can be environmentally helpful, but most are not.) Both the quantity of this waste and the way it is managed affect the quality of the natural environment. Pollution thus feeds back onto our ability to consume ecological benefits, and the availability of natural inputs to production. The environment can absorb some pollution, but eventually it begins to deteriorate. In some cases that deterioration is experienced locally (such as garbage or industrial waste). In some cases it is experienced regionally (such as smog or water pollution). In some cases it is experienced globally. Differences between where pollution originates and where it is experienced greatly complicate efforts to control pollution – especially when pollution crosses borders. Figure 15.1 indicates pollution as originating at the stage of production; it can also occur, however, when products are consumed (such as the pollution caused by the use of private automobiles). Either way, pollution is an unwanted side-effect of the basic economic cycle.

Economists, and the public as a whole, have been concerned with the relationship between the economy and the environment since the beginning of capitalism (and probably before). For example, the classical economist David Ricardo worried deeply about the supply of arable land. He developed a whole theory of economic stagnation based on his belief that land would eventually "run out." Early neoclassical economists worried about shortages of coal. The appalling environmental consequences of early unplanned capitalist development motivated policies to manage the environmental effects of growth – through urban zoning, garbage collection and sanitation, air and water pollution regulations, and conservation programs (protecting specified natural places from economic development).

In recent years, however, public concern with the environment has become very intense – and with good reason. And the most pressing environmental challenge facing global civilization is clearly the problem of CLIMATE CHANGE.

Because of the massive growth in fossil fuel consumption (coal, oil, and natural gas) over the past two centuries, emissions of carbon dioxide and other chemicals (byproducts of energy use) into the earth's atmosphere have exploded (see Figure 15.2). The resulting concentration of these gases (called GREENHOUSE GASES because of the "greenhouse" warming effect they produce) causes the atmosphere to retain more heat energy from the sun, and has produced a visible increase in average global temperatures. Worldwide average temperatures have risen by more than a full degree Celsius in the last half-century (and more than that on land); that may not sound like much, but it is already causing dramatic changes in weather patterns, ecosystems, and human activity. Unfortunately, this warming will continue for decades as a result of pollution that has *already* occurred.

The urgent challenge for humanity now is to quickly reduce greenhouse gas pollution, in order to stabilize carbon dioxide concentrations and slow down and eventually stop the rise in global temperatures as soon as possible. The implications of climate change for quality of life, settlement patterns, and geopolitical stability are potentially catastrophic. Consequences will include rising sea levels, drought, severe weather (including disastrous storms), mass dislocations of people, and the extinction of species that cannot adapt to rising temperatures. These terrible consequences, and the global scale of the problem, make climate change probably the most daunting environmental challenge humans have ever faced.

Aggressively reducing greenhouse gas emissions to avoid the worst effects of climate change will require powerful efforts to reduce fossil fuel use, and limit other sources of greenhouse gas pollution (such as methane gas and nitrous oxide emissions from agricultural and chemical industries). It is now clear that the world will also have to invest heavily in *adapting* to warmer temperatures, and assisting the victims of climate change – including residents of low-lying and

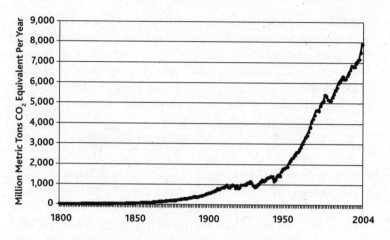

Figure 15.2   **Global Greenhouse Gas Emissions**
1800–2004

Source: Carbon Dioxide Information Analysis Center.

island nations fleeing rising sea levels, and those harmed by dramatic changes in rainfall patterns.

In addition to the incredible challenge of climate change, many other environmental problems also need attention, including:

- Controlling and reducing other kinds of pollution.

- Protecting important natural spaces (such as sensitive rainforests and marine areas), and the plants and animals that live there.

- Developing ways of harvesting timber, minerals, and other natural resources that do not disrupt ecosystems.

- Recycling raw materials used in the economy.

- Investing in systems to conserve and recycle water.

- Cleaning up and restoring past environmental damage, such as former industrial, mining, and toxic waste sites.

A key concept motivating all of these efforts is the vision of environmental SUSTAINABILITY. The general principle of sustainability is to manage interactions between the economy and the environment so that the economy can continue functioning *without* causing ongoing degradation of the environment. Sustainability for the environment is thus similar to reproduction for people (as we studied in Chapter 9): making sure that the planet (like the people who live on it) can continue to provide us with the ecological benefits and resource inputs we need to keep producing. Sustainability will require weaning the economy from non-renewable energy and minerals; extensive recycling of materials to reduce the need for resource extraction; aggressive protection of natural spaces and habitats; and strict limits on pollution of all kinds.

Environmental inequality

As with everything else under capitalism, poor people bear the worst costs of pollution. They have little power to prevent or avoid the garbage, polluted water, and filth that are the byproducts of unregulated capitalism. To confirm this, just take a walk through a poor neighbourhood in any Third World city.

Well-off people, in contrast, can afford to live in more pleasant neighbourhoods, and to invest in mitigating many of the consequences of pollution – purified water, good trash collection, private parks and other recreation facilities. They also enjoy more political clout to prohibit polluting activities in their own particular neighbourhoods. Economic studies have confirmed that pollution tends to be worse in poorer regions and neighbourhoods.

Perhaps the greatest environmental injustice of all is the distributional effect of climate change. The poor residents of low-lying tropical countries will bear the greatest costs of climate change, which was caused mostly by fossil fuel consumption in richer countries located thousands of miles away. Even in the developed countries, poor people will suffer the worst consequences of environmental degradation – as illustrated by the horrifying impact of Hurricane Katrina on poor people in New Orleans in 2005. On the other hand, the effects of climate change will clearly not be limited to poor people. No-one will be able to fully escape the global and potentially catastrophic consequences of climate change – not even the wealthy.

Markets and the environment

Many economists have argued that environmental problems result from an "imperfection" in the operation of free markets. Pollution

imposes a real cost on those who experience its negative effects. But that cost is not paid by the polluting company; they can pollute for "free," because of the absence of regulations and the inability of affected people to collect compensation for the costs they bear. In economics, this is called a market EXTERNALITY. Market-oriented environmentalists suggest forcing companies to absorb (or "internalize") the costs of pollution, through various fees (such as a CARBON TAX on greenhouse gas pollution) imposed on polluting activities. Market mechanisms (like emissions trading schemes) would then ensure that pollution reduction occurred in the most "efficient" manner – more effective, supposedly, than simply mandating lower emissions through government standards or regulations.

This approach places an awful lot of faith in the efficiency of markets and competition. In reality, price signals (even "correct" ones, incorporating pollution costs) are not always effective in changing behaviour in desired ways. Think of alcohol consumption: even in countries with high alcohol taxes, people still drink a lot, and alcoholism is still a problem. Relying only on the price mechanism to reduce pollution also has negative distributional effects: the burden falls disproportionately on lower-income households, whereas well-off people can continue to "buy" as much pollution as they want. Stringent pollution fees could undermine profit rates in some industries, with consequent implications for business investment spending (although they would also stimulate new investment in some other industries). This doesn't concern free-market economists, who believe that supply and demand forces will naturally ensure continuing full employment and maximum prosperity; in the real world, however, we do need to worry about falling investment or unemployment.

Environmental taxes and other market-friendly mechanisms can surely play some role in encouraging energy conservation and other goals – not to mention raising valuable funds to pay for government-sponsored environmental programs and investments. But these measures must be backed up with direct pollution regulations and efficiency standards (which are more powerful than price signals in reducing pollution), and the direct expansion of environmental investments by businesses, government, and households.

Some environmentalists also hope the market can encourage environmental progress through "green" choices by consumers. They urge consumers to purchase environmentally-friendly products, and assume that companies will respond to consumer opinion by improving their environmental performance. Consumers can best help the environment by altering or "down-shifting" their lifestyles, spending and consuming less, and buying environmentally preferable brands. All of these individual, personal decisions, presumably, will translate into a more sustainable economy.

Here, too, some environmentalists naïvely credit market forces with more integrity and power than they deserve. Businesses shape consumer sentiment as much as they cater to it; they often respond to "green" consumerism with shallow advertising trumpeting the often-phony environmental virtues of their existing products. Consider the car rental company in Australia that advertised itself as the "green" alternative – because it donated A$2 to an environmental charity for each completed car rental! (The truly green alternative, of course, is to use public transport – something the car rental company doesn't want you to do.)

Sometimes consumers are presented with more genuine environmental choices: for example, buying an energy-efficient but more expensive home appliance. But many consumers will be more concerned with the immediate purchase price (often because they have limited income), rather than longer-term operating cost savings. Hence they will purchase the cheaper (but more polluting) product. This is why direct government energy efficiency regulations, which *force* each industry to produce less polluting products, are more effective.

And if consumers ever did decide, in sufficient numbers, to significantly cut back overall spending, the inadvertent outcome could be a recession. Consumer spending accounts for half of GDP in advanced economies. If we're going to have less of it, then we'll need a lot more of other kinds of spending (perhaps like big increases in government spending on environmental programs or relatively non-polluting public services) – or else we'll need ways to manage the resulting employment downturn in an equitable, socially sustainable manner (for example, by reducing average work hours). None of this will occur through the operation of market forces alone. And it is clearly unreasonable to ask many of the world's people (including people in low-income countries, and poor people in rich countries) to consume less. They deserve, and need, *more* goods and services, not less. The challenge is finding ways to meet those genuine needs without degrading the environment.

Is growth the culprit?

Many environmental activists blame economic growth for environmental problems, and it is certainly clear that the dramatic expansion of global output over the last 200 years is the ultimate cause of the environmental crisis we are now grappling with. But the implication of this "anti-growth" view (and sometimes its explicit conclusion) is that growth must be reduced or stopped, to protect the environment. This implies an outright opposition between economic progress and environmental protection that I suspect will help neither the economy nor the environment.

Part of the problem here may be a lack of clarity in terminology. As we discussed in Chapter 1, economists define "growth" as an increase in the real (after inflation) value of GDP. That can consist of many different things, with very different environmental implications. More strip mines, or more child care centres. More private automobiles, or more public transport. An increase in the *quantity* of total output. Or an increase in the *quality* of total output. In GDP terms, this all counts as "growth."

Some environmentalists, on the other hand, interpret growth more narrowly as an increase in the material quantity or scale of economic production – and not necessarily as an increase in its quality or value. For them, growth is equated with the production of more "stuff." In this view, growth is clearly and directly damaging to the environment, since a greater quantity of output implies the use of more natural inputs, and more pollution (unless offset by improvements in how efficiently we use natural inputs and how successfully we prevent pollution). Improving the quality of output, or expanding the production of services, is not considered "growth." In this chapter, however, I will continue using "growth" in its broader, generic meaning: an expansion of real value of marketed goods and services. Part of meeting the sustainability challenge will undoubtedly involve managing and directing that growth into less damaging activities (like child care centres and public transport).

Don't Wait

"The evidence shows that ignoring climate change will eventually damage economic growth. Our actions over the coming few decades could create risks of disruption to economic and social activity, later in this century and in the next, on a scale similar to those associated with the great wars and the economic depression of the first half the 20th century. And it will be difficult or impossible to reverse these changes. Tackling climate change is the pro-growth strategy for the longer term, and it can be done in a way that does not cap the aspirations for growth of rich or poor countries. The earlier effective action is taken, the less costly it will be."

Sir Nicholas Stern, British economist (2006).

Some pollution problems clearly get better as economies grow and living standards improve. This is true for some localized forms of pollution – such as garbage, local air pollution, and polluted water – which are consistently worse in poor countries than in rich. People with higher incomes are more willing to devote resources to localized environmental protection in order to improve their quality of life.

Moreover, advanced economies produce less polluting kinds of output (including more services), and use less polluting technologies and fuels. For these reasons, higher living standards (based, in part, on economic growth) can contribute to the reduction of many kinds of pollution. In other ways, however, economies do more harm to the environment as they get richer – especially by consuming more energy, and hence emitting more greenhouse gases.

By the same token, poverty and desperation clearly drive poor people to do environmentally destructive things – like clear-cutting rainforests, using highly-polluting fuels (like wood and coal), or poaching endangered animals. Meeting basic needs and enhancing economic security will thus be essential to any successful effort to limit and eventually prohibit these destructive activities. Again, this requires economic growth.

Growth alone won't guarantee either environmental protection or human progress, as has been emphasized throughout this book. Growth must be managed and controlled to ensure that its benefits are realized by masses of people. But it is very difficult, verging on impossible, for mass living standards to rise appreciably *without* economic growth. And under capitalism, when growth *stops* (as during a recession), economic and political conditions change in ways that clearly undermine both the well-being of working people and prospects for environmental progress: mass unemployment, growing poverty, a "zero-sum" distributive struggle (in which one group's gain is necessarily another group's loss), and a focus on meeting immediate income and consumption needs (rather than addressing longer-term challenges like sustainability).

Strictly speaking, the problem here is capitalism, not a lack of growth. It is possible to imagine a no-growth economy which avoids those negative outcomes (unemployment, poverty, and desperation), but I suspect it won't be a capitalist one. As we have seen, capitalism relies on the hunger for growing profits, enforced through competitive pressure, to motivate the business investment that drives the whole system. Therefore, capitalism and growth are two sides of the same coin. So while we are working to manage capitalism in a more environmentally responsible manner, we may also wish to think about alternative ways of organizing the economy to avoid this head-on collision with the environment (something we consider, tentatively, in Chapter 27).

But even under capitalism, there are clearly ways in which growth – properly defined, and properly managed – need not harm the environment, and can even help the environment. Some of these are summarized in Table 15.1.

Table 15.1 "Good Growth" and the Environment

Growth that Does Not Harm the Environment:
Improving the quality rather than the quantity of manufactured products.
Providing more child care, youth services, education, elder care, neighbourhood recreation, and other human services.
Production of many private services.

Growth that Helps the Environment:
Building expanded public transportation.
Retro-fitting homes and buildings for energy efficiency.
Production of fuel-efficient and alternative-technology vehicles.
Investment in non-polluting machinery and equipment.
Investment in clean energy generation.
Cleaning up industrial waste sites.
Construction of new parks.

Improving Living Standards Without Producing More:
Consume more "leisure" and less "stuff," by equitably reducing working hours (per week, per year, or over a lifetime).

One form of environmentally neutral growth is the production of higher-quality products, instead of larger quantities of products. For example, producing 100,000 luxury compact cars instead of 100,000 base-level compact cars need not utilize additional material inputs or cause additional pollution – yet could triple the GDP associated with that work. Better yet, higher-priced vehicles allow auto-makers to more readily build in extra costs for innovative energy-saving technologies (like high-tech transmissions, fuel-efficient tires, and lightweight materials). Of course, all this depends on consumers being able to *afford* higher-quality goods – which is another reason why mass prosperity can be good for the environment, not bad.

Growth can also involve producing services instead of goods. In particular, a major expansion of public and caring services (like child care, education, elder care, and other life-affirming programs) would generate huge increases in GDP and incomes, with virtually no impact on the environment. Even many private service industries – like restaurants, cultural facilities, household renovations, and personal services – have relatively small environmental impacts.

And investing in environmental protection is itself a form of economic growth that obviously benefits the environment. After all, environmental investments create work, generate incomes, and contribute to GDP as surely as any strip mine or chemical factory. In this regard, there's no shortage of things to do. Trillions of dollars could be invested worldwide in coming years on energy-efficient transportation, clean energy technologies, energy-saving retro-fits of homes and buildings, the clean-up of waste sites, and the expansion of parks and conservation areas. These investments would generate massive, positive gains for workers and communities.

In this context, the ultimate conflict is not between the economy and the environment. The ultimate conflict is over who is going to pay for those needed investments, how, and why.

Of course, there are forms of economic growth that clearly do damage the environment: activities that exploit and consume more natural resources, consume more fossil fuels, and emit more pollution. The challenge is finding ways to close off these profitable activities (or else make them unprofitable), while simultaneously stimulating more beneficial or benign forms of growth.

Declaring "war" on pollution

At the outset of World War II, the countries that fought fascism suddenly and dramatically invested huge resources in their military effort. These investments were not made because of a hunger for profit. They were made because of a deep, shared conviction that this battle had to be fought and won. These investments, therefore, completely sidestepped the usual motivation for growth under capitalism. (Of course, private companies on both sides of the war profited mightily from military spending, but it was not the profit motive that elicited that spending in the first place.) The huge investments were financed in unusual ways, too: by massive government spending, large deficits, and the issuance of "war bonds."

Notwithstanding the death and destruction on the battlefields, the war produced nothing short of an economic miracle. Economies which had languished in deep depression for a decade, plagued by mass unemployment, poverty, and falling incomes, sprang suddenly to life. Full employment was quickly attained, and new sources of labour supply (notably women) were recruited. Incredible innovation was demonstrated: not just in the technology of war, but in transportation,

logistics, the organization of work, and even in creative financial and social innovations which helped maximize the war effort. Incomes rose dramatically, and so did material living standards (despite wartime shortages of some goods). Workers became more confident and demanding, despite the wartime culture of mutual sacrifice. Strikes were common, and unions grew. This wartime experience (along with other economic and political factors) left workers confident and empowered, and thus helped them win mass prosperity during the postwar Golden Age.

Man on the Moon, or a Liveable Planet?

A coalition of concerned US unions and citizens groups has argued that if America could develop technology to put a man on the moon, they can also find technology to produce needed energy without damaging the environment. The "Apollo Project" calls for a US$300 billion investment by the US federal government in renewable energy projects, with a special emphasis on maximizing the spin-off effects of these investments for environmentally-advanced manufacturing industries.

This program would not only be good for the environment – it would be great for the economy. The Apollo Project estimates that the investments would ultimately create over 3 million jobs and US$1.4 trillion in new GDP.

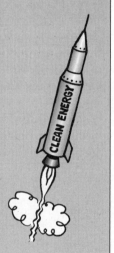

How ironic that something as destructive and horrific as world war should generate such remarkable economic and social benefits – precisely because the usual incentives and constraints that typify capitalism were deliberately bypassed. And imagine if humanity could now mobilize both its collective willpower and its economic resources with just as much determination, but to an end purpose that is constructive rather than destructive.

Climate change quite possibly poses a challenge to human well-being comparable to (if more gradual than) fascism in the 1930s and 1940s. It will take much more than fiddling with market mechanisms, or encouraging consumers to "think green," to arrest this fearsome process.

We should protect the environment by doing *more*, not by doing *less*. We should declare a peaceful "world war" on climate change, and mobilize large investments (significantly, though not exclusively, through government) in environmentally beneficial activities. The resulting stimulus to spending power would offset any deterioration in profitability resulting from stricter environmental regulations, and would simultaneously open up profitable business opportunities in "green" industries (like building and installing energy-efficient machinery and clean-power systems).

Where consumption is actually reduced (in societies prosperous enough to do this), this could be attained through widespread and equitable reductions in working hours (shortening the working week; expanding holidays; and improving family leave, education leave, and early retirement opportunities). In this manner, the higher productivity generated by ongoing economic development translates into greater opportunities for leisure – rather than greater material consumption.

Like the war effort, this campaign against pollution would imply a significant expansion of government, public investment, and regulation – all justified by the urgent collective need to slow and stop climate change. But this would occur in a manner that enhances economic well-being (and boosts growth, properly defined), rather than undermining it.

Part Four

The Complexity of Capitalism

16

Money and Banking

What is money, and what is it good for?

In this book, we've tried to discuss economics in very concrete, real terms. Production is how we make useful goods and services. Work is the human effort that goes into that production. Consumption is the use of some of those goods and services to keep us alive, and make life enjoyable. Investment is the use of some of that output as "tools," allowing us to produce even more output in the future. All of these things are *real*: they all consist of actual goods and services. None of them need be measured in terms of money. They are all real stuff.

But just look around at the actual economy: there are dollar signs *everywhere*. Prices in stores. Amounts in bank accounts. Values on stock markets. GDP in statistical reports. All measured in terms of money.

A visitor from Mars would quickly conclude that the economy is *totally* about money. Yet underneath, the economy must be more real and tangible. Underneath, the economy needs to produce concrete goods and services, to meet concrete needs.

Explaining money, and linking the real activities at the core of the economy with the money that represents them (prices, revenue flows, wealth) has bedevilled economists for centuries. What is money, anyway? How are money prices determined? Why do they change over time? How does money affect real economic activity?

Very broadly, money is anything that allows its holder to purchase other goods and services. In other words, money is purchasing power. Early forms of money were tangible objects with an inherent value (usually official coins minted by government from precious metal). Today, money is very different: it is usually intangible, and its value depends on social convention and government pronouncement. What's more, in a modern economy money is constantly changing – mostly because of the creativity of financial companies (like banks) who seek more profitable ways to facilitate financial transactions, and accumulate and store financial wealth. Indeed, in modern capitalism those private companies control the *creation* of money.

Modern money comes in many shapes and sizes:

- **Currency**　Currency is no longer minted from precious metal. Instead, currency consists of paper money and non-precious coins officially issued and sanctioned by the government. Most people think of "money" as "currency." But in fact currency accounts for a very small share (around 5 percent) of total money in an advanced modern economy.

- **Deposits**　Most people don't keep a lot of cash on hand. They deposit extra cash in the bank, so they don't lose it and can earn interest. But money in the bank is still money. And with modern electronic-banking, deposits can quickly change hands, without ever touching hands. These deposits come in many different forms: standard savings and chequing deposits, term deposits, foreign currency deposits, and even money market investments (like short-term government bonds).

- **Credit**　Today customers can make many purchases without paying anything at all – simply by promising to pay in the future. Think of the furniture store offering a great bargain on a new sofa: "Don't pay anything until next year!" Strictly speaking, credit is not money, but it does allow spending to occur, and it is the most important way that money is *created* in modern capitalism. Credit gives a person or company purchasing power, even when they don't yet own the funds to pay for their purchases. No longer does an individual have to save all the money required before making a major purchase (like a sofa, a home, or a car). Even more importantly, no longer does a business have to save all the money required (from their profits) before making a major new investment. Instead, a bank or other financial institution provides borrowed purchasing power: through a loan, a line of credit, a deposit into a chequing account, or the issuance of a credit card. In return, the borrower promises to pay the loan back later – with interest. Credit accounts for most new money in a modern capitalist economy. When a new loan is issued, new money is created. When a loan is paid back (without a corresponding new loan being taken out), then money is destroyed. The emergence of this credit system fundamentally changed the way capitalism works.

Money has many economic uses:

- Money is a **means of payment**. It allows people to buy products or services. It also allows them to make other kinds of payments (like taxes or loan repayments).

- Money is a **unit of account**. It provides a common way for companies, households, and governments to measure income and wealth, evaluate different products or assets, and determine whether a firm is profitable.

- Money is a **store of value**. Money allows individuals or companies to store some of their wealth in a flexible, convenient form. Few people get intrinsic value from money, purely for its own sake. True, it must be thrilling for rich people to see all those zeros in their bank statements. But in general, money is useful only for what it can buy. However, when they can't find anything better to do with it, or when they fear losses on other types of assets, individuals or firms will simply set aside some of their wealth as money (in cash, bank accounts, or term deposits). Holding onto money in this way is called HOARDING, and it can cause major problems for the overall economy. Money's use as a store of value is the most complicated, unpredictable, and potentially troublesome aspect of its multifaceted personality.

- Thanks to its usefulness as both a means of payment and a store of value, money is an excellent way to **facilitate exchange** between different buyers and sellers. Without money, all trade would have to occur on a BARTER basis – where one product or service is traded directly for another. This is tremendously inefficient: no deal can be made until a seller finds a buyer who has something to offer that the seller also wants. Imagine trying to sell a used car this way. You'd have to find someone who wanted to buy your used car, but also wanted to part with something you wanted – like a month's rent on a vacation cottage, a large-screen television set, or whatever else you were interested in purchasing with the money from your car. It would be very hard to consummate such a deal. Money is thus essential for effective exchange.

Because of its obvious economic benefits, money has been used for thousands of years, in various forms. But the specific *form* that money takes is less important than the fact it must be accepted as a valid form of payment by most participants in an economy. Money is thus a *social* institution. Its usefulness relies on the political and legal authority of the official body (usually some branch of national government) that endorses it. It also requires the trust, even the faith, of the people who use it. Anyone who accepts money payment for something must be confident that they'll be able to spend that money when they want to buy something else.

Economies in which money is not widely accepted (due to war, political instability, extremely rapid inflation, or other catastrophes) generally suffer severe economic disruption. Usually, people in those economies try to find something other than the official currency (like the US dollar, gold, or even commonly-used commodities like cigarettes) to serve as a replacement form of money.

Capitalism and money

While money has a very long history, under capitalism money takes on a new and particular importance, for three broad reasons:

1. For the first time in economic history, accumulating more money becomes the *goal* of production. Companies initiate production in order to make a profit, and that profit is always measured in money.
2. In the act of initiating new production, companies actually *create* money. The financial system provides credit to companies to allow them to pay for capital investments, and for their initial purchases of labour and other inputs. Business credit is the main source of new money in capitalism, and that money is essential for economic growth and job creation.
3. Private profit-seeking financial companies (like banks) control the creation and destruction of money through their lending (that is, credit-creating) activities.

For all these reasons, capitalism is an *inherently* monetary economy. It is impossible to imagine a capitalist economy in which money does not play a central role. And thus, to understand how capitalism works, understanding money is a central priority. Money clearly matters.

Controlling and creating money

In modern capitalism, credit is the main source of new money. Who issues credit? Banks and other private financial institutions – and hence they have replaced government as the most important players in the monetary system.

Of course, government still plays a crucial role. Government endorsement is essential to the widespread acceptance of money. Governments closely control the printing and distribution of hard currency (supplied to the economy through the banking system) to prevent counterfeiting and other crimes. And government regulators oversee the money-creating activities of private banks, injecting extra funds into the banking system when needed, and trying to prevent bank collapses and other financial crises.

But the day-to-day creation and destruction of money is now the domain of the private banks and other financial institutions which control credit. And their actions, in turn, are driven by the same motivating force that propels capitalism as a whole: the pursuit of private profit.

> ## Sleight of Hand
>
> "The modern banking system manufactures money out of nothing. The process is perhaps the most astounding piece of sleight of hand that was ever invented."
>
> Sir Josiah Stamp, President of the Bank of England (1927).
>
> "The process by which banks create money is so simple that the mind is repelled."
>
> John Kenneth Galbraith, Canadian-American economist (1975).

Modern banks are the product of a centuries-long process of corporate evolution. Early customers deposited currency in the bank for safe keeping, and withdrew it when needed to make a purchase – paying a fee for the service. Bankers realized that most of their clients' money was sitting idly in their vaults, most of the time. Why not lend it out to borrowers, generating interest for the bank? This would allow the banks to make profit on their lending, so long as the bank's depositors were happy to leave most of their money with the bank. If a lot of them came to withdraw their money at the same time, then the bank would be in trouble. (From time to time this actually happens, usually when customers lose faith in a bank's stability; the result is a "run" on the bank, as panicked customers withdraw funds, and the bank soon collapses.)

Banks compete with each other to entice depositing customers. Banks are equally aggressive in recruiting new borrowers, since only by lending can they earn a profit. The opportunity to earn profit on new loans, however, must always be balanced against the credit-worthiness of the borrowers (banks need to be confident their loans will be repaid). Banks earn their profit in two main ways: by charging higher interest rates on loans than they pay out on deposits, and by imposing service charges and fees for bank transactions.

The banks' balancing act between "greed" (for profits on loans) and "fear" (that loans won't be paid back) tends to evolve in cycles, and these cycles can affect the whole economy. When economic times are good, fewer borrowers go bankrupt, and banks become less sensitive to the risks of loan default; they thus push new loans more aggressively, stimulating new purchasing power and faster economic growth. The reverse occurs when times turn bad: banks become hyper-sensitive to the risks of loan defaults, they pull back their lending, and this causes a CREDIT SQUEEZE which reduces overall purchasing power and growth even further. Ironically, banks' *fear* of defaults can actually *cause* defaults – since their lending restrictions produce an economic downturn and hence bankruptcies (among both businesses and households). This cyclical, profit-driven process is called the BANKING CYCLE, and it is a major cause of the boom-and-bust cycle visible under capitalism. As this book went to press (spring 2008) the US economy was entering a credit squeeze recession.

Of course, it takes two to tango, and every loan needs two willing participants: a borrower who wants to borrow, and a bank which is willing to lend. Banks can be quite aggressive in "pushing" loans into the economy – by reducing interest rates, or offering loans to increasingly risky customers. But they can't *force* anyone to borrow. For credit to expand, borrowers (both businesses and households) must *want* to borrow. The desire to take on new credit will depend on the level of interest rates, and on borrowers' degree of confidence about their future. If businesses and consumers are very pessimistic about future economic prospects, then even very low interest rates might not be effective in stimulating new credit and hence new spending (see box below).

Ultimately, then, the expansion of credit money (and hence the expansion of purchasing power) depends on the willingness of companies and consumers to borrow, overseen by the profit-maximizing judgements of private banks and other financial institutions.

No-Interest Loans!

In the 1990s, Japan's economy experienced a long, painful recession, following the meltdown of an overblown real estate "bubble." In response to the recession, Japan's central bank cut interest rates to zero: borrowing money became *free*. Despite this, credit (and hence spending) grew very slowly for several years, because Japanese businesses and consumers remained very pessimistic about the economy's future prospects.

The fragility of finance

Private bank lending is a lucrative business: private banks, quite literally, have a license to create money. But it is an inherently fragile business, too – always hanging on the hope that depositors will remain confident in the stability of their bank, and never collectively demand their money back at the same time. If that happens, a bank never has enough currency on hand to make those payouts, and the bank collapses.

In response to periodic bank failures (and the immense economic and social damage they caused), government regulators gradually instituted rules limiting how aggressively private banks can expand their lending. Initially, they utilized a FRACTIONAL RESERVE system: banks had to keep a certain fraction (usually less than 10 percent) of their total loans on hand at all times as hard currency, to guard against a rush of withdrawals. Governments also used other tools (including requiring banks to keep certain amounts of their own money on deposit with the government's CENTRAL BANK) to further stabilize the banking system, and also to try to smooth out the ups and downs of the private banking cycle.

Today, those rules have been relaxed considerably, and the private financial industry functions in a largely unregulated environment. Banks must meet very broad CAPITAL ADEQUACY requirements, maintaining enough internal resources (including the bank's own invested capital) to handle (with some safety margin) any foreseeable surge in withdrawals. But finance is still inherently fragile. Throughout its history, capitalism has experienced periodic episodes of collapse and crisis in private banking, and there's no reason to expect that this has changed. In Chapter 18, we will discuss the more sophisticated, and even more fragile, ways which private financiers have developed to extract extra profit from the buying and selling of paper assets.

Putting money on the map

Let's review the key features of the capitalist credit money system:

- The financial industry itself is not directly productive. You can paper your walls with currency, stocks, and bonds, line your birdcage, or even use them (in a pinch) as toilet paper. But the real value of money is not the paper it is printed on; it comes from the things it can buy. Likewise, the financial industry is a "paper economy." It does not produce goods or services that are inherently useful. It produces money. In doing so, finance provides a service which allows (when it works well) genuinely productive companies and households to work, consume, and invest. Finance is economically valuable only to the extent that it stimulates and facilitates this real production and growth. And private finance doesn't always do that job well.

- The money-creating and money-destroying actions of banks are guided by their private profits, not by the needs of the broader economy. When credit expands rapidly, spending expands rapidly, and – to a point – the economy grows rapidly. When credit does not grow, or even contracts (as when banks "call in" existing loans), the economy stagnates or shrinks. Banks oversee how and when this happens, in line with their efforts to maximize their own profits. There are times when these private interests of banks, and the interests of society as a whole, diverge dramatically. For example, during an economic downturn fearful banks reduce lending, just when the economy needs *more* purchasing power, not less.

- The emergence of credit has broken the link between savings and investment. In pre-credit societies, producers had to physically save surplus production before it could be re-invested in new, more ambitious projects. Today, however, companies just take out loans to pay for new investment – and then repay those loans with a portion of the profits from future production. All the company needs is a credible business plan and a willing banker. In a credit system, investment *leads* economic growth; savings, meanwhile, are *produced* by economic growth.

Essentially, then, finance plays a subsidiary, helping role to the real economy, by providing credit for productive, growing, non-financial companies.

Figure 16.1 incorporates this subsidiary role into our map of the economy. Finance sits "above" the real economy. It provides credit (new money) to capitalists, allowing them to invest sooner and faster than if they had to pre-save all their investments. This flow is labelled D (for debt) on the map. In return, the banks receive a share of profits in the form of interest and loan repayments (the original debt D, plus i

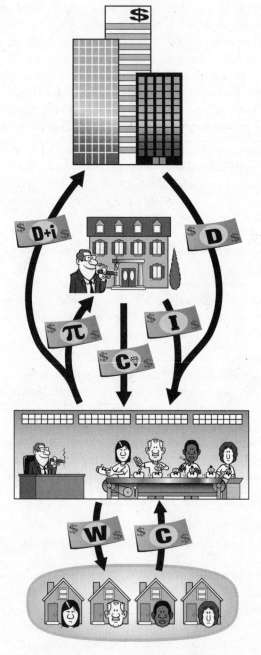

Figure 16.1   Economic Road Map: Banks

for interest) from the companies they financed. The remaining residual profit is retained by the actual owners of the company.

This sets up a potential conflict of interest between the financial sector and real, productive companies over how the profit pie is divided. If the banks' share becomes too large, then the incentive for companies to undertake real investment is reduced. On the other hand, both financiers and "real" capitalists have a shared interest in increasing the *total* return to capital. This explains why they have both strongly supported the overall direction of neoliberal economic policy. Indeed, it was a coming together of financial interests (appalled at the losses experienced in the 1970s) and real businesses (fatigued at the difficulty of extracting work effort from an increasingly uppity workforce) that was the crucial precondition for the political triumph of neoliberalism at the end of the 1970s.

In real-world practice, the financial industry also provides credit to households to facilitate major purchases, and recycles personal savings from those lucky households which do not spend all their income. But since households as a whole do not significantly save, this role is less important to overall economic growth than business lending; hence we have not portrayed it on this map.

Bankers, like capitalists, live very comfortable lives, and a portion of their interest income (which was siphoned off from capitalists' profit income) is devoted to the same luxury consumption patterns as the capitalists they lend to. For simplicity, then, Figure 16.1 includes bankers' consumption spending within overall capitalist spending.

17

Inflation, Central Banks, and Monetary Policy

Prices and inflation

Every marketed product has a money price, measured in units of currency (dollars, pounds, and so on). These prices help buyers to compare one commodity to another. When a shopper goes looking for a bargain, they compare prices of different brands to see which one offers (in their judgement) the best deal. When comparing prices of different commodities, we are examining RELATIVE PRICES: that is, the price of one commodity relative to another. In this comparison, it doesn't really matter what currency is used, or whether we measure prices in dollars or cents. It is the *ratio* of prices, not the prices themselves, that is most interesting. A bottle of fine chardonnay costs three times as much as the cheap house white; a passenger car costs 20 times as much as a high-definition TV set; a detached home costs four times as much as a small condominium. For this purpose, you can choose any standard of measure.

Relative prices change over time, reflecting the changing conditions of production of different commodities. Technological breakthroughs which make it less costly to produce certain commodities usually lead to declines in their relative prices. For example, prices have declined quickly for personal computers and other electronic products in recent decades for this reason. Changes in the intensity of competition in particular industries can also change their relative prices, by affecting the "normal" rate of profit paid out in those industries.

In contrast, absolute prices are simply the actual numbers attached to prices. And the PRICE LEVEL is the overall level of absolute prices prevailing in an economy. Suppose that suddenly, every store in the country began to label prices in cents (or pence), rather than dollars (or pounds). Prices would suddenly *seem* much higher. But at the same time everyone now receives their income in pennies. Suddenly, their wages and salaries look much bigger, too.

Has anything changed? Not really. All relative prices are the same. And the purchasing power of wages and salaries is the same. So people aren't any richer (by virtue of their "high" incomes), nor are they any poorer (because of "high" prices). But the absolute price level (quoted in cents now, rather than dollars) is 100 times higher than it used to be – since the absolute number describing each price is 100 times larger.

The most common reason for a change in the absolute price level is INFLATION. Inflation occurs when the average level of prices in the economy increases over time. Even as overall prices are increasing, particular *relative* prices will change. Prices of some commodities will increase more slowly than average (thus becoming less expensive in relative terms), while others increase more rapidly (becoming relatively more expensive). For a few commodities (like electronics), prices might decline in absolute terms despite the rise in the overall price level. These products thus become doubly inexpensive in relative terms – since their absolute prices are falling while most other prices are rising.

DEFLATION is also possible if the absolute price level *declines* over time. Deflation usually occurs during severe economic recession or crisis, when banks contract credit and businesses are desperate to sell products. Deflation has disastrous consequences, including escalating debt burdens for households, businesses, and government.

The real price of any commodity is its price adjusted to reflect any change in the overall price level. A commodity's real price is therefore its particular relative price compared to the general level of *all* prices. A commodity's real price goes up if its absolute price (measured in dollars) rises faster than the overall price level.

Other economic variables can also be measured in real terms. For example, suppose that workers receive a 5 percent increase in their wages. But at the same time, suppose that overall consumer prices also grew by 5 percent. REAL WAGES – that is, the purchasing power of wages – haven't changed at all. Wages measured in dollars (known as NOMINAL WAGES) must grow faster than consumer prices for workers to experience any improvement in real purchasing power.

Interest rates, too, should be measured in real terms, as the difference between the nominal interest rate (in percent) and the rate of inflation. If a bank charges 5 percent annual interest for a loan when overall prices are also growing at 5 percent, the bank's wealth doesn't change – because the loaned money, once repaid with interest, has no more purchasing power than it did when it was loaned out. If interest rates are *lower* than inflation, then the REAL INTEREST RATE is *negative*: the borrower, not the lender, is better off at the end of the loan because the money they pay back is worth less than the money they borrowed. The higher is inflation, therefore, the lower is the real interest rate. That's why financial institutions hate inflation more than any other sector of society.

The costs of inflation – and its benefits, too

Governments, financiers, businesses, and even ordinary citizens often wring their hands over inflation. And under neoliberalism, the never-ending fight to reduce and control inflation has become the top economic priority: more important than reducing unemployment or alleviating poverty.

It is true that inflation can be painful. At very high levels, it can be downright destructive. But the social costs of inflation are often exaggerated by those (like bankers) who have vested interests in a low-inflation environment. And at moderate levels, inflation can actually be good for the economy – serving as a kind of lubricant to grease the economic wheels.

If every price and every flow of income experienced inflation at the same rate, it would have no real economic impact, and no winners or losers. This was true in the preceding example of an economy which converted from dollars to cents. The absolute price level grew by 100 times, with no real effect whatsoever.

In real life, however, inflation is never so even-handed or predictable. Some prices rise faster than others. Some incomes keep up with inflation, or even surpass it; others lag behind. Inflation (or more precisely, changes in the rate of inflation) creates uncertainty in the minds of companies, investors, and households; this can be stressful, and in some cases can impede investment.

Individuals or groups try to protect themselves against inflation by indexing their incomes to the price level. Labour contracts or social programs which provide for automatic cost-of-living adjustments are a common way to do this.

Some sectors of society, meanwhile, actually benefit from inflation (and from an increase in inflation). Borrowers are the biggest winners: the real burden of their loan is eaten away by higher prices. Governments are large debtors, so in theory they should

Measuring Inflation

The most common measure of prices is the CONSUMER PRICE INDEX (CPI). This is a weighted index of inflation in all the things that consumers buy, including shelter, food, transportation, personal services, and household products and appliances. Statisticians gather detailed information (usually each month) on the prices of all products included in a specified "basket" of typical consumer purchases. Each product is then weighted according to its importance in overall consumer spending. The index is phrased in terms of prices in a certain base year (when the CPI is set to 100). Annual inflation in consumer prices then equals the percentage rise in the CPI index over one year. Since the CPI is based on the most detailed and frequent statistical research, and is widely reported in the media, it receives the most attention from policy-makers (including central banks).

There are other measures of inflation, too. Special price indices are calculated to measure average inflation in producer prices (like raw materials, parts, and other supplies), or commodities (such as oil, other forms of energy, minerals, and bulk foods). Somewhat different is the GDP DEFLATOR: this measures inflation as the difference between the increase in nominal GDP and the increase in real GDP (both of which are separately estimated by statistical agencies). Deflators can also be calculated for any particular component of spending in GDP (such as consumer spending, investment, and exports and imports).

be relatively unconcerned about inflation. This makes it especially ironic that neoliberal governments pushed so hard for strict anti-inflation remedies in the 1980s and 1990s. A major side-effect of those measures (lower inflation and higher real interest rates) was a dramatic escalation in government debt.

On the other hand, some sectors lose from inflation:

- Individuals who live on incomes that are fixed in dollar terms lose purchasing power when overall prices rise.

- Workers who are unable to win wage increases to keep up with inflation also lose real purchasing power.

- Lenders who loan money at a fixed rate of interest will see the real value of their loan (and future interest payments) reduced by inflation. It is possible to index loans to inflation, but this is rare.

- Owners of financial wealth lose some of their real wealth with every increase in prices.

These latter two sectors – financial institutions and wealth-owners – constitute an immensely powerful and influential bloc in favour of reducing and tightly controlling inflation. Their very negative experience during the 1970s, when accelerating inflation produced negative real interest rates and destroyed trillions of dollars of private wealth, led them to forcefully demand (and win) strict anti-inflation policies under neoliberalism.

In terms of the impact of inflation on overall economic performance (as opposed to its varying distributive impacts on different sectors of society), there's no conclusive evidence that moderate inflation undermines real investment, growth, or productivity. Higher rates of inflation can indeed cause significant economic and social stress, as individuals and companies take drastic measures (including the removal of capital from the country) to protect their incomes and wealth. And very high inflation (called HYPER-INFLATION) is usually associated with economic and political breakdown.

But there's no reliable evidence that single-digit inflation (under 10 percent per year) harms real economic progress. If anything, there seems to be a positive connection between single-digit inflation and growth: not because inflation *causes* higher growth, but simply because faster-growing economies tend to experience somewhat faster inflation. Some economic evidence suggests that modest inflation (in the range of 2–4 percent) is actually beneficial. It allows sellers of various commodities (including workers, who sell their labour) to reduce relative prices when necessary, without actually cutting nominal prices (in dollars). Modest inflation thus lubricates the ongoing relative price adjustments that are necessary in any evolving economy.

Beyond this low rate, however, there's no convincing evidence that there are any economic benefits to inflation, either. In particular, there's no predictable relationship between unemployment and inflation. Economists once believed that an economy could "trade" a slightly higher rate of inflation for a slightly lower rate of unemployment, but empirical evidence has refuted this theory, as well. In fact, there's no reliable relationship at all between inflation and unemployment.

The causes of inflation

Inflation is a complex, unpredictable phenomenon. Over the years, many economists have developed one-size-fits-all theories of inflation, its causes, and its remedies. But these simplistic theories have failed.

For example, the ultra-conservative monetarists who became so influential with the advent of neoliberalism (led by Milton Friedman) believed inflation was caused solely by an excess supply of money. This was proven wrong in the 1980s. Others argued inflation would take off whenever unemployment fell below its so-called "natural" rate. This was proven wrong in the 1990s. Today's central bankers have a more nuanced but still one-dimensional view: inflation results when overall spending exceeds the economy's vaguely-defined "potential output." Restraining spending (through higher interest rates, when needed) is the latest one-size-fits-all prescription for controlling inflation. Eventually this theory will be proven wrong, too.

In reality, there are many potential causes of inflation. Policy-makers should take a pragmatic, flexible, and balanced view of these various causes – because the appropriate cure for inflation (when one is deemed necessary) depends on its cause:

- Inflation can indeed result from excess spending; this is called "demand-pull inflation." If consumers and businesses are increasing spending too aggressively (fuelled, probably, by a rapid expansion of credit) relative to the quantity of goods and services available to purchase, then prices may be bid up as purchasers compete for scarce supplies. Curing this kind of inflation could involve reducing demand (through *higher* interest rates). But it could also involve stimulating additional supply (including measures to encourage investment – which would require *lower* interest rates).

- Inflation can result from higher labour costs. If wages grow faster than productivity, then unit labour costs (the ratio of labour costs to productivity) will increase. Companies will try to pass on those higher production costs in higher prices. Depending on competitive conditions, they may or may not be able to do this. Potential responses to this kind of inflation include deliberately promoting unemployment (as neoliberal central banks have done), finding ways to moderate wage increases when unemployment is low (perhaps through economy-wide bargaining arrangements, as exist in some European countries), or trying to prevent companies from passing on higher prices (through price controls, more competition, or increased imports).

- Higher profits can cause inflation, too – not just higher wages. If companies feel that they can increase prices without losing customers (perhaps due to a lack of competition, or a willingness of customers to tolerate higher prices), they will do so.

- Another kind of inflation arises from increases in raw material prices, especially for crucial commodities used as inputs throughout the whole economy. Energy costs are an important example of this problem: higher oil prices were a major cause of the inflation of the 1970s. This type of inflation usually arises from global changes in commodity prices, which makes it hard for individual countries to control.

- Inflation can become self-fuelling: once it starts, then the actions of various economic players to protect themselves (such as companies passing on higher prices, or workers demanding cost-of-living adjustments) reinforce inflation at that rate. For this reason, inflation rates tend to demonstrate a natural *inertia*: inflation next year will likely be similar to what it was this year, unless some significant change in economic conditions "knocks" the inflation rate off its mooring.

Real-world experience has indicated two additional insights regarding changes in the inflation rate:

- Reducing the inflation rate is a very painful process, usually involving recession, high unemployment, and lost economic opportunity. On one hand, this suggests extreme caution in deciding to reduce the inflation rate: the costs of doing so are very high, and the benefits (when inflation is moderate, anyway) are questionable. On the other hand, it also suggests caution in allowing inflation to increase – because the cost of bringing it back down, if that is ever deemed necessary, will be painful.

• Increases in employment and purchasing power can be associated with higher inflation, for obvious reasons. When more people are working, earning more money to spend, they willingly pay more for the things they buy, and companies willingly pump up prices. Experience has shown, however, that if economic expansion is gradual and steady, then the inflationary impacts of growth and employment are muted. Companies have time to respond to strong purchasing power with more output, rather than higher prices, and competition will be more effective in restraining prices. Sudden surges in growth or employment, on the other hand, are more likely to lead to outbursts of inflation.

Central banks

CENTRAL BANKS are probably the most important single actors on the economic stage. They have an immense impact on the economy – more than governments. They have the power to closely regulate everything from prices to job creation to incomes. And in most countries, central banks perform their duties without any direct accountability whatsoever to the broader population, or even to government ... even though the central bank itself is a government agency!

The first central banks (like the Bank of England) were created in Europe in the early days of capitalism, to provide banking and credit services for national governments. In the twentieth century their role evolved, partly in response to problems encountered in the private banking system. Central banks took on additional tasks: supervising private bank lending, imposing limits on especially risky bank activities, and stepping in during times of crisis and panic to provide emergency loans and forestall bank collapse. Because of this role, the central bank is often called the "lender of last resort."

More recently, these supervisory functions have become less important as private finance has been mostly deregulated. But central banks must still be ready to act quickly in times of crisis. For example, in 1998 the US Federal Reserve bailed out several large private financial firms (including Long Term Capital Management, a notorious investment fund) to prevent an all-out financial panic when their speculative investments suddenly collapsed. It did the same thing again a decade later (joined by other leading central banks) in response to severe problems in the US mortgage lending industry.

More important today than regulating private banks, however, is central banks' role in regulating the "temperature" of the whole economy. Central banks are in charge of MONETARY POLICY: using interest rates (and, occasionally, other policy instruments) to either stimulate or discourage growth and job creation. Low interest rates stimulate credit creation and spending across many sectors of the economy: including home-building and construction, cars and other major consumer purchases, business investment, and even exports (low interest rates tend to reduce a country's exchange rate and thus stimulate more foreign sales). High interest rates have the opposite effect.

Central banks directly control interest rates on short-term loans they provide to private banks, as part of the normal day-to-day clearing and accounting operations that occur in the financial system. In turn, private banks use this interest rate as a guide in setting the rates they charge customers for everything from home mortgages to business lines of credit. (Of course, the banks add a generous profit margin for themselves.) In turn, longer-term interest rates (like long-term bond rates) tend to follow the (longer-term) direction set by central banks. Central bank policy, therefore, is the crucial determinant of interest rates across the financial spectrum.

The impact of interest rates on economic growth is relatively slow to be felt: a change in interest rates can take up to two years to have full effect on spending. And monetary policy can be undermined or even overwhelmed by other factors – such as changes in consumer or investor sentiment, exchange rates, or government taxes and spending. Unfortunately, interest rates are also a very blunt instrument: they're a one-size-fits-all policy tool, which can't take account of unique conditions or problems faced in specific regions or specific industries.

Nevertheless, interest rates are a powerful tool with which the central bank influences the overall path of the economy. And the criteria on which central banks make their decisions are not "neutral" or "technical." They reflect central bankers' views of the economy, their ranking of the importance of different economic goals (holding inflation as more important than unemployment, poverty, and other economic problems), and their susceptibility to the influence of different sectors within society. Central bankers like to pretend they are neutral technocrats, merely helping to guide the economy to some mythical point of maximum efficiency. But in reality they are political institutions – and like other political institutions, their actions reflect judgements regarding which priorities are more important than others.

Neoliberal monetary policy

During the long Golden Age expansion, central banks generally supported efforts to keep the economy as close to full employment as possible. However, both the direction of monetary policy and the ways in which it is implemented changed dramatically with the advent of neoliberalism. Indeed, the change in monetary policy that began in the late 1970s was the first and most important indicator of the dramatic U-turn being engineered at the economy's highest levels. And monetary policy remains one of the most powerful and entrenched features of the broader neoliberal agenda.

Blood on the Floor

"The Federal Reserve had to show that when faced with the painful choice between maintaining a tight monetary policy to fight inflation and easing monetary policy to combat recession, it would choose to fight inflation. In other words, to establish its credibility, the Federal Reserve had to demonstrate its willingness to spill blood, lots of blood, other people's blood."

Michael Mussa, former Research Director, International Monetary Fund (1979), cited in Andrew Glyn, *Capitalism Unleashed: Finance, Globalization, and Welfare* (Oxford: Oxford University Press, 2006), p. 24.

Initially, neoliberal monetary policy was heavily influenced by the monetarist ideas of Milton Friedman and other ultra-conservative economists. They weren't concerned with unemployment, arguing that it reflected laziness or the perverse impact of labour market "rigidities" (like unions, unemployment insurance, and minimum wages). In their extreme interpretation of neoclassical theory, the only impact of money is to determine the absolute price level. Therefore, to control inflation, central banks simply had to control the growth of the money supply. If they allowed an annual 5 percent increase in the total supply of money, and if they stuck to that rule for a long time, then inflation would eventually settle at 5 percent. Thus began an experiment in MONETARY TARGETING (trying to directly control the expansion of money) that was a colossal failure.

The vicious global recession of 1981–82 was caused directly by monetarist policies. Their effort to link inflation to money supply growth failed, because in a credit banking system central banks *cannot* control money supply. Rather, money expansion is determined by the credit-creation activity of private banks and the willingness of borrowers to take on new loans.

However, that deliberate recession was ultimately successful in signalling the beginning of a new era in global capitalism. It disposed of the notion that full employment was the top economic priority. And it began the long, painful process of ratcheting down popular expectations, regarding what average people can (and can't) expect from the economy.

Since then, central banks have fine-tuned their approach to controlling inflation. Like the original monetarists, modern central bankers still believe the free-market economy is largely efficient and self-adjusting (see Table 17.1). The only long-run impact of monetary policy, they still believe, is on the rate of inflation; free-market forces in the real economy determine real output, employment and productivity. Central banks should therefore have tunnel vision: focusing only on controlling inflation, ignoring other goals (like job creation). ▪ *

However, modern central banks have altered their operational strategy for pursuing this common vision. They no longer try to control the money supply directly, recognizing that money expansion depends on the creation of credit. Instead, most central banks now directly target a certain inflation rate. To attain the targeted inflation rate, central banks influence credit creation and hence spending by frequently adjusting interest rates. It is clear that the fundamental assumptions of the monetarists have been inherited by today's central bankers, who can therefore be considered "quasi-monetarists." (Neoclassical economists arrogantly call this approach the "New Consensus" in monetary policy – ignoring the criticisms made by heterodox thinkers.) They still believe that controlling inflation is the

* See the Economics for Everyone website for statistics, www.economicsforeveryone.com.

Table 17.1 Monetarism and "Quasi-Monetarism"

Areas of Agreement:

Monetary policy should focus solely on controlling inflation, not reducing unemployment.

Apparent unemployment is either voluntary (people who don't want to work) or due to labour market frictions and rigidities.

The only long-term way to reduce unemployment is to eliminate labour market frictions and rigidities.

Near-zero inflation will assist the real economy to reach its natural full-employment equilibrium.

The central bank should be independent and "apolitical," free from political interference or democratic oversight, to insulate its inflation-controlling mandate from popular pressure.

Areas of Disagreement:

Monetarism (Milton Friedman, 1980s)	Quasi-Monetarism (modern central banks)
Inflation is caused by too much money.	Inflation is caused by too much spending.
Central banks should directly control money supply.	Central banks should indirectly manage money supply via the interest rate.
Central banks should target growth in the money supply, to control inflation indirectly.	Central banks should target the inflation rate.
Economic fine-tuning doesn't work; government should stand back and let markets re-create full employment.	Constant fine-tuning of interest rates guides the economy to its full-employment equilibrium.

central, even exclusive goal of central banking; all they have changed is their view on how that goal should be pursued.

Another important feature of neoliberal monetary policy has been an emphasis on entrenching the so-called "independence" of central banks. In most developed countries, central banks have been granted day-to-day freedom to pursue their goals without oversight or interference from government. To varying degrees, national governments still participate in determining the banks' broader objectives – most importantly, setting formal inflation targets (where they exist). But they are prohibited from influencing the banks' regular interest rate adjustments or other actions.

The deliberate goal of this structured independence is to insulate the powerful, often painful interventions of central banks from popular pressure. Of course, central banks are not really "independent" at all:

the elevation of inflation control to the top of the economic agenda, regardless of what else is sacrificed in the process, is a non-neutral and highly political choice that imposes uneven costs and benefits on different segments of society. The financial industry and owners of financial wealth have benefited most clearly from neoliberal monetary policy. And they continue to have huge influence over the day-to-day actions of central banks. But by erecting central banks as an independent, supposedly apolitical authority, elected governments pretend that choices regarding the fight against inflation are out of their hands.

Central bank "independence" is explicitly and deliberately anti-democratic. It removes a crucial element of public economic policy from the realm of public deliberation and control. By pretending that monetary policy is a neutral, technical, and hence apolitical activity, governments hope that public debate over monetary policy will evaporate.

Evaluating quasi-monetarism

Neoliberal monetary policy has been highly successful in several of its stated goals. Global inflation rates have subsided notably since the early 1980s (see Figure 17.1). In recent years, inflation throughout most of the developed capitalist world (and many developing countries, too) has been remarkably stable at around 3 percent – despite relatively low unemployment rates, and the sharp energy price increases which occurred early in the new century.

In broader political terms, too, the new agenda has been highly effective. In most countries, there is very little public debate about interest rate policy. The notion that interest rates should be used to control inflation, and nothing else, has gained wide currency, even among centre-left political leaders (whose acceptance of this strict regime is usually motivated by a desire to impress powerful financial lobbyists with their "realistic" economic views). And the former belief that the economy can and should be managed in order to maintain full employment seems dead and buried.

Dig deeper, however, and the completeness of this triumph is not quite so clear. While broad consumer price inflation has declined, this is not solely due to monetary policy. Other factors – like shrinking unit labour costs, the rise of low-cost imports from China, and other time-limited effects – also played a role. Moreover, periodic bouts

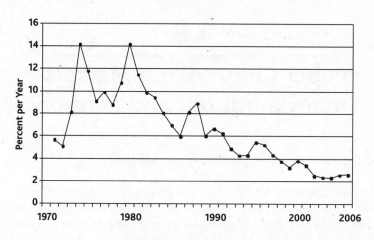

Figure 17.1 **Consumer Price Inflation**
OECD Average

Source: Organization for Economic Cooperation and Development.

of inflation in asset prices (including unsustainable bubbles in stock markets and real estate) have been a regular and at times disastrous feature of life under the quasi-monetarists, proving that they haven't truly achieved "price stability."

More fundamentally, the promised boost to real investment, growth, and productivity which was supposed to accompany low inflation has been very hard to detect. GDP growth rates are consistently slower than they were even in the latter, troubled years of the Golden Age expansion, and real business investment has slowed noticeably. This failure to stimulate stronger improvements in the real economy is the most important crack in the apparent triumph of quasi-monetarism.

18

Paper Chase: Stock Markets, Financialization, and Pensions

Corporate finance: putting it all together

In earlier chapters, we described a simple process of business lending between a productive company and a bank. The bank creates credit. The productive company uses this purchasing power to invest in capital goods, hire workers, and expand production. This lending-and-investment process is essential to economic growth and job creation under capitalism.

In practice, however, companies have access to a wide range of financial resources to pay for their investments, not just bank loans. In fact, most established companies can usually pay for ongoing real investment needs internally (from profits on existing business), with no need for outside financing sources at all. Indeed, in recent years the business sector has generated far more profit than it needs to pay for new investments. As a result, a strange reversal of traditional financial channels has occurred: instead of turning to financial markets to finance new investment, companies now use financial institutions to recycle surplus cash.

Quickly-growing companies, however, do need help to finance new investments. Troubled or loss-making companies, too, need to borrow – often as they struggle to turn around their operations. And all companies need routine financial tools (like lines of credit) to pay their day-to-day bills, while minimizing the idle cash they keep on hand.

The various financial resources available to productive companies include:

- **Bank loans** These are the simplest form of finance, but usually the most expensive. Loans can be short term or long term, depending on how quickly the borrower must pay back the money (with interest, of course). Loans are usually backed up with some kind of real collateral from the borrowing company.

If the company stops paying interest, then the bank gets that property as compensation.

- **Corporate bonds**   These allow companies to borrow directly from investors, cutting out the bank as the "middleman." Like loans, companies must pay interest on a bond. Riskier companies have to pay higher interest rates. Very risky companies issue "junk" bonds, which pay interest several percentage points higher than normal loans. Investors, in turn, can buy and re-sell corporate bonds on bond markets. Through this trading they can make extra profit (or reduce potential losses when a borrowing company is in financial trouble). Bond prices rise when interest rates go down, or when a company's financial stability improves.

- **Equities**   Companies can also raise new funds by issuing small "pieces" of ownership, called equities, SHARES, or stocks. These assets do not normally pay interest, although special shares (called "preferred shares") may pay interest. And many companies pay cash dividends (usually every three months) to shareholders, which are similar to interest. But even if no interest is paid, issuing new equity is costly for a company. Administration costs (like brokerage fees) eat up a tenth or more of all new funds raised, and companies which issue shares must comply with complex government regulations regarding financial disclosure, accounting procedures, and internal management practices. If a company goes bankrupt, shareholders are the last to receive any compensation from selling the company's remaining assets: this is the risk they must take, by becoming part-owners of the company. Company shares are bought and re-sold on the STOCK MARKET. Professional analysts and investment brokers monitor stock market trends very carefully, hoping to profit from the ups and downs of share prices; they put incredible pressure on corporate executives to manage their companies with a strict focus on maximizing profitability and hence shareholder wealth.

Companies try to balance their financial needs across these different sources: loans, bonds, and equity. Interestingly, no corporate executive would ever claim (as conservative politicians do) that company debt should be eliminated altogether. Effectively used, debt allows a company's owners to enhance their own profit. If the company's real investments generate a higher rate of profit than the interest that must be paid on its debt, then the company can "magnify" bottom-line profit by increasing its debt.

But big risks come with debt, too. In tough times, heavily-indebted companies face greater risk of outright bankruptcy (since they must continue to pay interest, whether they have any profits or not). With little internal equity to fall back on as a cushion, the company might be unable to pay its interest costs – in which case it collapses.

Speculation, financialization, and fragility

Unlike normal bank loans, bonds and equities can be bought and sold on "second-hand" markets (like the bond market and the stock market). In theory, these paper markets have a productive underlying purpose: they make it easier for companies to mobilize financial resources (from individual investors) to finance real investment projects. And the ability to sell their bonds or stocks when needed makes investors more willing to invest their money in a company in the first place.

Bubbles and Whirlpools

"Speculators may do no harm as bubbles on a steady stream of enterprise. But the position is serious when enterprise becomes the bubble on a whirlpool of speculation. When the capital development of a country becomes a by-product of the activities of a casino, the job is likely to be ill-done."

John Maynard Keynes, British Economist (1936).

However, once they've been issued, the useful "real" life of stocks and bonds is over. The borrowing company has received the initial finance, and (hopefully) done something productive with it. The subsequent secondary buying and selling of those assets has no direct impact on the company which issued them. And all that second-hand buying and selling is fundamentally divorced from the real production that real businesses undertake. Instead, the enormous paper chase which occurs every trading day on financial markets is motivated by a very different goal.

Productive profit is generated by a company which purchases inputs (including labour), produces a good or service, and sells it for more than it cost to produce. The pursuit of productive profit has many unfortunate side-effects, but at least it results in production and employment.

Speculative profit, on the other hand, involves no production. It is motivated by the age-old adage: "Buy low, and sell high." No jobs are created (except for the brokers who handle the trading, pocketing a lucrative commission on each sale). Investors simply buy an asset, and then hope that its price rises, allowing them to sell it for more than they paid. SPECULATION is the act of buying something purely in hopes that its price will rise.

Any asset can be bought and sold for speculative purposes: including "real" things like real estate, fine art, and commodities (from oil to pork bellies). But today paper financial assets are the major tool of the speculative trade. And the dramatic expansion of financial trading under neoliberalism – both the variety of financial assets traded, and the amount of selling that takes place – means that financial speculation now plays a dominant, wasteful, and often destructive role in the economy.

To make matters worse, clever financial experts are constantly developing new kinds of financial assets, and new ways of trading them for profit. Some of these assets (called DERIVATIVES) depend, often in very complex ways, on the performance of *other* financial assets. Example of derivatives include futures, options, and swaps. Money itself can be traded for speculative reasons, especially on foreign exchange markets (where one country's money is converted into another country's money). And whether it's stocks, bonds, or derivatives, every trade generates a juicy commission (typically 2 or 3 percent) for the brokers who conduct it – giving them a massive interest in frenetic trading for its own sake.

The development of secondary financial markets has thus opened up a Pandora's Box of speculative financial activity. Investors become less concerned with companies' real businesses and more concerned with their paper assets. And the profits from innovative financial "engineering" – developing and selling new types of paper assets – can be immense. Individuals and investors can become far wealthier, far faster, by successfully playing the financial markets rather than through the gradual, often boring process of building a successful productive business. Unfortunately, speculative bubbles – which occur when the price of a certain asset is driven quickly higher by exploding investor interest, creating fabulous (but surreal) wealth in the process – are always followed by speculative crashes.

A typical speculative cycle begins with the "discovery" of some new asset: perhaps a new product, a new technology, or even just some amazing new kind of financial derivative. In the 1600s, in one of capitalism's first speculative episodes, Dutch investors drove the price of new breeds of tulips to astronomical highs – peaking in 1635 at as much as several thousand Dutch florins for a single tulip bulb (equivalent to as much as US$75,000 today). Initial investor interest, concentrated among insiders, drives up the price of that asset. Other investors see rising prices (and the associated speculative profits), and pile in for a piece of the action. This in turn drives the price even higher.

No matter what the initial spark for the upward motion, it is soon overwhelmed by purely speculative pressure. Investors' hopes for quick trading profits become self-fulfilling, driving the price still higher ... for a while, anyway. But eventually something shocks the confidence of investors. Insiders, smelling trouble, sell out first. That produces an initial price decline. Suddenly greed turns to fear, and other investors sell their assets en masse. Once again, the herd mentality of investors becomes self-fulfilling – but this time in a downward direction. The end result is a faster rise, and a deeper fall, than could be justified by any "real" economic factors. In the interim, the bubble produced an immense waste of resources, and untold losses for those who didn't reach the financial exits in time.

In many economies (especially those in the Anglo-Saxon world), this endless paper chase has come to dominate economic news and economic moods. It's assumed that if the stock market is rising, the economy must be healthy. Indeed, pompous executives commonly describe their efforts to boost the wealth of their shareholders as the "creation of value." And they can seemingly create billions of dollars of "value" overnight, if their company's shares catch a rising speculative tide. How utterly miraculous this must seem in contrast to the daily grind and drudge of average working people who toil to create smaller bits of genuine value every day. But in concrete economic terms, there's no value at all in the hyperactive and pointless flight of paper assets around the markets. Well over 95 percent of trading on major stock markets simply represents the recycling of already-issued assets. Where's the value in that?

Today there's an incredible diversity and flexibility of financial assets, and those assets (and the specialized financial experts who create and manage them) play a larger role in the operations of real businesses. The shift to an increasingly finance-intensive mode of economic development is called FINANCIALIZATION. One simple way of measuring financialization is to compare the stock of financial assets in an economy, with the stock of real capital assets which underlies it. Figure 18.1 does this for the US economy – the largest and most financialized in the world. Until the late 1970s, there was roughly a dollar in real capital (buildings, property, equipment) for every dollar in financial wealth (stocks, bonds, or other paper assets). ▮ * One could have some confidence that each financial asset was backed by something tangible and lasting.

With neoliberalism, however, that ratio dramatically grew – due partly to the deliberate slowdown in the accumulation of real wealth and partly to the explosion of financial activity. Today there are over two dollars in financial assets for every dollar of tangible capital. This ratio peaked in 1999 (at the height of the dot-com stock market bubble), declined during the subsequent financial downturn, but has started to grow once again. Clearly the financial tail has come to wag the economic dog. And investors should quite rightly worry about what, if anything, underlies their financial wealth.

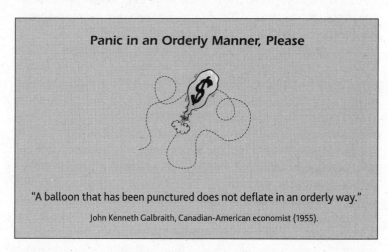

Panic in an Orderly Manner, Please

"A balloon that has been punctured does not deflate in an orderly way."

John Kenneth Galbraith, Canadian-American economist (1955).

* See the Economics for Everyone website for statistics, www.economicsforeveryone.com.

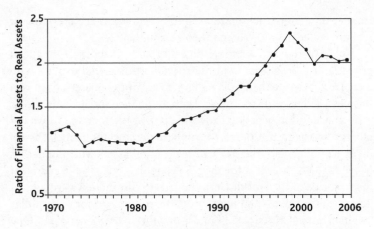

Figure 18.1   **Financialization in the US Economy**
1970–2006

Source: Author's calculations from US Federal Reserve Board of Governors data.

The complex layering of financial assets on top of each other, constant speculative trading in those assets, and the normal tendency of companies (including financial companies) to leverage their investments with debt, together gives rise to a deep-rooted financial fragility in modern capitalism. Financial assets have expanded much faster than real capital. Investors don't fully understand the diversity and complexity of new financial assets, and their unpredictable dependence on other economic trends. Yet they continue to take on more debt, so long as their bankers are willing to lend them the money.

The rupture of any link in the long financial chain of modern capitalism can set a crisis in motion. For example, when speculative investments are financed with borrowed money (as is often the case), sudden speculative losses can force the investor to default on those loans; this can cause trouble for the bank or other lender which made those loans, and the losses begin to cascade from one player to another. At the beginning, these losses may have little impact on the real economy. Eventually, however, a financial downturn can impact on real investment, production, and employment. This is especially ironic – since the rapid expansion of finance which created the fragile conditions in the first place had little positive impact on the real economy. But a quick and severe financial downturn can undermine real production, investment, and employment, for various reasons:

- Companies worry about their ability to sell additional output in the future, and hence postpone planned investments.

- Banks suddenly become very worried about default risk, and pull back the amount of new credit on offer (even for routine business and consumer purchases).

- Consumers may become infected by the negative headlines, and postpone their own purchases (especially major, discretionary ones, like homes or cars).

Any of these outcomes, if strong enough, could cause a recession in the real economy.

On the other hand, the fragility of modern finance should not be overestimated. For the most part, neither the ups nor the downs of the paper economy have much impact on the real economy. Proactive central banks generally respond to episodes of financial crisis and contracting credit with quick reductions in interest rates and injections of emergency funds; these help to restore spending power and confidence. It is unlikely, at least in the developed economies, that outright financial collapse could cause dramatic or long-lasting damage to the real economy. On a day-to-day basis, however, the waste and distortion arising from the excesses of financialization give plenty of reason to try to curtail the paper chase.

Pensions and stock markets

Most financial assets are owned by the small minority of very well-off households which composes the modern capitalist class. As discussed in Chapter 7, a clear majority of corporate wealth is owned by the very richest households in every leading capitalist economy. Financial wealth is especially concentrated at the top in the major Anglo-Saxon economies.

Some analysts have argued, however, that ordinary households are sharing in the benefits of capital ownership through pension funds. Large pension funds have been among the most active and sophisticated players in the paper markets, always with an eye on maximizing their own speculative profits. However, their importance should not be exaggerated, and it is not remotely true that capitalism is being gradually "socialized" through the expansion of pension funds. As indicated in Table 18.1, collectively-managed pension plans account for a very small share of total stock market wealth, and that share is declining over time (mostly due to the shrinking share of workers who have workplace pension coverage in the first place).

Table 18.1   **People's Capitalism?**

	Pensions and Stock Markets, 2006	
Country	*Pension Fund* Equity Holdings as Share Total Equity Wealth*	*Change Since 1990*
US	6.7%	−3.2 points
UK	12.7%	−19.0 points
Canada	13.5%	−2.6 points

*   Collectively managed trusteed pension plans.

Perversely, pension funds have helped to impose a tighter degree of financial discipline over real companies. That discipline typically involves more intense efforts to minimize operating costs – including labour costs, through wage cuts, downsizing, and resistance to unionization. Pension funds' efforts to maximize returns can thus badly undermine the immediate economic well-being of workers whose future security is entrusted to those same funds!

By allowing workers the opportunity to retire at a decent age and enjoy their last years in some comfort (free from the compulsion to work), pensions are a crucial underpinning to workers' quality of life. They reduce lifetime working hours and have helped reduce poverty among the elderly. The first pensions were negotiated by unions at the workplace level. These workplace-based pensions are called occupational pension plans.

Later, workers fought for and (in most countries) won public pension systems. These pensions are paid by governments or government agencies. In some programs, public pensions are universal, paid to all elderly citizens. In other programs, pensions are paid only to those who were employed for a sufficient number of years during their working lives. In most cases, workers are required to contribute to public pensions via deductions from their paycheques. In a few cases, public pensions are funded directly from the government's general tax revenues.

Pensions can be financed in two main ways. A PAY-AS-YOU-GO PENSION (or "paygo")* is financed directly from the plan sponsor's ongoing revenues. Most paygo systems are run by national governments. They allocate a share of current and future tax revenues (including targeted pension premiums) to pay for promised pension benefits. This is the simplest way to organize a pension, with very low administration costs. The stability of these plans, however, depends on the continuing economic viability of the sponsoring organization. This explains why they are used mostly by governments (since companies can't credibly promise that they'll stay in business forever, and hence be able to fund far-off pension benefits from future revenues). Most public pensions in developed countries are organized on a paygo basis.

In contrast, in a PRE-FUNDED PENSION the plan sponsor accumulates financial wealth over time to pay promised pension benefits in the future. Typically, premiums are collected from plan members and/or their employers. These premiums are invested in a range of financial assets (trying to maintain a balance between high rates of return and low risk). On the basis of complex and uncertain actuarial assumptions (regarding everything from wage rates to interest rates to life expectancy), the plan is supposed to have enough disposable funds on hand to pay promised pensions when the time comes. Most workplace pensions are organized on a pre-funded basis, as are public pensions in some countries.

The advantage of a pre-funded pension is the somewhat greater certainty that a fund will be able to live up to its promises (although even pre-funded pensions are never truly secure – since financial markets can perform badly, and actuarial assumptions can miss the mark). This is essential with private companies, which can go bankrupt at any time. And if a plan sponsor (especially a government) is committed to investing pension monies according to some criteria other than maximum profits, the pool of capital created by pre-funding can be a useful economic tool. The disadvantages of the pre-funding model include much higher administration costs (mostly for the well-paid professionals who manage the fund's investments), and the risk that the fund won't accumulate enough assets to pay out promised benefits.

---

* Examples of this pay-as-you-go system are the US Social Security system, the Canada Pension Plan, the Basic State Pension and Second State Pension in the UK, and South Africa's Social Pension.

Pre-funded pensions, in turn, come in two main forms. DEFINED BENEFIT plans are group programs which specify the level of benefits to be paid, based on the number of years a retiree worked, their retirement age, and other factors. The onus then falls on the plan sponsor to ensure that sufficient funds are available to pay those benefits.

DEFINED CONTRIBUTION plans, on the other hand, simply deposit a specified annual premium (typically shared between a worker and their employer) into personalized accounts for each worker. These accounts are then used to "buy" individual pensions for each worker when they retire. The pension received by each worker depends totally on how much was deposited into their account, how much profit the account earned while it was invested, the level of interest rates prevailing at the time they retired, and other variables completely beyond the worker's control. There's little difference between a defined contribution pension and an employer-subsidized personal savings account.

The choice between these two kinds of pre-funding mostly hinges on who should bear the risks related to investment returns, life expectancy, and other key variables. In a defined benefit plan, the sponsor bears the risk; under defined contribution rules, that risk is transferred to the individual pensioner. No wonder, then, that employers have pushed hard in recent years to convert defined benefit pension plans into defined contribution schemes. Especially in the private sector, the overall importance of defined benefit plans is currently shrinking rapidly. The downside is that many pensioners will be left with inadequate pensions if their individual savings accounts should run out before they die.

Financial lobbyists argue strongly that pre-funded pensions are superior to paygo plans, even for public pensions. However, they have a huge vested interest in moving to a pre-funded system: namely, the massive trading commissions they earn for managing those funds, and investing them in various financial assets. Chile was one of the first countries to organize a pre-funded, defined contribution national pension system; while this model is endorsed by financial professionals and right-wing economists, it has been very ineffective in providing secure retirement incomes.

From a broader economic perspective, pre-funding offers no benefits and many risks. It contributes significantly to the financial-ization of the economy, with all its associated waste and instability. For public pensions in particular, paygo systems are preferable. Concerns

that these funds will be bankrupted by the ageing of the population have been deliberately exaggerated by the financial industry. In fact, while premium rates must be adjusted over time to reflect changing demographic factors, public paygo pension systems are clearly the most financially stable type of pensions in existence.

19

The Conflicting Personalities
of Government

Does size matter?

Many political debates between "right" and "left" seem to be about the optimum *size* of government. Conservatives want smaller government; they propose cutbacks in public programs, privatization of government agencies, and lower taxes. Progressives want bigger government; they demand more public programs, and higher taxes to pay for them. The main debate is whether government should be "small" or "big."

Conservatives also argue that governments over time have been moving from "small" to "big," and that this is a major reason for poor economic performance. According to this storyline, capitalism supposedly began as an idealized, individualistic society, organized around self-governing free markets. But then governments began to disrupt that libertarian ideal – with taxes, regulations, public ownership, and other intrusions. These expanding intrusions supposedly undermined the efficiency of the market system, and conservatives have been fighting hard to roll back government ever since.

To support this argument, conservatives invoke the writings of Adam Smith, the founder of classical economics (see Chapter 4). He argued that the state should play no economic role other than establishing a safe, secure framework for markets (by enforcing property rights; preventing individuals from stealing, or injuring others; and defending against internal or external threats). Everything else should be left up to markets, guided automatically by the self-interest of individual entrepreneurs. Today many neoclassical economists still adhere to that vision of minimalist government. And critics of that view are understandably tempted to distil their argument down to a demand for "bigger" (rather than "smaller") government.

The only problem is that capitalism *never* resembled that free-market, minimalist-state ideal. And merely having a "bigger" government is no guarantee that capitalism will become fairer or more responsive to the needs of its citizens. Sex therapists have a motto: "It's not what you've got, it's how you use it." This theory could just as well apply to the economic role of government.

Taking care of business

Even in its early days – perhaps *especially* during its early days – capitalism was guided by a strong, focused, central government. In fact, the state played a crucial role in the very emergence of capitalism. It enhanced and protected the profits captured by the new class of capitalists, and provided essential functions and services without which capitalism could never have been born.

Recall that industrial capitalism was born in Britain in the eighteenth century. Britain's relatively centralized and powerful state, which was willing and able actively to support private-sector investment and production, was a key reason why capitalism began there – rather than in continental Europe, China, or India.

Britain's government created a unified market at home: breaking down barriers between feudal enclaves, standardizing weights and measures, and providing passable and safe transportation routes. It did the same thing globally: using military might to forcibly access raw materials and markets. It provided early capitalists with tariff and patent protection. It helped to establish private ownership rights over agricultural land (through the ENCLOSURES process), creating the new class of landless, desperate workers that industrialists needed.

In short, far from reflecting the spontaneous energy of unplanned private enterprise, the early success of British capitalism wouldn't have occurred *without* the state's active support. Measured as a share of GDP, the state's various and far-flung activities consumed about as much of Britain's total output then (around a third) as it does today.

And if anything, capitalism's subsequent expansion to other jurisdictions – first to continental Europe, then America, then around the world – was even more dependent on powerful state leadership. Governments in all these places used tariffs and trade policies, capital subsidies and public ownership, extensive regulations, aggressive labour market measures, and (surprisingly often) military force to foster the establishment and growth of capitalism. In Germany, deliberate state planning, public investment, and tariffs were essential to early industrialization. Early American capitalism relied

The Long Arm of the Law

In the early days of capitalism, protecting the private property of wealthy investors was a fairly straightforward matter. Police kept the uncouth masses far away from the estates of the rich, protected banks and other stockpiles of financial wealth, and defended the capital equipment of factories (sometimes against the actions of their own workers).

As the system became more complex, however, private property became harder to define and protect. Now the law intrudes into our lives in new, far-reaching ways in order to protect the wealth of investors and companies:

- **Intellectual property** Complex laws and patents protect the monopoly powers of software companies, pharmaceutical firms, cultural producers, and other firms, regardless of the social benefits that could be generated by the wider distribution of those products. And governments devote vast resources to hunting down patent violators – hounding farmers who use privately-patented seeds, or health care providers distributing life-saving copycat drugs.

- **Financial wealth** In today's computerized financial system, "money" is a fluid, flexible commodity. And it's become harder and harder to police and protect that system against abuse or theft – from white-collar crime, fraudulent investment schemes, and other financial shenanigans.

- **Trade laws** Many international trade agreements contain provisions giving special legal powers to companies to challenge government measures, even in foreign countries, which undermine their profits.

It is very wrong to conclude that the state has become powerless under neoliberalism. In these and other ways, it is as ambitious and active as ever in its efforts to protect private wealth.

on huge government investments in railroads and other infrastructure, enormous giveaways of public land and resources, and highly protectionist trade policy. American tariffs on imported industrial products remained extremely high (averaging nearly 50 percent) until World War II. In nineteenth-century Japan, to nurture early entrepreneurs, the government directly established companies which were then (if they survived) handed over to private investors. Later, the Japanese pioneered the use of state industrial planning, through which key industries were selected for targeted assistance and promotion. This recipe has been re-used with great success in Korea, China, and the other late-industrializing Asian economies.

Table 19.1   **Ten Ways Governments Serve Business**

Protect private property (including intangible property, like patents).	Pay for basic economic infrastructure (roads, communication, utilities).
Pay for essential training of workers.	Keep workers "in line" by managing and policing labour relations.
Maintain business-friendly macroeconomic conditions (inflation, interest rates).	Enforce stable rules and standards (quality standards, competition laws, etc.).
Support business investment through tax incentives or subsidies.	Open up new markets for businesses (privatization, trade agreements).
Provide tax loopholes and subsidies to high-income financial investors.	Rescue businesses (especially financial companies) in times of crisis.

This noble tradition of governments nurturing capitalists (like a nanny nurtures a baby) carries on, even in developed countries (see Table 19.1). Governments continue to intervene to regulate and create markets, support private investment, protect private property, and facilitate the actions of capitalists in many different ways.

Whose economy? And whose government?

So even today, the real question is not whether government should be big or small (although clearly, proposals for improved social programs and other progressive reforms would require more public funding and hence a "bigger" government). And there is no real debate over whether governments should "intervene" in the economy: they always have, and always will. The real questions are rather different. *How* does government intervene in the economy? And in *whose* interests?

We have learned throughout this book that the capitalist economy is a dramatically unequal place. The decisions by profit-seeking companies to invest in production are essential to setting the whole economic machine into motion. Without those decisions, the system grinds to a halt. All other economic actors (including workers, small businesses, and – yes – even governments) are fundamentally dependent on the continuing willingness and ability of capitalists to "do their thing." Meanwhile, ownership and control over wealth (and hence over investment) is concentrated among a shockingly small and powerful elite.

This fundamental economic inequality naturally and inevitably translates into an equally fundamental, although partly disguised, political inequality. Because of their economic power, capitalists demand (and usually win) immediate attention from governments. Governments know they must cater to businesses' overall demand for a hospitable, profitable economic and social climate, or else businesses will stop investing and the economy will experience a crisis. Unless it is prepared to challenge the basic logic and structures of capitalism (by reorganizing the economy so that it is no longer dependent on private investment), no government can risk that kind of crisis. Hence, when business talks, government – virtually regardless of its political stripe – listens. In this manner, businesses (and the people who own them) ensure that governments continue to play the proactive, supportive economic role described above.

Trickle-Up

"The idea that conservatives trust the market while progressives want the government is a myth. Conservatives simply are not honest about the ways in which they want the government to intervene to distribute income upwards."

Dean Baker, US economist (2006).

In earlier eras, capitalist societies were not very democratic (in fact, only property owners had the right to vote), and the links between economic and political power were easier to see. In analyzing this relationship, Karl Marx painted the state under capitalism with a broad, black brush: it was nothing more, he argued, than the "executive committee" of the ruling class, and he considered capitalism to be a dictatorship (even after nominally democratic institutions, like parliaments, were established).

Today, however, that simplistic stereotype is clearly wrong (in most countries, anyway). Thanks to centuries of popular struggle for fundamental rights (including the right to vote, to organize political parties, to form unions, and to go on strike), capitalism has become more democratic. Working people have won considerable opportunity to air their views and concerns, and to demand that governments and businesses alike modify their actions and policies. These grass-roots efforts always face an uphill battle against the vested interests and economic power of private capital. But it is wrong to conclude that capitalists automatically call all the shots. When they are sufficiently motivated and organized, working people and their allies can clearly force governments to respond to *their* demands, too – instead of listening only to business.

In this regard, the state in modern developed capitalist economies demonstrates a kind of "split personality." Its natural tendency is to focus on the core function of protecting and promoting private wealth and business. And businesses (and the wealthy people who own them) have many sophisticated ways of ensuring that governments continue to respect their interests, first and foremost, including:

- Ownership and control over most of the mass media (and other cultural industries). This ensures that a broadly pro-business message is delivered constantly to all of society.

- Direct influence over the electoral process through candidate and campaign financing. Political candidates cannot succeed without massive financial resources; obviously this gives wealthy people (and their favoured candidates) a substantial headstart.

- Structures and practices which discourage political participation by working and poor people – the ones who have the most to gain from political change. In the US, for example, less than half of poor people vote. But more than 80 percent of high-income people do.

- Pro-business ideas are further strengthened through corporate and wealthy funding of think tanks, academic research, private schools, and other educational and ideological activities.

When push comes to shove, businesses can exert enormous political influence simply through their investment decisions. Investors and executives can "vote with their wallets" in response to unfavourable political or policy changes – cutting back investment (we might call this "disinvestment"), and slowing down overall growth. This threat does not require any deliberate, planned "conspiracy." It can merely reflect the combined impact of many individual decisions to shift investment to other jurisdictions (or just hoard capital, rather than investing it) until more business-friendly conditions emerge. In any event, the economic consequences of disinvestment are frightening, to both governments and voters. Usually the mere threat of disinvestment is sufficient to shift policy back onto a pro-business track. Indeed, to forestall this kind of problem, most left-wing political parties today (at least those with any realistic chance of winning an election) go out of their way to pacify business – pledging not to undermine profits, to prevent the economic damage that would otherwise occur from disinvestment.

This array of political weapons is intimidating, to say the least, and ensures that business interests remain predominant in most political debates. But it's not a done deal. There are times when, thanks to popular pressure, a different personality of government can come to the fore. Popular pressure can force governments to use their power to enhance economic security and quality of life for the rest of society – namely, those who do not own companies. There are several different ways for working people and their allies to enforce their preferences on the actions of government:

- At the ballot box, by fighting to advance key issues during election campaigns, and supporting progressive political parties. Money carries disproportionate influence in elections, as discussed above. But by their sheer numbers (after all, wage-labourers and their families make up around 85 percent of the population of advanced capitalist countries), working people can demand that their issues and concerns be addressed – if they are sufficiently organized and motivated.

- Between elections, by campaigning for particular reforms through lobbying, pressure campaigns, advertising and information efforts, and protests.

- In the workplace, fighting for specific demands through collective bargaining and other union actions.

- Engaging in a longer-term "battle of ideas," to challenge the power of pro-business thinking. This requires the development of alternative media, cultural, and educational resources and activities. (Developing a more democratic, grass-roots approach to economics is one part of that ongoing battle of ideas.)

Democracy or dictatorship?

No capitalist country is truly democratic so long as those with wealth and power are able to exert such disproportionate influence over political decisions – hence ensuring that government policies continue to reflect the imperatives of private profit. Workers can try to level the democratic playing field by fighting for improvements in democracy (such as limits on private political financing, or the establishment of publicly-run media outlets). And they will naturally use whatever democratic space they can open up to advance their demands for fairer treatment in the economy, and in society as a whole.

In some countries, however, even these limited democratic levers are not available to workers. In these places, the state acts more directly and blatantly in the interests of the local elite. Perhaps surprisingly, however, dictatorships (even pro-business ones) are not usually favoured by capitalists. They worry about long-run political instability, the arbitrary seizure of their property, bad publicity, and other risks. So in general, businesses prefer a modern, stable, liberal democracy as the most secure political context for their investments.

But capitalists are certainly not above partnering with dictators when they offer a stable, productive, pro-business climate. Corporations offered crucial support to past dictatorial regimes in places like Chile, South Korea, South Africa, and Indonesia. That deplorable pattern continues today in other countries (from Myanmar to Colombia to Iraq) – where democratic rights range from shaky to non-existent, but where local and global companies alike scrabble for as much profit as they can make, while the getting's good.

Consider the massive foreign investments (over US$500 billion worth in the decade ending in 2006) that global corporations made in

China, undeterred by that country's obvious democratic shortcomings. Cheap, productive, repressed labour; powerful government support for technology and productivity; low business taxes; access to what will soon be the world's largest market – these advantages easily overcome any lingering "guilt" business executives might have experienced over supporting such a fundamentally anti-democratic regime. And corporate promises that investments in China would be used to leverage democratic reform have proven utterly hollow. Instead, business works actively to *maintain* the current, immensely profitable state of affairs – for example, by shamefully opposing the modest labour law reforms that were proposed and debated in China in 2006.

Under the Bridge

"The law, in its majestic equality, forbids the rich as well as the poor to beg in the streets, steal bread, or sleep under a bridge."

Anatole France, French author (1894).

So, contrary to the claims of philosophical libertarians like Milton Friedman (who equate "freedom" with the right to accumulate private wealth), there is no inherent link whatsoever between capitalism and democracy. Quite the reverse: capitalism actually demonstrates a natural anti-democratic streak (by virtue of the inherent tendency for private wealth, and hence political influence, to be continually concentrated in the hands of a very small proportion of society). Therefore, fighting to protect and expand democratic rights, and rolling back the undue political influence of private wealth, is an essential part of workers' broader struggles for a more just economic order.

The agenda, and the toolkit

If and when workers are able to force governments to protect and advance the interests of the "little people," rather than society's fat cats, there is a long list of *goals* which they will want to demand. And governments possess an equally diverse set of policy *tools* to use in order to pursue those goals.

Some of the economic and social goals that governments might pursue when pressured by the working majority of their population include the following broad categories:

- **Redistribute income,** to partially offset the inequality that is the normal outcome of private markets, and establish minimum living standards for all citizens.

- **Stimulate employment and overall economic activity,** to offset occasional downturns in private-sector activity, and resulting unemployment. (Issues related to recessions and depressions are discussed in detail in Chapter 24.)

- **Provide certain products** (mostly services) that private companies do not produce – often because they cannot be supplied profitably as a result of flaws or quirks in private markets. Examples here include things that are useful to everyone in society, not just those who privately agree to pay for it – such as free radio and television broadcasts, safe streets, or national defence; economists call these PUBLIC GOODS. Governments may also take charge of NATURAL MONOPOLIES: industries in which it is economically inefficient to have more than one producer (such as pipelines or electricity utilities).

- **Provide more equitable or efficient access to certain products** – even those that *could* be produced by private firms. For example, private firms can supply education and health care services (and in some countries, they dominate these industries). But most countries have found that governments can provide these types of services more efficiently (for lower cost and/or higher quality), and more accessibly to the whole population (rather than just higher-income customers).

- **Regulate** the activities of private business. Some of the most damaging side-effects of private-sector production can be curtailed through government laws and regulations which set minimum standards for corporate behaviour. Regulations can govern health and safety practices in workplaces, labour standards (such as hours of work or minimum pay), product safety, pollution, and other corporate sins. Businesses complain loudly about the burden of complying with all this "red tape." But in practice, many regulations are enforced weakly, if at all; most businesses are left essentially to self-regulate their behaviour.

While government actions in all of these areas hold potential to improve the security and quality of life for working people, not all of them would necessarily be *opposed* by business. In some cases, businesses might actually consider some of these goals beneficial. For various reasons, business might decide it is preferable to guarantee minimal living standards (*very* minimal), mass education, strong overall economic conditions, and equitably-enforced regulations. So long as the essential prerequisites for successful capitalist production are maintained (including the ability to hire workers, and extract work effort from them, at profitable labour costs; and the ability to generate profits through the production and sale of goods and services), then businesses may grudgingly accept some of the foregoing intrusions into their realm. In other words, there is room to negotiate. But if you go too far for the comfort of business, watch out: business will push back, and hard (as it did, successfully, at the end of the postwar Golden Age).

Governments have an array of tools at their disposal to try to attain whatever economic and social goals are ultimately impressed upon them by political circumstances. Several of the more important policy levers are listed below:

- **The legal system**   Basic personal security and property rights are protected through the operation of the police and legal system. Business laws (regarding patents, securities laws, liability, and related topics) can also have important economic effects.

- **Monetary policy**   This refers to adjustments in interest rates, and the use of regulations governing the financial system, to influence the rate of inflation and/or the level of overall economic activity (see Chapter 17).

- **Fiscal policy**   This refers to the spending and taxing functions of government (discussed further in the next chapter). How much tax is collected, and from whom? How are those revenues spent? Government spending typically includes both redistribution (through TRANSFER PAYMENTS) and the direct production by government of specific goods and services.

- **Services delivery**   High-quality human services (like education, child care, and health care) can promote stronger economic and social participation and achievement by all parts of society. They are especially important for those who face limited employment and income opportunities (such as low-income households, women, immigrants, and racialized groups).

- **Labour market and social policy**   Labour market policies address the whole spectrum of employment conditions: minimum wages, trade unionization and collective bargaining, pay determination, income security, hours of work, employment security, training, and other aspects of employment. These policies determine whether the employment playing field tilts in favour of employers or in favour of workers. Social policies (such as family income supplements, child benefits, parenting supports, pensions, and disability policy) play a complementary role in influencing the labour market participation and income levels of specified groups – including women, seniors, and the disabled.

- **Competition policy**   Most countries have rules aimed at fostering more competition between firms and preventing companies from abusing a dominant market position. As we saw in Chapter 11, competition can produce negative economic effects, as well as positive ones. In some industries, governments prefer to *limit* competition (to prevent economic damage resulting from excess supply and over-competition).

- **Technology policy**   Most governments have developed special policies to foster innovation (such as research and development spending) and the adoption of new technology. The ultimate goal is to encourage productivity growth and competitiveness.

- **Industrial policy**   Governments may design special policies to promote industries with particular value for the overall economy. For example, many governments take special measures to stimulate investment and exports in high-tech industries such as automotive products, aerospace, biotechnology, defence, and computer technology.

- **Public ownership**   In some cases (outside of traditional public services) government may directly undertake production – by nationalizing an existing private company, or building a publicly-owned company from the ground up. State-owned enterprises are used to pursue many different goals: to expand particular industries, to enhance domestic control, to capture a share of profits, to prevent private monopoly, to support employment, to force companies to undertake activities that private owners reject. Public ownership expanded in most countries during the Golden Age, but has been dramatically scaled back under neoliberalism. The proportion of GDP produced by state-owned enterprises in the OECD countries has been roughly cut in half under neoliberalism, from around 10 percent in 1980 to below 5 percent by 2005.

- **Foreign policy and trade policy**   Managing economic and political relationships with other countries are an important government responsibility. Foreign policy (including military activity) can be important in opening or preserving international economic opportunities for domestic businesses. Trade policy is aimed at influencing exports, imports, and foreign investment flows (see Chapter 21).

Obviously, there are a great many ways in which government can aim to influence economic and social conditions: how much is produced, what is produced, how it is produced, and how output is distributed and ultimately used. Each of these major policy tools can affect various dimensions of economic performance. The policy challenge facing governments is to design and implement the right combination of these levers in order to attain the desired mix of outcomes. A rough rule of thumb suggests that each policy goal requires a distinct lever to make it happen. It is rare that multiple objectives can be satisfied simultaneously with a single policy instrument.

But for working and poor people, the *political* challenge is more daunting than the technical *policy* challenge. If government is willing to limit the power of private business and wealth, and enhance the well-being of the broader population, there are abundant tools in its toolkit to do the job. The big hurdle, however, is for working and poor people to organize enough power to force government to act that way. Unfortunately, it is on that score – with workers' collective strength and influence eroding substantially since the 1970s – that neoliberalism has been carrying the day.

20
Spending and Taxing

The fiscal role of the state

Conservatives often deride government as a "tax-and-spend" operation – implying that politicians' goal in life is to find new ways to collect taxes from hard-working citizens, and then invent new (and presumably wasteful) projects to spend that money on. This stereotype is wrong on many counts.

First, no government (even "big-spending" ones) collects taxes just for the sake of collecting taxes. Taxes are collected to fund the complex mixture of government activities and programs described in the previous chapter. If a government no longer feels compelled to provide a program, it stops performing it. Generally it will then give back the taxes. (In fact, some neoliberal governments actually cut taxes first, and *then* cut spending – using intervening deficits to politically justify the subsequent painful cuts.)

I prefer to reverse the order of the conservative epithet. Government is actually in the business of spending and taxing. First it decides (in the context of the conflicting and contradictory political pressures described in the last chapter) what programs it will provide. Then it figures out how to fund those programs. The government's overall spending and taxing strategy is called its FISCAL POLICY.

Spending

Government expenditures contain many line items, which together may account for up to 50 percent (in highly developed welfare states) of a country's GDP. Several broad categories of spending can be defined. ▓ *

- **Interest payments** Like businesses and consumers, most governments have debt (more on this below), and they must

---

* See the Economics for Everyone website for statistics, www.economicsforeveryone.com.

service that debt with regular interest payments. Interest costs are perhaps the least useful type of government spending.

- **Program spending**   All spending other than interest payments is called the government's PROGRAM SPENDING. Overall program spending, measured as a share of GDP, is a good indicator of the overall size or intrusiveness of government. Program spending, in turn, can be divided into two major categories: transfer payments and government production.

- **Transfer payments**   Many government programs involve collecting money (via taxes) with one hand, and then giving it back (to someone else) with the other. These programs are called TRANSFER PAYMENTS, since they involve no government function or expenditure other than shifting income from one group or sector to another. Transfer payments can be made to individuals (via social programs like unemployment insurance, welfare benefits, and public pensions). Transfer payments can also be made to businesses (through business subsidies), or to other countries (as foreign aid).

- **Direct government production**   A portion of government program spending actually involves government "doing" something – that is, financing the production of some concrete function or service (rather than simply redistributing income). Some of this productive activity is undertaken directly by governments. Other functions are undertaken by independent or semi-independent non-profit agencies which receive much or all of their funding from governments (such as hospitals or school boards). Governments hire labour to perform this production, and they purchase inputs from private companies (sometimes including outsourced programs and services). Government production can be further divided into two more categories: consumption and investment.

- **Public consumption**   Most governments provide a range of public services that are used (or "consumed") by the public. These programs are economically equivalent to consumption, since they involve the use of output to meet a current human need or desire. But this consumption occurs in a public form: instead of paying for it through their private purchasing power, the users of public services are entitled to this consumption by virtue of their status as citizens.

- **Public investment** Not all government production is consumed, however. Some is invested, in order to facilitate more public production in future years. Governments allocate a portion of their revenues to long-lasting investments in infrastructure and other forms of physical capital (like buildings, schools, hospitals, roads, machinery and equipment). PUBLIC INVESTMENT is thus an important contributor to broader economic growth and productivity. Unfortunately, however, public investment was scaled back especially badly during the neoliberal era, and so the public capital stock has been badly run down in most countries – as evidenced by crumbling infrastructure, buildings, facilities, and water systems. In many cases, the neoliberal policy-makers who starved public facilities of needed capital now point to their decrepit state as justification for further privatization.

Taxing

In order to pay for the programs and services which their voting constituents have demanded, governments collect revenues in a variety of ways. ▦

- **Income taxes** An income tax is collected as a proportion of an individual or company's income. Individuals pay personal income taxes; businesses pay corporate income taxes. Most countries impose PROGRESSIVE personal income taxes, in which the rate of tax rises with a person's income. In this manner, well-off people pay a higher proportion of their income to support government programs. An alternative system, used in more conservative jurisdictions, is a FLAT-RATE personal income tax, which collects income tax at a constant rate (regardless of a person's income).

- **Sales taxes** A larger share of total tax revenues in recent years has been provided by SALES TAXES (also known as value added, or indirect, taxes). When a consumer makes a purchase, they pay a certain additional proportion in sales tax. Businesses may also have to pay sales taxes on their purchases; in many countries, however, business sales tax payments are refunded.

- **Payroll taxes**   Employment is also taxed, via a PAYROLL TAX imposed as a proportion of wages paid to an employee. The tax may be paid by the employer, by the employee, or shared between the two. Payroll tax revenues are often channelled to particular social programs – like pensions, health care, or unemployment insurance.

- **Wealth taxes**   Taxes can also be collected on the accumulated wealth of an individual or a business. This is morally appealing: a WEALTH TAX allows governments to target taxes at the most privileged members of society. However, they have fallen out of favour in recent years – mostly because wealthy people (whose political influence has grown so much under neoliberalism) strongly oppose them. Annual wealth taxes, inheritance taxes, land or property taxes, and capital taxes on business are all examples of wealth taxes.

- **Environmental taxes**   In recent years, environmentalists have proposed taxes on the use of certain polluting inputs (like energy), or taxes on the amount of pollution emitted. One example of an environmental tax is a CARBON TAX, which collects taxes on different types of energy according to their contribution to climate change.

- **Non-tax revenues**   A share of government revenue is generated through non-tax measures. For example, many governments impose USER FEES for the use of certain programs and services (like public transit, garbage collection, or even health care). Governments also generate income from their own investments (such as interest on financial investments, rent and other income from government-owned properties, or the profits of state-owned enterprises).

Fiscal policy on the economic map

Government is a major player in the economy, largely (but not exclusively) because of its fiscal actions. Figure 20.1 presents the next incarnation of our economic map, this time including government.

Government collects taxes from various stakeholders, at various points in the economic chain. We have bundled all those taxes into two categories, depending on whether they are ultimately paid by

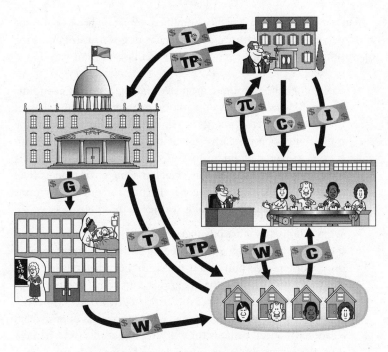

Figure 20.1   **Economic Road Map: Government**

either workers or capitalists. Income and other taxes paid by workers are labelled T. Taxes paid by capitalists are distinguished with the same subscript (a luxurious diamond!) that we used to identify their consumption: $T_\diamond$.

Government uses this revenue to undertake many different functions, two of the most important of which are shown on our map. Transfer payments (TP) are given back to specified households (as unemployment insurance, income security, and pensions). Most transfer payments go to worker households, but some are received by capitalists as well.

Meanwhile, direct government production involves the public (or non-profit) production of goods and services (mostly services). This provision establishes a second, parallel channel of production in the economy. In addition to private, for-profit production, there is now a segment of production undertaken for other motives – namely, to directly meet some perceived public need (like education, health care, or infrastructure).

Once again, this map is highly simplified, yet is still brings out some extremely important features. The presence of government alters the operation of the capitalist economy in several important ways:

- Taxes alter the economic incentives facing different economic players. Usually this isn't a major problem. But in terms of the system's overall energy level, the impact of taxes on the profitability of private investment and production is important. If taxes are too high on businesses, their investment spending is likely to weaken. That is why even left-wing governments (like those in Nordic countries) generally pay for public programs with high taxes on individuals (rather than on businesses).

- Worker households are no longer exclusively dependent on what they can earn through employment; government transfers now offer workers a certain degree of economic independence. This can dramatically alter the economic and social relationships which underpin capitalism. Not surprisingly, workers generally support strong transfer programs, while employers oppose them – especially social benefits for working-age adults (which make it harder for employers to attain desired wage costs and labour discipline).

- Direct government production establishes an entire, dual chain of economic output that supplements the productive activity of private companies. Society as a whole is now somewhat less dependent on private investors to set the whole economic cycle in motion. Moreover, public production helps to stabilize the economy in the face of fluctuations in private investment and production. In most developed countries, direct government production makes up a small share of total production (generally about 10–20 percent of GDP), and business lobbies hard to prevent the further expansion of the public sector. Nevertheless, the mere fact that production can and does occur successfully outside of the core profit relationship of capitalism opens up intriguing possibilities for future economic change.

- Another consequence of direct government production is that government itself becomes a major *employer*. A significant segment of workers (again, typically between 10 and 20 percent of the total labour force) is employed by public and non-profit

Design Your *Own* Budget

In the early 1990s, Canada's government (like so many other countries) was imposing a historic series of spending cutbacks that badly damaged many public programs and services. The government claimed these cuts were an inevitable and necessary response to large budget deficits.

So a broad group of community and labour organizations came together, in a project called the Alternative Federal Budget, to show that there were alternatives to the cutbacks. They developed their own government budget, showing where they would collect the revenues necessary to maintain and even expand public programs.

You can try this, too. Consult with concerned groups and individuals in your city, region, or country. Identify the programs that are most important, and estimate their cost. Identify potential revenue sources. Show that the bottom line of your budget "adds up" – either to a balanced budget (that is, zero deficit), or to a bottom-line deficit that is consistent with your country's ability to service its ongoing public debt.

Now you have shown that society can indeed provide public services and programs that improve the quality and security of life for its members – so long as it is willing to allocate the resources necessary to pay for them.

In most countries, it is not a shortage of resources that prevents governments from providing necessary services. It is a shortage of political will.

providers, rather than private-sector employers. The nature of work in public-sector agencies is usually (although not always) better-paid and somewhat more secure than in private companies – since the employer (government) is not motivated by the same relentless pressures (the profit motive and competition) that drive private employers to cut costs. At the same time, public-sector workers (and their unions) face a constant challenge to improve working conditions and compensation, and public-sector unions have historically played a crucial role in labour movements and other progressive struggles.

Deficits and debt

Fiscal debates in many countries over the past quarter-century have
been dominated by concern – much of it exaggerated, but some of it
legitimate – over big government deficits and rising government debt.
Conservative politicians have seized on these concerns to justify painful
cutbacks in public programs. Yet ironically, conservative governments
often wracked up the largest deficits of all. The record is held by the
Republican government of George W. Bush, which incurred the largest
US federal deficit (measured as a share of GDP) since World War II
– largely due to enormous tax cuts which Bush implemented in 2003
for wealthy investors. And in general, the broad fiscal decline that was
experienced in most developed economies during the 1980s and 1990s
was clearly caused by neoliberal economic policies – especially by
higher interest rates (which produced higher unemployment, slower
growth, and higher debt-servicing charges). Those neoliberal policies
were far more damaging to governments' bottom line than public
spending on social programs.

A government DEFICIT occurs when incoming tax revenues
are insufficient to pay for outgoing expenses. A SURPLUS, on the
other hand, occurs when tax revenues are larger than expenses. A

BALANCED BUDGET is achieved when tax revenues perfectly match government spending.

It is normal for budgets to tend toward deficits when the economy experiences a slowdown or recession. This is because government revenues decline during a downturn (tax revenues fall as workers lose their jobs and reduce their spending); meanwhile, expenses for unemployment insurance and other social programs automatically increase. Even without any change in policy, therefore, a recession makes a deficit worse. Likewise, strong economic growth automatically improves the government's budget balance. Tax and spending programs which produce this response to broader economic trends are called AUTOMATIC STABILIZERS.

A short-term deficit, especially one resulting from an economic downturn, is no cause for concern. In fact, such a deficit can actually help the economy recover more quickly from the recession (by supporting spending levels). Perversely, trying to eliminate a cyclical deficit through proactive restraint (like spending cuts or tax increases) only makes the recession worse (by further undermining consumer and business spending).

On the other hand, large chronic deficits that persist year after year are indeed a cause for genuine concern. A deficit in any given year must be financed by government borrowing (which can occur in many different forms: issuing bonds to investors, borrowing from private banks, or even borrowing from the government's own central bank). A deficit, therefore, increases a government's outstanding DEBT, by the amount of the annual deficit. Large consecutive deficits produce an ongoing and rapid accumulation of public debt, which can have negative economic and financial consequences.

There is great controversy in economics regarding the appropriate level of public debt. Productive projects funded by public debt can enhance overall economic performance, and can even stimulate stronger private investment. Government bonds are typically among the most stable and reliable financial assets – much safer than corporate shares or private bonds. A sizeable stockpile of public debt (large, but not too large) can thus help to stabilize financial markets. And during times of economic weakness, government debt-financing can stimulate spending and hence employment.

At the same time, there are costs to public debt, too. The biggest cost is the burden of interest payments made to service the debt. If public debt is growing, then interest costs eat up a larger proportion of total government revenues. Interest payments play no productive economic or social role. Worse yet, they are received by financial investors, who tend to be among society's richest households. Interest payments thus constitute a "reverse Robin Hood" redistribution – shifting resources from average taxpayers to well-off investors. If debt grows too quickly, or becomes too large, investor confidence in government bonds, or even in a country's currency, can become rattled. This produces financial and economic instability (including higher interest rates, exchange rate instability, and – in severe cases – an outflow of financial capital from the country).

So government debt is quite acceptable, within limits. The true constraint on public finance is the need to curtail the debt from rising too far, too fast (rather than any imaginary compulsion to balance the budget, every single year). The best way to measure the DEBT BURDEN in this context is as a proportion of nominal GDP (since it is government revenues derived from that GDP that determine a government's ability to service its debt). The European Union's Maastricht Treaty (signed in 1992) imposed a debt ceiling on countries joining the euro common currency zone. It was supposed to cap debt at a maximum of 60 percent of GDP – but the rule has been weakly enforced. It is quite feasible for countries to take on even larger public debt (perhaps up to 100 percent of GDP), but at the cost of higher debt-service charges. Any higher than that, and the government's debt-service charges will become crushing (unless the government imposes dramatic measures to reduce interest rates and regulate financial flows), and the country is likely to experience financial instability.

Counter-intuitively, a government can maintain a stable debt burden (measured as a share of GDP) while still incurring *annual* deficits. So long as GDP is growing, a government can experience a small deficit each year with no growth in the debt burden (measured as a share of GDP). The "allowable" deficit equals the rate of GDP growth times the desired, stable debt burden. For example, if nominal GDP grows at 5 percent per year, and the government wishes to maintain a stable debt burden equal to 60 percent of GDP, then it can safely budget for an annual deficit of 3 percent of GDP (60 percent times 5 percent). If the economy suffers a recession, however, then the debt burden will rise above the desired level (due both to a larger deficit and to the decline in GDP). So to play it safe, the government might wish to plan for a slight decline in the debt burden during years of stronger growth, leaving room for an increase in the debt burden during years of economic slowdown. Nevertheless, quite significant annual deficits can be incurred by governments, with no long-run increase in the debt burden.

In sum, it is clear that conservative anti-deficit and anti-debt campaigns of the past quarter-century were motivated more by politics than economics. Neoliberals used fear of public debt to politically justify the elimination of public programs (like income security programs) which they wanted to get rid of anyway. More recently, they have used similar arguments to justify the stealthy privatization of public investment through PUBLIC–PRIVATE PARTNERSHIPS. These initiatives nominally transfer the debt associated with major public projects from government to private investors – yet governments (and taxpayers) are still left holding the bill for future, long-run interest costs (paying interest rates *higher* than the government would have paid itself). These so-called "partnerships" are in reality a gigantic taxpayer-funded giveaway to private investors, justified by a phony phobia of public debt that is the legacy of a quarter-century of anti-government ideology.

On the whole, it's usually best (barring national emergency) for governments to avoid increasing debt too rapidly. But government budgets do not need to be balanced every year (or even on average over periods of expansion and recession). And it is quite wrong to assume that government debt is inherently "bad" and must be eliminated.

Fiscal policy under neoliberalism

As we saw in the previous chapter, even capitalists want a strong central state to perform many important functions – like protecting private property, managing social relationships, and paying for helpful government services (like training, roads, or utilities). These functions require money, and hence taxes, that can amount to a considerable portion of GDP. Even in the US (the role-model for many neoliberals), government activity consumes over 30 percent of GDP – and this figure hasn't declined under neoliberalism.

Nevertheless, a redirection of fiscal policy has played an important role in the broader neoliberal agenda. Likewise, debates over those fiscal choices have been important in resistance to neoliberalism. Here are some of the key fiscal priorities that have been pursued by neoliberal governments:

- **Cutting income security programs**, especially for working-age adults. There is no more hated form of government spending, from an employers' perspective, than income security programs. They give working-age people a degree of independence from having to offer their labour for hire in the labour market. And across the capitalist world, income security programs for working-age adults – unemployment insurance, welfare benefits, even disability benefits – have borne the deepest proportionate spending cuts. The goal is to once again firmly compel people to work, and work hard.

- **Privatizing once-public functions**   Privatization is doubly beneficial, in neoliberal eyes: it reduces government spending, and it opens potentially lucrative new terrain for private, profit-seeking investment.

- **Abandoning counter-cyclical fiscal policy**   Fiscal policy was once used to deliberately offset the ups and downs of the private sector economy: boosting spending in lean years, pulling back in better times. This approach has fallen out of favour more recently, and governments now rely mostly on MONETARY POLICY to smooth out economic fluctuations.

- **Reducing income, wealth, and business taxes**   When fiscal conditions allow, and governments have sufficient funds to perform the functions that businesses support, neoliberal governments will happily cut taxes. In general, the first taxes cut are those which impose the maximum burden on businesses, and the well-off individuals who own them. Personal income taxes, wealth taxes, and corporate taxes of all kinds, have been reduced aggressively by neoliberal governments. Taxes on investment income (like dividends and capital gains) have been cut most of all.

Spending, taxing, and redistribution

Despite these negative shifts in fiscal policy, the spending and taxing activities of governments still have a broadly positive impact on the overall distribution of income and opportunity in capitalist societies. Despite neoliberal efforts, most taxes are still PROGRESSIVE: that is, they impose a relatively higher burden on higher-income individuals. (A

REGRESSIVE tax, on the other hand, imposes a proportionately larger burden on lower-income individuals.)

Meanwhile, many forms of public spending make a significant contribution to the well-being of working and poor people. Of course, well-off people and businesses also benefit from many government activities. But some programs (like income security transfers) clearly benefit poor people proportionately more than rich people. Table 20.1 summarizes the distributional impact of different kinds of taxing and spending.

Table 20.1 Redistributive Impacts of Spending and Taxing

Spending:	
Interest payments	Regressive
Transfer payments	
To individuals	Progressive
To others	Mixed
Government production	
Health care	Progressive
Basic education	Neutral
Higher education	Mildly regressive
Infrastructure	Neutral
Military and police	Mixed
Overall spending	**Neutral**
Revenues:	
Income taxes	
Personal	Strongly progressive
Corporate	Strongly progressive
Sales taxes	Mildly regressive
Payroll taxes	Regressive
Wealth taxes	Strongly progressive
Other taxes	Mixed
User fees	Mildly regressive
Overall taxing	**Mildly progressive**

Assume for now that the overall tax system imposes a mildly progressive burden (with well-off people paying a proportionately higher share of their income in tax). Assume that transfer payments to individuals are also progressive: poor people get somewhat more than "their share" of those payments. Finally, assume that all individuals consume, on average, an equal share of the value of government-produced public services. These services add measurably to everyone's standard of living (supplementing the value of privately-purchased goods and services). But they make a *proportionately* larger contribution to the total standard of living of lower-income people.

The overall impact of government spending and taxing on income distribution can then be measured at three distinct stages, as follows:

1. **Market income**   If we consider only the total income (before tax) which individuals "earn" in the economy (including through employment, investment income, and other private sources of income – but excluding government transfers), the distribution of income in most capitalist countries is highly, and increasingly, unequal.

2. **After-tax-and-transfer income**   We then adjust each person's income for the taxes they pay and the personal transfer payments they receive from government (which were not counted in market income). Higher-income people pay more tax, and generally receive less transfer income. So the distribution of income after taxes and transfers is much more equal than the distribution of market income.

3. **Real consumption**   Next we adjust distribution to account for the actual consumption opportunities provided by direct public services (like health care, education, public facilities, and so on). These services supplement the standard of living that is possible for each household (above and beyond what they can buy with their money income). This further reduces the proportionate gap between the richest and poorest households.

Despite the regressive effect of neoliberal fiscal policies, therefore, the overall spending and taxing activities of government continue to considerably narrow the gaps between rich and poor under capitalism. The difference between the richest and poorest households at stage 1 above, is many times larger than the difference at stage 3. This positive impact of government taxes and programs is not as strong as it used to be, nor as strong as it could be. But the positive distributional effect of government budgets is still very powerful, and it is important to understand the different ways in which it is felt.

21

Globalization

Global, global, global

There's probably been no more controversial aspect of economic policy in the last two decades than globalization. Some of the greatest policy weapons in the neoliberal arsenal have been aimed at enhancing global economic linkages, and granting more global power to companies and investors. These include regional FREE-TRADE AGREEMENTS; the unilateral opening of many countries (especially developing and former Communist countries) to international trade and investment; and the creation in 1995 of the WORLD TRADE ORGANIZATION (WTO).

On the other hand, some of the fiercest battles against neoliberalism have been waged by citizens concerned about the one-sided nature of those global policies and institutions. Indeed, at the turn of this century a youthful, worldwide movement targeted globalization as the main enemy of social and economic justice. That movement succeeded in blocking some important aspects of globalization – for example, by defeating the proposed Multilateral Agreement on Investment in 1998, and derailing the proposed European Union constitution through referendum defeats in France and the Netherlands in 2005.

To some extent, the preoccupation of both neoliberals and their opponents with these global debates has been sensible and justified. Over the past quarter-century, changes in both the global economy and global economic policy have been massive. The economic and political power of businesses and investors has been strengthened immensely by globalization. And developing ways to manage the global economy differently will be crucial to any alternative, progressive economic vision.

At the same time, however, it is important to keep the "global" dimension in context. Many of the negative consequences of neoliberalism would clearly have occurred anyway, even without globalization. And we could conceivably dismantle specific aspects of globalization (for example, cancelling free-trade agreements, or even disbanding the WTO) without substantially altering the functioning of modern capitalism.

Try this: say the words "global, global, global" aloud to yourself several times, as fast as you can. You'll find yourself sounding like a turkey ("gobble, gobble, gobble").

We have to keep our eyes on the whole barnyard, not just the turkey; we can't become unduly obsessed with the global dimension of economics. The vast majority of the goods and services produced in a modern economy never cross a national boundary (see box opposite); these products are produced strictly by and for the residents of each country, and we can reform the conditions of their production without worrying much at all about global constraints on those reforms. Most of the decisions affecting how the economy evolves, for better or worse, are still made at home. Yes, globalization is a very important piece of the modern economic puzzle – but it is still just one piece.

Globalization: what's really new?

What's more, if we define globalization (at its simplest) as the strengthening of economic linkages between countries, then it's not even *new*. People from different countries, even different continents, have been trading with each other for centuries. And capitalism has always had a global dimension. International trade in raw materials and finished products was important to early merchants and industrialists. Using brute global force to open captive, colonial markets allowed British capitalists to make the most of the awesome productivity of their new factories. And the inherent expansionary impulse arising from the drive to maximize profits spurred an ongoing global quest for markets and investment opportunities, right from the beginning of capitalism. By the turn of the twentieth century (before colonial rivalries exploded in World War I, and world trade subsequently declined), international trade and investment were probably nearly as important (relative to GDP) as they are today.

While globalization (in this sense) has been around for centuries, it is certainly clear that there has been a dramatic, more recent expansion of international commerce. In 2006, some US$12 trillion worth of tangible merchandise crossed national borders – and merchandise trade has been growing faster than GDP since the end of World War II. Another US$3 trillion worth of services was traded across borders. Meanwhile, multinational corporations undertook US$1.3

Not So Global?

Table 21.1   How Big is Global?

Sector	Approximate Share Total GDP (OECD Average)	Share Exported
Primary*	5%	Over half
Manufacturing	15%	About half
Construction	5%	None
Private services	60%	Well under 10%
Public services	15%	Almost none
TOTAL	100%	Well under 20%

* Primary includes agriculture, forestry, and minerals.
Source: Author's summary of OECD data.

Some very misleading statistics imply that international trade accounts for most or even all of a country's GDP. But in reality, foreign trade accounts for only a small minority of GDP – even in the smallest, most trade-dependent economies. We can see this by examining the sectoral composition of GDP, and considering how much of each sector's true output is exported. About 80 percent of GDP in a developed economy is produced by sectors (construction, private services, and public services) which experience very little foreign trade. Moreover, those "non-tradeable" sectors make up a growing share of total GDP – which means that the relative importance of foreign trade may *decline* over time.

trillion worth of new foreign direct investment projects in 2006. And the volume of cross-border financial flows is impossible to measure – certainly exceeding US$1 trillion every business day. 🖩 *

Many factors have contributed to this quantitative expansion of international business. Policy changes (like free-trade agreements) explain some of that growth, but not all:

- **Communications technology**   New computer and communications technologies have reduced the cost, and enhanced the capacities, of global communications. Technology has opened up incredible possibilities for performing and coordinating work across long distances.

* See the Economics for Everyone website for statistics, www.economicsforeveryone.com.

- **Transportation technology** Similarly, international transportation (including merchandise shipping and travel) has become easier and cheaper. This has also facilitated global business.

- **Improvements in management** Business executives have become more adept at identifying far-flung supply, production, and marketing opportunities; outsourcing particular functions to reliable suppliers (including those in far-off places); and implementing strategies to maximize global profits. This evolution in management skill has been very important to the expansion of international commerce.

- **Unilateral opening** Quite apart from the impact of international agreements and institutions (like the WTO and regional free-trade agreements), many countries have unilaterally reduced barriers to foreign trade and investment during the neoliberal era. For various reasons – including the failure of previous, more inward-oriented economic strategies; pressure from international agencies like the World Bank and the International Monetary Fund (IMF); and sheer desperation for investment – governments (especially in developing countries) have dismantled regulations which once limited foreign trade and capital flows. This opened up fantastic new opportunities for global businesses to take advantage of the natural resources, labour, and markets of these countries.

- **Political "stability"** Companies once worried about investing in other countries (especially developing countries) because of potential political turmoil that could result in lost profits (and even, in many cases, lost businesses). Today, a pro-business welcome mat has been firmly laid out by most countries, and companies can globalize their operations with much less political risk.

- **Free-trade agreements** The growth and deregulation of global commerce would have occurred anyway as a result of these changes. But globalization has been mightily reinforced, and given a starkly pro-business character, by international agreements which cement free-trade rules and limit government powers to interfere with trade and capital flows. Some of these agreements are regional (like the European Union and the North

American Free Trade Agreement); some are global (like the WTO). They promote freer trade in merchandise and services – for example, by eliminating TARIFFS (taxes imposed to limit imports) and other trade barriers. Less obvious, but ultimately more important, are provisions aimed at opening and protecting investment flows, granting special legal protections to foreign investors, and generally limiting government intrusions into the private sector. For example, the General Agreement on Trade in Services (GATS), which is a trade treaty overseen by the WTO, has a blanket provision which limits governments' ability to regulate service industries, even if exactly the same regulations are applied to local and foreign companies.

All these factors have contributed to the growth of global commerce. However, it is clear that modern globalization is more than just the *quantitative* expansion of global linkages. Under neoliberalism, globalization has taken on a particular *qualitative* dimension. Yes, the global economy has become more integrated and connected – but in a very one-sided way, governed by a one-sided set of rules and practices. Trade and investment policies grant freedom and protection to companies and investors; they limit governments' ability to interfere with profit-maximizing business decisions; and they are virtually silent on protecting workers, regulatory powers, and the environment.

Free-trade advocates claim that globalization is "inevitable," and there is no point opposing it. Certainly, the fact that international commerce, communications, travel, and the transfer of knowledge are all faster and easier than ever is not something we can reverse – nor would we want to. There are many benefits from living in a more closely integrated world: for the economy, for culture, for global cooperation, for peace.

But the particular character of globalization under neoliberalism is not remotely set in stone. Yes, countries will trade, capital will flow, and people will travel. But this does not have to occur under neoliberal rules – which grant unprecedented rights and security to businesses and investors, but no protection for employment, social conditions, or the environment. Working individually and multilaterally, countries have the power to change the current rules of the global game: balancing the interests of business and investment against the

Kangaroo Court

One of the most offensive aspects of modern trade agreements is their creation of alternative "dispute settlement mechanisms" which give private businesses and investors special legal powers to challenge unfavourable government policies.

An example of this system is provided in Chapter 11 of the North American Free Trade Agreement (NAFTA). It created a new, parallel legal system – that can only be used by businesses and investors. If a NAFTA member government implements a new law or policy which reduces the profitability of a business investment, the owner can use this special court to sue the government for compensation. Similar mechanisms have since been included in other regional trade agreements and bilateral investment treaties.

In the first decade of its use, almost 50 Chapter 11 lawsuits were launched, challenging everything from limits on polluting additives in gasoline, to laws prohibiting the export of bulk fresh water, to the operation of Canada's public post office. Total damages claimed in these suits exceeded US$30 billion[*] – and companies won enough judgements to force governments to take the process very seriously. Hence this bizarre corporate court has had a chilling effect on government policy-making: politicians fear that anything they do that harms corporate profits could result in another NAFTA lawsuit.

Chapter 11 proves that free trade agreements are intended to do much more than promote trade. Their true goal is to enforce a pro-business bias in all areas of government policy.

[*] "NAFTA Chapter 11 Investor-State Disputes," Canadian Centre for Policy Alternatives, Ottawa, 2007.

desire to promote employment and economic security. But this would require the citizens of the world to successfully demand a change of approach from their respective governments – and that, in turn, will require more of the energetic campaigns and protests that we saw at the dawn of this century.

Forms of globalization

Economic activities can be conducted across a national border, and hence become international, in several different ways. Here are the major forms of global commerce:

- **Merchandise trade**   Tangible goods are the easiest thing to ship back and forth between countries, and international merchandise trade has been occurring for centuries. EXPORTS are products which a country produces and then sells to purchasers in another country; IMPORTS are products that are made elsewhere, but purchased and used at home.

- **Services trade**   It is not as easy to buy and sell services across a national border, because usually the service producer must be near the service consumer. (It is hard to conduct international trade in haircuts, for example!) In some specialized service industries, however, international trade is important. Customers may purchase services from providers in another country, in order to access unique features or skills which can't be purchased closer to home. Service industries which sell their products internationally include higher-level financial and business services, cultural industries (like movies and music), higher education, and specialized health care. Technological changes are facilitating more international services trade, including many lower-wage functions (like call centres). Tourism is another form of services trade: when a foreign tourist visits another country (spending money on travel, accommodation, and meals), it is equivalent to that country "exporting" tourism services.

- **Foreign direct investment**   A MULTINATIONAL CORPORATION is a company which operates productive facilities in more than one country. And the act of investing in those real foreign facilities is called FOREIGN DIRECT INVESTMENT (FDI). Incoming FDI can be very useful to the receiving (or "host") country: it supplements domestic investment spending, and the multinational firm usually brings along some unique technological or managerial advantages not possessed by domestic firms. For this reason, most countries welcome FDI, and have reduced or eliminated barriers to incoming FDI. The bigger concern for many countries is not trying to control incoming FDI, but rather trying to limit *outgoing* FDI – capital heading to more profitable foreign jurisdictions. But even incoming FDI comes with a price tag. Countries which are too reliant on incoming FDI face many risks, including: a long-run outflow of profits from foreign-owned businesses; the loss of head-office jobs (like management, marketing, and engineering positions, which tend to be clustered around a company's global headquarters); and the loss of domestic control over major investment decisions.

- **International financial flows**   The global flow of finance dwarfs flows of international trade and investment. For every dollar in real trade or direct investment that crosses a border, at least $100 in purely financial flows also cross a border. Indeed, sophisticated financial institutions now operate 24 hours per day, using branch offices around the world, trading non-stop in an infinite variety of assets (currencies, stocks, bonds, and derivatives), and seeking to profit from short-term changes in prices and market sentiment. In most countries, investors can freely convert financial wealth from one currency into another; the "price" of buying another country's currency is its EXCHANGE RATE. Like other prices, a currency's exchange rate tends to rise (or "appreciate") when more investors want to buy it; it falls ("depreciates") when investors prefer other currencies. This overdeveloped, hyperactive network operates without much supervision or oversight. International institutions (like the INTERNATIONAL MONETARY FUND, or the BANK FOR INTERNATIONAL SETTLEMENTS in Switzerland) try to impose certain rules on global finance; national financial regulators (like central banks) do the same, where possible. But the system is largely unregulated, and very prone to destructive mood swings on the part of global investors – who can do incredible economic damage to countries or even entire continents.

- **Migration**   Cross-border human flows, motivated by both economic and non-economic factors, have been important throughout human history. Workers move from one country to another in search of better employment or income prospects. Capitalists may encourage those migrations when they face uncomfortably tight labour market conditions in particular countries (in which case immigration is a convenient way to keep a lid on wages). But migrant workers usually face difficult economic and social challenges in their new lives. Prejudice, racism, and labour market segmentation undermine their earning opportunities, and often prevent them from fully utilizing their skills and education. Migrants are treated as temporary, second-class citizens, often forced to return to their country of origin when their jobs are finished, and subjected to social and legal abuses in the interim. Their migration can also harm the countries they leave – especially since it is usually the best-educated, most capable people who are allowed to migrate to better-paying opportunities in other countries. Many migrants send regular remittance payments home to support their families; these payments are economically important to many developing countries.

- **International institutions** The globalization of governance and policy is another important dimension of the current world economy. And unfortunately, this aspect has been utterly dominated by neoliberal, pro-business ideas. At the conclusion of World War II, the leading capitalist economies, led by the US, established the IMF and the WORLD BANK. The former was to focus on stabilizing and freeing international financial flows; the latter's job was to assist poor countries with economic development. At the time, the British economist John Maynard Keynes argued for the IMF to function like a global central bank – supporting growth and employment, and helping resolve trade imbalances. But Keynes' vision was rejected, and instead the IMF and the World Bank worked to impose free-market, pro-business structures on the world economy. Since the 1980s, both have become very aggressive in using their financial leverage to force countries (especially desperate developing countries) to follow the neoliberal economic recipe book. Using a strategy called CONDITIONAL-ITY, they required dozens of countries to unilaterally open their markets, deregulate capital flows, privatize industries, and cut back government spending – in return for short-term financial aid to weather economic and financial crises that were, more often than not, caused by neoliberal policies in the first place. Today even World Bank officials admit their dictates to developing countries were wrong. Meanwhile, the WTO, founded in 1995, became the third member of the global neoliberal trio. It has a special "dispute-settlement system" which can order countries to dismantle policies and programs which violate free-trade principles.

What's wrong with free trade, anyway?

Free-trade advocates claim that globalization is an unequivocally positive force. Freer global trade and investment flows will allow every country to specialize in what they do best. Efficiency and output will grow, and every country will benefit. They argue that globalization is especially beneficial for poor countries, which can finally escape their lower status and become full, prosperous players in a more inclusive global system.

Indeed, this faith in the automatic, mutual benefits of free trade has been a guiding principle of mainstream economics since the birth of capitalism. In the early nineteenth century, David Ricardo postulated his theory of COMPARATIVE ADVANTAGE to celebrate (and intellectually justify) the expansion of international trade. He supported free trade for pragmatic, political reasons: it would reduce labour costs (through imports of cheaper foodstuffs), supplement the profits of industrialists (who he viewed as the most dynamic force in society), and reduce the power of unproductive landlords.

Trade and the Environment

Free trade can be bad for the environment, too. In some polluting industries, companies may be lured to locate in countries with lax environmental rules. This undermines global efforts to reduce pollution.

Also, the long-distance transportation associated with globalization consumes vast quantities of fossil fuels. Many products now use more energy being transported to far-off markets than they do being produced. Intercontinental ocean shipping, which relies on heavily-polluting bunker oil, is one of the most polluting industries on the planet. In fact, ocean shipping produces more carbon dioxide emissions than all but ten of the *countries* which adopted initial Kyoto targets for emissions reduction. And because ocean shipping operates beyond the reach of national governments, it avoids environmental regulations. (For the same reason, labour standards in the shipping industry are also horrendous.)

Ricardo's theory worked like this: imagine two countries (he chose England and Portugal). Each can produce two products: wine and cloth. Suppose that Portugal can produce *both* wine and cloth more efficiently (that is, with fewer hours of required labour) than England. Portugal's advantage is greatest in wine – but even in cloth production it bests the English factories. England might fear that both its wine and cloth sectors would be wiped out by free trade with Portugal. But Ricardo showed that it was still better (under certain, restrictive conditions) for England to trade with Portugal (sending English cloth, its *relatively* most efficient product, in return for Portuguese wine), than to try to produce both products itself. Portugal, too, is better-off to specialize in wine and trade it for English cloth (rather than making its own cloth).

This theory is much-beloved by economists, who love to expound on its counter-intuitive beauty at policy forums and cocktail parties alike. And the argument that international economic integration must always benefit both sides is still tremendously influential. Neoclassical economists adapted Ricardo's approach to fit their own, more complex theories. They still argue that countries (even high-wage countries) have nothing to fear from expanded trade and investment ties with other countries (even low-wage countries). They have constructed computerized economic models to predict, in stunning detail, the economic gains from further globalization, and have used those predictions to politically support the expansion of the WTO and the implementation of more free-trade agreements.

There's only one problem: the theory is wrong. Even in theory, but especially in practice, the conditions and assumptions that must prevail in order for free trade to be *guaranteed* to benefit both sides, simply do not apply. In reality, free trade produces both winners and losers – just as capitalism itself produces winners and losers. There are several scenarios (summarized in Table 21.2) which disprove the conviction of Ricardo and his descendants that free trade necessarily benefits everyone involved:

- Ricardo's model assumed a supply-constrained system, in which all resources are used in production. In essence, everyone will be employed doing something after free trade, and market forces will ensure they are employed doing what they do best. In reality, however, unemployment exists – in large numbers, and for long periods of time. If it leads to higher unemployment in a particular country or region, then free trade is clearly damaging.

Table 21.2   **Six Ways Free Trade Can Do Damage**

Unemployment: Trade will result in job losses when an economy's products are not competitive.

Capital flows: If a country loses more investment than it gains under globalization, it will experience slow growth or recession.

Transitional costs: The movement of labour from one industry to another is costly, and old capital is destroyed in the process. These costs can outweigh the efficiency benefits of trade.

Perverse specialization: Globalization can lead a country to specialize in less desirable, low-productivity industries.

Terms of trade: As a country produces more of a particular good under free trade, its world price can decline – offsetting the efficiency gains of specialization.

Distribution: A country's GDP may grow under free trade, but the income of particular groups (e.g. workers) may fall.

- Ricardo also assumed that capital could not flow from one country to another. If capital was mobile, in his example, all investment would likely flow from England to Portugal, devastating England's economy. In the real world, capital flows can overwhelm efficiency gains from trade. Any country which loses investment spending as a result of globalization will experience major economic losses.

- When trade is opened up, market pressures will lead to a reallocation of capital and labour from one industry to another – reflecting a country's specialization in its relatively most productive industries. But that economic transition is not costless. Workers lose their jobs, may be unemployed for long periods of time, and may not earn as much when they find new jobs. And in most cases, it is not possible to physically move capital from one industry to another: capital in old industries is simply left to rust, while new investment gradually occurs in growing industries. This loss of capital in the old industry can outweigh the efficiency benefits of trade.

- The issue of which countries get to specialize through trade in which industries is very important. Some industries (such as advanced manufacturing and higher-end services) are especially beneficial: they utilize cutting-edge technology, produce innovative products, and generate higher-than-average productivity and incomes. Other industries (such as many agricultural, minerals, and lower-technology manufactured goods) demonstrate stagnant technology and low productivity. If free trade leads a country to abandon its foothold in more desirable, cutting-edge industries, in order to specialize in less appealing sectors, then that country's future development prospects will be undermined.

- Even when a country specializes in an industry with growing productivity, the efficiency gains from trade can be offset through a complex interaction involving the relative prices of a country's exports and imports (called the TERMS OF TRADE). A country (or countries) might specialize so much in producing a certain product, with so much added efficiency, that it can literally drive down its own price. As a result, the more the country produces, the lower the price falls – and the specialization is self-defeating. This risk is especially acute for agricultural and natural resource products.

- Finally, comparative advantage theory is all defined in terms of national economic benefits. It doesn't say anything about how the benefits of trade, even if they were realized, are *distributed* within a country. Even neoclassical models raise important distributional questions. For example, if a relatively high-wage economy opens trade with a relatively low-wage economy, wages in the richer economy should fall – even under neoclassical assumptions. In theory, the whole country may be better off (measured by GDP), but large groups within the country (namely, the workers) are worse off.

Honest neoclassical economists will admit that if any of these circumstances prevail then free trade can indeed be damaging. But free-trade theory holds such a powerful sway over the economics profession that few are willing to explore the policy implications of those theoretical issues. And so the false impression persists that economists universally agree on the virtues of free trade – even though actual economic theory (even *neoclassical* theory) indicates nothing of the sort.

At the same time, however, none of this discussion implies that free trade is necessarily harmful, either. In reality, globalization introduces a combination of opportunities and threats to economies (and to particular groups of people). New exports and incoming foreign direct investment can add positively to an economy's growth and employment prospects. The ability to produce specialized varieties of manufactured products for a larger international market can enhance productivity. But for every winner, there can also be a loser: an economy that loses production and employment as a result of a failure to compete internationally for market share and investment. Worst of all, the neoliberal rules of globalization as we know it preclude governments from managing those trade and investment flows to enhance the broader benefits, and reduce the costs, of participation in the global economy.

Putting the world on the map

This core conclusion – that globalization introduces risks and costs, as well as benefits, to a national economy – can be illustrated with another edition of our economic map. Figure 21.1 adds the "world" to our economic map, and indicates (in highly simplified form) the different ways in which the domestic economic "circle" is now hooked into a global economic system.

Companies have an opportunity to sell some of their output as exports (X) into other countries' markets, to supplement what they are able to sell to their own consumers and investors. However, their own domestic sales (again, to both consumers and investors) may now be undermined by imports (M) from other countries. There's an opportunity, but also a risk. If its imports are larger than its exports, the country experiences a trade deficit which undermines overall output and employment (Figure 21.1 shows imports as entering the country through a private business, perhaps an import–export company.)

Total investment spending in the economy, meanwhile, may be amplified or reduced by cross-border flows of FDI. But if more FDI leaves than enters, then investment spending is reduced by globalization. Once again, there's both an opportunity and a risk.

The overall prospects of the real economy, therefore, will be enhanced or hampered by globalization, depending on whether exports exceed imports, and on whether the inflow of FDI exceeds the outflow.

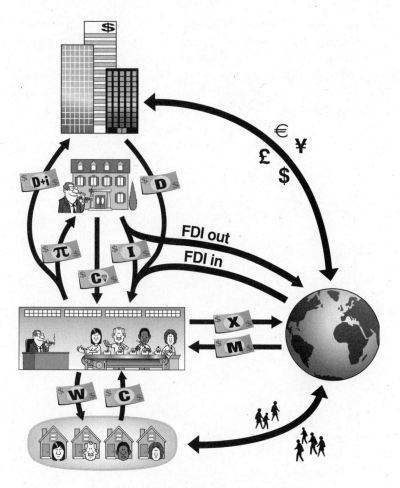

Figure 21.1 **Economic Road Map: Globalization**

International financial linkages are also portrayed, symbolized by the diverse currency symbols linking domestic banks to their global counterparts. The potential benefit from these purely financial flows is harder to identify. Domestic banks should be able to create all the purchasing power they need to finance domestic investment; global linkages are not required for this. If an international financial flow helped to lubricate a real international trade or investment flow, then it could be genuinely useful. But most financial flows have nothing to do with real trade and investment, so their concrete value is not at all clear. On the other hand, financial linkages certainly carry major risks: a large or sudden financial outflow can send an economy into crisis, and even large financial *inflows* can be damaging.

Finally, the global map also illustrates the potential flow of human beings – migration – that can supplement labour supply in particularly vibrant economies, when employers find it necessary.

22

Development (and Otherwise)

The greatest inequality of all

By far the most extreme inequality in the global economy is between the rich and poor countries. This schism is called the "North–South" gap – since most rich countries are located in the Northern hemisphere, and many poor countries in the Southern hemisphere. But the dividing line isn't based on geography: it is based on economic condition. Within many well-off Northern countries are pockets of poverty and exploitation that are more typical of the global South than an advanced economy. By the same token, there are rich and powerful people in poor countries whose lives are as privileged and comfortable as that of any Northern capitalist.

Over one-third of the world's people live in economic conditions that can only be described as appalling. The WORLD BANK estimates that more than 1 billion people live in "extreme poverty," surviving on less than US$1 of income per day. Another 1.5 billion people live in mere "moderate poverty," with just US$1–2 of income per day. Some 40 percent of humanity therefore must support themselves on less income in a year than a global chief executive earns in an hour – collectively consuming only about 2 percent of total global GDP (or one-twentieth of their "fair" share). An estimated 800 million people in the world are malnourished; 1.1 billion lack access to safe water.

Because of this deprivation, lives in the global South are both harsh and short. At least 10 million children under five years of age die every year from entirely preventable disease and malnutrition (accompanied by many millions of adults). United Nations programs have demonstrated that much of this hardship could be alleviated with a shockingly modest redirection of resources. For example, an international project called the Measles Initiative achieved a stunning 70 percent reduction in worldwide deaths from measles between 2000 and 2006, saving over 500,000 lives per year (mostly children) on a budget of just US$300 million. UN agencies have estimated that as little as US$100 billion (one-fifth of 1 percent of global GDP) could

> ### 385 million to 225
>
> "My calculations, albeit they are very crude, tell me that the world's richest 225 people, having a combined annual income of $50 billion (US), earn more than the combined annual incomes of the people of the world's twelve poorest countries, or about 7 percent of the world's population (385 million)."
>
> Partha Dasgupta, Indian-British economist (2001).

pay for the provision of water, basic nutrition, and basic health and social services to everyone on the planet.

Clearly, then, the immense and mind-numbing hardship that prevails across so much of the South does not reflect any genuine economic *shortage*. The world possesses ample resources, food, and know-how to alleviate most of this hardship and prevent most premature deaths. If the global economy is capable of installing a refrigerated soft-drink vending machine in a remote African village, it is also capable of supplying basic foods and medicines to that village – and every other community on the planet.

The problem is not scarcity; the problem is power. Who has the power (both economic and political) to demand that productive resources be devoted to *their* favoured uses (whether it's high fashion, video games, or medicines to treat erectile disfunction)? And who lacks this power? The fact that this inequality is experienced via supposedly "neutral" global market forces should not obscure the fact that it is still rooted in *power*.

The nature of development

Poor countries face an overarching challenge to develop their economies. This process of DEVELOPMENT requires more than just increasing the total size of GDP (although that is a big part of it). There are also many qualitative and structural changes that must occur as an economy develops. These include:

- **Capital accumulation** An economy that uses more "tools," broadly defined, will be more productive, and capable of producing more goods and services. An increase in the stockpile of physical capital is a crucial indicator of development; developing countries must attain a rapid rate of real investment.

- **Investing in knowledge, skills, and health** Productive economies need well-trained workers and managers, to make the most of the physical capital that they are accumulating. Major investments in education – from early childhood through to post-graduate – are a prerequisite for successful development. In poor countries, improving health outcomes (again, starting with children) is also essential for improving human capacities and productivity.

- **Changing sectoral balance** As an economy develops, it experiences a series of important structural changes. Agriculture and other resource-based sectors tend to decline, sparking a population migration from rural areas to cities (that itself poses huge social and economic challenges). Manufacturing expands; exports may be particularly important at this stage. Eventually services production becomes dominant, and the economy gradually becomes more self-reliant. Throughout this process, there is normally a parallel expansion in the FORMAL sector of the economy (the portion that produces goods and services for money), and a decline of the INFORMAL sector (individuals producing food and other products in small quantities, largely for their own use).

- **Institutional development and stability** Improved institutional and political conditions are another key feature of economic development. Institutions (including the legal system, regulatory agencies, and parliaments) need to become more developed, stable, and corruption-free. Investors, businesses, and individual households need certainty and confidence in the economic and political "rules of the game," so that they will be willing to make long-lived commitments to capital projects, education, home-ownership, and communities.

- **Rising incomes** If all of these ingredients come together, then productivity will improve, and GDP will expand – potentially quite quickly. Rapidly developing economies can attain real GDP growth rates of 10 percent per year, or more – sufficient to double total output every seven years. A healthy share of that

growth must show up in rising personal incomes, to ensure that
the bulk of the population shares in the gains of development.

These broad qualitative prerequisites apply to a developing
economy whether it follows a neoliberal, business-driven approach,
or an alternative path to development.

Table 22.1   United Nations Millennium Development Goals

In September 2000, 147 heads of state met in New York to sign the United Nations
Millennium Declaration, which they hoped would symbolize a new global commitment
to reducing global poverty. The Declaration formulates eight broad goals to meet by
2015 (defined in terms of 18 specific quantitative targets). While progress has been
made in a few areas, most of the goals will not be met without a dramatic reorientation
of global policy and an expansion of foreign aid.

1. Eradicate extreme poverty and hunger.
2. Achieve universal primary education.
3. Promote gender equality and empower women.
4. Reduce child mortality.
5. Improve maternal health.
6. Combat HIV/AIDS, malaria and other diseases.
7. Ensure environmental sustainability.
8. Develop a global partnership for development.

Development, undevelopment, and *under*development

To some extent, the poverty and stagnation which typify the South
simply reflect a failure in those countries to attain the preceding
preconditions, and successfully start the development process. In other
words, poor countries suffer from a *lack* of development: we might
call that a state of *un*development. Their challenge is to assemble
the necessary ingredients (capital, human capacities, sectoral mix,
and institutional stability), in order to get the development process
really cooking.

But to some extent, the plight of the global South is more sinister
than just an absence or failure of development. To some extent, their
condition is actually the *result* of the same economic processes which
produced successful development in the North. In this view, it is
not that poor countries failed to develop – rather, it's that global
economic development has assigned them this particular, undesirable
role. These countries, therefore, are not just undeveloped; they are
*under*developed. They have not been "sidestepped" by growth and

progress. In fact, they are an integral part of the global economy. In some ways, poor countries might actually be worse off as a result of this underdevelopment, than if they had been ignored completely by the global economic system.

Several historical and economic factors help to explain underdevelopment – that is, the process through which the global economic system actually pushes poor countries backward:

- **Colonialism**   Strictly speaking, there are not many formal colonies left in the world (mostly small islands). But the violent and disruptive legacy of colonialism continues to undermine development in much of the South. National borders rarely reflect genuine cultural or linguistic realities, causing unending political and ethnic strife. Former colonial powers retained huge economic and political influence, which allowed them to keep exploiting resources and labour in a new guise. Southern governments never had a chance to achieve stability or democracy, given the turmoil (and often war) that accompanied decolonization.

- **Specialization in resources**   Another legacy of colonialism, reinforced after decolonization, has been the specialization of most poor countries in PRIMARY PRODUCTS (including agriculture, minerals, forestry, and other resource-based industries). The growth of primary industries can play a supporting role in kickstarting development. But there are drawbacks to relying too much on primary goods. In the long run, resource prices tend to decline (relative to manufactured goods and services); primary industries face risks of depletion and environmental destruction; primary industries have limited potential for productivity growth; and powerful developed countries have an annoying tendency to invade whenever the security of key resources (like oil) is threatened!

- **Foreign ownership**   FOREIGN DIRECT INVESTMENT can provide a "host" country with capital investment, technological know-how, and management expertise. But here, again, too much of a good thing can become harmful. Countries which are highly dependent on FDI suffer from a long-run failure to develop home-grown technological and managerial expertise. And they often end up paying more profit back to foreign investors than they received in incoming investment in the first place. Foreign debt is even worse: it carries an obligation to pay interest back to Northern lenders, but without any improvement in the borrowing country's productive capacity. Far from constituting a form of "assistance" to poor countries, foreign loans have been a massive economic dead weight around their necks.

- **Uneven development and cumulative causation** Free-market forces have an inherent tendency to imbalance that works against countries in the South – simply because they entered the development process later. The developed countries established an early lead in the production of more advanced products. That initial advantage was reinforced through ECONOMIES OF SCALE and other efficiency gains. The early leaders became even more dominant through competition, making it even harder for newcomers to enter these industries. Unless Southern governments deliberately disrupt market forces in order to counter the North's widening advantage (through the use of interventionist investment and trade policies), free trade can "trap" Southern economies in a state of underdevelopment.

- **Neoliberal policy** One of the most important ways that globalization (as currently practiced, anyway) holds back the countries of the South is via the often-dictatorial advice given to poor countries by officials of the INTERNATIONAL MONETARY FUND and the WORLD BANK. In return for needed financial aid, these institutions have enforced a "hands-off" policy approach in most of the South: cementing free trade, free capital mobility, and government spending cuts. Unfortunately, this has generally made it even more difficult for these countries to escape underdevelopment.

For these reasons and more, poor countries face an uphill struggle to successfully launch the development process. Yes, wages are low in poor countries, and this can provide an incentive for Northern businesses to relocate some investment to the South (a process which evens out North–South differences somewhat – although at the expense of Northern workers). But this only occurs in certain conditions: if Southern governments successfully establish the broader economic and political preconditions for productivity, profitability, and stability. The South's poverty (which explains its low wages) is never, on its own, a recipe for *escaping* poverty.

Wrong Turn

"The application of mistaken economic theories would not be such a problem if the end of first colonialism and then communism had not given the IMF and the World Bank the opportunity to greatly expand their respective original mandates, to vastly extend their reach. Today these institutions have become dominant players in the world economy. Not only countries seeking their help but also those seeking their 'seal of approval' so that they can better access international financial markets must follow their economic prescriptions, which reflect their free-market ideologies and theories. The result for many people has been poverty and for many countries social and political chaos. The IMF has made mistakes in all areas it has been involved in."

Joseph Stiglitz, former Chief Economist of the World Bank (2003).

Recent development successes ... and failures

So in general, the economic deck is clearly stacked against poor countries. Assembling the right conditions and ingredients to launch development remains a daunting, often overwhelming task. The many advantages enjoyed by developed countries tend to strengthen their position in dealing with the global South, thus amplifying the grim inequality that already typifies the world economy.

But development is not impossible. A few countries have managed to do this in recent decades, proving that development can still occur under globalization (despite the roadblocks noted above). However, far from vindicating neoliberal policies, these success stories reflect a rather surprising departure from orthodox economic prescriptions.

By far the most important examples of successful development in recent years have been the East Asian economies. Japan's spectacular growth after World War II blazed the trail. Other regional economies followed suit (including Korea, Taiwan, Hong Kong, and Malaysia), each putting their own stamp on the recipe that Japan pioneered.

All of these countries relied on strong state intervention to guide the development process. (As we learned in Chapter 19, this was also true of Britain and the other early capitalist economies.) Very rapid investment was supported by government tax policy, capital subsidies, and financial regulations. Exports played a crucial role, but not in the manner imagined by neoclassical free-trade theory. Like the eighteenth-century Mercantilists, the Asian countries generated large trade surpluses through aggressive exports (reinforced by strict limits on imports). They welcomed foreign investment and foreign technology, but required that the know-how be quickly transferred to domestic firms. Soon the imitators became the imitated, as Asian firms set global benchmarks in productivity, quality, and innovation. Incomes grew rapidly (for workers, too), thanks in part to a cautious, paternalistic form of CORPORATISM: a system in which income distribution is managed jointly by government, businesses, and unions.

The East Asian model is not without its problems. Attempts to regulate finance in order to accelerate real investment have been undermined by recurrent financial crises (such as Japan's decade-long real-estate meltdown that began in 1990, or the shorter-lived Asian financial crisis of 1997). Asia's export success, meanwhile, directly contributes to lost production and employment in its trading partners (whose chronic trade deficits are the other side of Asia's export-led coin). It is an open question how long those countries (especially in North America) will tolerate huge trade deficits.

The history of this state-led development strategy is being rewritten, in very large letters, in modern China. Beginning in the late 1980s, China's government reintroduced an explicitly capitalist economic policy in which growth is led by private investment (including from new domestic capitalists, as well as multinational companies lured by China's ultra-low labour costs and massive market). Like the East Asian economies which preceded it, China's strategy deviates fundamentally from the neoliberal vision of a minimalist state and free markets. The state is the conductor of this economic orchestra, using a whole set of active measures including:

- Channelling finance to support extremely rapid capital investment (amounting to 30 percent or more of GDP).

- Paying special attention to specific industries (including high-tech sectors like automotive, aerospace, electronics, and pharmaceuticals) and "national champions": companies which the government expects will become globally successful.

- Welcoming foreign investment, but with strings attached – including the requirement to share technology with Chinese companies.

- Investing massively in public infrastructure and services to meet growing needs for utilities, transportation, and skilled workers.

- Actively managing foreign trade to generate large, ongoing trade surpluses – including by controlling the EXCHANGE RATE.

- Tightly regulating labour relations (independent trade unionism is banned) to ensure discipline and productivity, and keep the growth of wages far below the growth of productivity.

China's economic transformation will have massive implications (economic, geopolitical, and environmental) for the future of our planet. China has become, amazingly quickly, a focal point for global capitalism. Many multinational corporations (like General Motors) now make more profit in China than in all their other global operations combined. At the same time, there is no doubt that hundreds of millions of Chinese have benefited substantially from this growth. Indeed, China is single-handedly responsible for the modest reduction in global poverty that has been achieved in the past decade. (If China is excluded, global poverty and inequality have *increased*, despite neoliberal promises that globalization would open the door to mass prosperity in the South.) On the other hand, the benefits of growth have been poorly shared within China: it is now one of the world's most unequal societies. And how long Chinese workers, and

---

Kicking Away the Ladder

"The developed countries used interventionist trade and industrial policies in order to promote their infant industries. The forms of these policies and the emphases among them may have been different across countries, but there is no denying that they actively used such policies. And ... many of them actually protected their industries a lot more heavily than what the currently developing countries have done. If this is the case, the current orthodoxy advocating free trade and *laissez-faire* industrial policies seems at odds with historical experience, and the developed countries that propagate such a view seem to be 'kicking away the ladder' that they used in order to climb up to where they are."

Ha-Joon Chang, Korean economist (2003).

citizens in general, will tolerate suppression of their democratic and labour rights, even as the economy grows by leaps and bounds, is an open question.

Excluding China and the other East Asian economies, there are few examples of successful development during the neoliberal era. India is also growing rapidly – although the benefits of that growth are distributed even less equally than they are in China. India's development is somewhat more business-directed than China's, although the state still plays a very important role. A few countries in Latin America have made notable progress in recent years, reflecting a range of policy orientation (from state-directed Brazil, to market-oriented Chile).

Most of the rest of the global South, however, remains mired in poverty, stagnation, and underdevelopment. Many of these governments followed the neoliberal advice of international institutions to the letter: unilaterally opening trade and finance to global markets, downsizing public programs and cutting taxes, and generally stepping back from an active role in directing development. That this advice has not worked (in glaring contrast to the East Asian experience) still hasn't spurred a sufficient rethinking within those institutions – although there are intriguing cracks in the wall of orthodoxy. Established development economists (like Joseph Stiglitz – see box, p. 275) now recognize that most neoliberal advice to poor countries was destructively wrong.

Mix matters: the economics of industrial structure

The sectoral make-up of the economy, and changes in that composition over time, have important implications for economic policy and strategy – even in developed economies. In other words, even developed countries need to keep worrying about their continuing *qualitative* development.

In this context, let's define an overarching distinction between two broad categories of output. TRADEABLE goods and services are those which can be purchased by customers located far from their site of production. Tradeable products include most kinds of merchandise (with the exception of perishable food, some other non-durable goods, and a few very bulky products). Some services are also tradeable (high-end business, education, and health services; a few lower-wage service functions, like call centres; and tourism). In contrast, NON-TRADEABLES are products which cannot be traded over long distances, and hence must be consumed near where they are produced. As discussed in the last chapter, non-tradeables include construction, most private services, and virtually all public services. (This distinction between tradeable and non-tradeable products is similar to the distinction between the formal and informal sectors in a developing country.)

To successfully "pay its way" in global trade (and hence to finance needed imports), every economy must be able to competitively produce a healthy range of tradeable products. And so having a core portfolio of tradeable industries, able to penetrate export markets, is a precondition for a region or country to have a healthy, sustainable economy. We'll refer to those core industries as the economic "base": they are the industries which generate initial production, employment, and income opportunities. Then, on the strength of that base, additional employment and income opportunities are generated as workers and capitalists alike spend and re-spend their incomes. Most of that "spin-off" activity occurs in non-tradeable sectors oriented around domestic consumers – like housing, private services (restaurants, retail, entertainment), and public services.

This relationship between a tradeable economic "base" and consequent spin-off jobs in non-tradeable sectors reflects the same circular pattern of income and expenditure that was described in our first economic map (back in Chapter 10). The initial export-oriented sales of the base industry play an economic role similar to an injection of investment in our simple economic "circle": they start the economic ball rolling. Then, the subsequent spending and re-spending of that income by various players keeps the ball rolling – ultimately supporting a total volume of production and income much larger than the initial injection.

For this reason, policy-makers need to pay special attention to the success of "base" industries – even in developed countries. They don't need to be nearly as concerned about the success of non-tradeable industries (although they should attempt to upgrade the quality of work and productivity in those industries). For example, the developer of a new shopping complex might claim the mall will create 500 new jobs, for the people working in its shops. But that claim is false. Unless the earnings generated by the region's base industries are expanding, overall consumer spending in the region cannot grow. The new shopping complex may attract consumers away from existing retail facilities in the region – but ultimately every job in the new complex will be offset by a lost job somewhere else.

Governments cannot expand output and employment by building shopping malls. More effective will be trying to ensure that the economy's base of tradeable industries stays healthy.

INDUSTRIAL POLICY refers to measures aimed at improving the sectoral mix of an economy, ensuring that a region or country has a strong set of base industries that allow it to compete successfully in global trade, and support non-tradeable spin-offs. Industrial policy uses a mixture of tax, subsidy, trade, and technology policies to attract a greater portfolio of high-quality tradeable industries. Successful industrial policy can strengthen productivity, incomes, trade performance, and even reduce inflation.

23

Closing the Big Circle

A complete system

In Part Two of this book, we described the basic capitalist "circle:" a cycle of income and expenditure that links capitalists who invest in a profit-making business, and the people who work for them. Our first economic map, in Chapter 10, described that circle and its main properties. Then, throughout Part Four, we've considered additional players, one at a time: banks, governments, and the global economy. Now we'll add all of them into the picture – painting a composite portrait of the real-world economy, in all its complexity.

Figure 23.1 portrays the main players and sectors in the modern economy: capitalists, workers, the environment, banks, government, and the global market. Still visible at the centre of the map is our core "little circle" that gives the system its capitalist character: investment, employment, production, profit, and reproduction.

Arranged around that core are the additional, complicating dimensions. Bankers supply investment finance, and in turn siphon off a share of business profits. Government production supplements the for-profit activity of capitalist enterprises, financed from the taxes (net of transfer payments) paid by workers and capitalists. Meanwhile, the global economy introduces new sources of potential demand (through exports), new competition (from imports), new investment (through FDI), and new labour supply (through migration). Underlying the whole system is the natural environment, which supplies both directly-consumed natural goods (like fresh air, open spaces, and pleasant surroundings) and raw materials for production.

Income and expenditure

As in our simpler circle, money flows in two directions around this system – representing the offsetting flows of income (received by the different players) and expenditure (spent by them). For the economy as a whole, those incoming and outgoing flows must balance. Table 23.1 (p. 285) reports those flows, organized by sector.

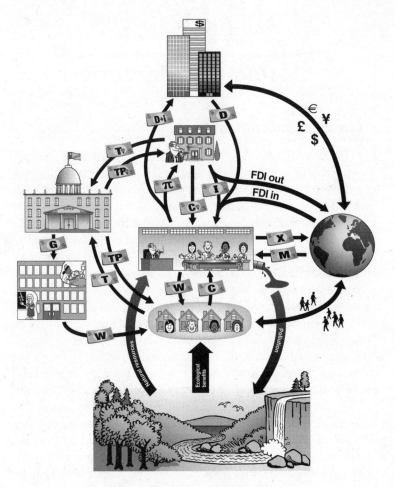

Figure 23.1   **Economic Road Map: Complete System**

Income flows are measured on the left side of the table. Workers' income equals wages (W), less their tax payments (T). (For simplicity, in this chapter we measure taxes *after* deducting the value of the transfer payments that go back in the other direction.) Capitalist income equals profits (Π), less their own tax payments (also net of transfer payments); we distinguish capitalist taxes using the "luxury" diamond (T_0). A portion of profit income is diverted from capitalists to financiers, to pay interest on outstanding loans. The government's income, meanwhile, equals the total flow of taxes (from capitalists

Who's Who?

To help the audience make sense of the often-convoluted plot, opera companies always provide a handy program summarizing who everyone is, and what they do to each other. In the same spirit, here is a summary of the major actors who appear on our economic stage, and the major ways they relate:

Key Players

Workers   Make up 85 percent of society; perform labour for wages and salaries.

Capitalists   Major owners and top managers of companies; make up less than 5 percent of society, but own most capital; initiate investment and organize production in pursuit of profit.

Environment   Source of direct ecological benefits and natural resources; dumping ground for pollution.

Banks   A special kind of company that creates credit for business, and captures a portion of profit in return.

Government   Produces services, financed with taxes received from workers and capitalists; also redistributes income through transfer payments, and regulates production.

World   Other countries linked to our economy via trade, investment, finance, and migration.

Key Flows

Investment (I)   Spending on new capital; starts production in motion.

Wages (W)   Received by employees in return for work.

Profits (Π)   The residual received by capitalists after selling their output and paying their bills (including labour costs).

Consumption (C)   Spending on goods and services needed for personal survival and well-being. Workers spend essentially all of their wages on mass consumption; capitalists spend some of their profits on luxury consumption (C_o).

Ecological Benefits   The essential and pleasurable things we derive directly from nature: fresh air, water, space.

▶

Natural Resources   Products harvested from the natural environment for use in production.

Pollution   Wastes expelled back into the natural environment as a side-effect of economic activity.

Debt (D)   Banks create loans to allow real businesses to expand their operations.

Interest (i)   Loans must be paid back with interest to the bank, siphoning off a share of profits.

Government Production (G)   Governments undertake direct production in certain industries (mostly public services) to meet public demands.

Taxes (T)   To pay for public services, governments collect taxes from workers (T) and capitalists (T_0). Some tax revenues are paid back to both classes as transfer payments (TP).

Exports (X)   A portion of our country's output is sold to purchasers in other countries.

Imports (M)   A portion of our country's spending buys products made in other countries.

Foreign Direct Investment (FDI)   Capitalists in one country may invest in a productive facility in another country; FDI can enter our country, or leave it.

International Financial Flows ($€£¥)   Banks lend to investors in other countries, and convert one country's money into another.

Migration   Workers cross national borders in search of employment.

and workers, $T + T_0$), minus transfers paid back to households. So the deduction of taxes from the worker and capitalist accounts is offset by their inclusion as income within the government account. For the economy as a whole, therefore, total income still equals simply the sum of *before-tax* wages and profits – and hence taxes disappear from the bottom line of our table.

The right side of Table 23.1, meanwhile, measures expenditure flows. As before, workers "spend what they get": essentially all their wages are devoted to mass consumption (C). Capitalists have more choice in spending their (much larger) incomes: on luxury consumption (C_0), or on re-investments in their businesses (I). (As in Chapter 16, we have lumped bankers' consumption in with the capitalists.)

Table 23.1   Income and Expenditure: Complete System

Class/Sector	Income	Expenditure
Workers	After-tax wages (W – T)	Worker consumption (C)
Capitalists	+ After-tax profits ($\Pi - T_0$)	+ Luxury consumption (C_0)
		+ Investment (I)
Government	+ Taxes ($T + T_0$)	+ Government production (G)
Rest of world		+ Net exports (X – M)
	= Total income	= Total expenditure
	(W + Π)	($C + C_0 + I + G + X - M$)

Government production (G) provides an additional spending boost. Internationally, foreign purchases of domestic products (via exports, X) add to total expenditure. But this is offset by domestic purchases of foreign-made products (imports, M), which divert a share of domestic spending away from domestic production. The difference between the two (exports minus imports) equals the trade balance (also known as "net exports"). If the trade balance is positive (a trade surplus), then foreign trade enhances total expenditure on domestic production; if it is negative (a trade deficit), then foreign trade undermines domestic production.

At the end of the day, an economy's income (received by workers and capitalists) will be fully allocated to those four primary forms of expenditure: consumption, investment, government production, and net exports.

(Table 23.1 does not list any "income" received by the rest of the world; strictly speaking, this should be required for other countries to pay for their net purchases of our exports. In practice, the rest of the world would need international capital flows to finance this trade deficit; to keep things simple, we have not shown this detail in Table 23.1, or on the map.)

Surpluses and deficits

While the economy as a whole must maintain a broad balance between income and spending, any particular part of the economy may experience an imbalance (for a while, anyway). If one sector takes in more income than it spends, it generates a surplus. If it spends more than it takes in, it experiences a deficit. In effect, sectors in deficit can borrow money from sectors in surplus, in order to finance their continuing "excess" spending. But for the economic system as a whole, all these surpluses and deficits will cancel each other out (since the whole economy's expenditure will equal its income).

Table 23.2   Sectoral Deficits

Class/Sector	Deficit
Workers	Spend more than their wages.
Capitalists	Invest (and consume) more than their profits.
Government	Spends more than its tax revenues.
International	Imports more than it exports.
Total Economy	**Sum of all deficits = 0**

Table 23.2 lists the same four major economic players: workers, capitalists (including bankers), government, and the rest of the world. Each player's potential deficit will equal the second column of Table 23.1 (its expenditure) minus the first column (its income).

We have generally assumed that workers can only spend as much on consumption as they earn in employment: that is, worker households "spend what they get." However, if worker households are willing to go into debt (via credit cards, second mortgages, or loan sharks), and banks are willing to provide that debt, then workers can consume beyond their income. This creates household deficits, and growing consumer debt, which can help to support production and employment for a while. But it can also cause long-term financial problems, if consumer debt grows too large. Recent turmoil in the US MORTGAGE industry (caused when lower-income households became unable to pay back their loans) reminds us that debt-financed consumption can be very unstable.

Other sectors may also experience deficits. The capitalist (or business) sector is in deficit when its new investment spending exceeds what it earns in profit (after deducting the costs of capitalist consumption). Government is in deficit when its spending (including transfer payments) exceeds its tax revenues. And any individual country experiences a trade deficit when it buys more imports than it exports. For the country as a whole, the deficits and surpluses must offset each other (unless the whole country goes into debt by borrowing from other countries).

Many conservative commentators follow the knee-jerk motto that "deficits are bad, and surpluses are good" – especially where governments are concerned. But Table 23.2 indicates that simply reducing the government's deficit (or any other single sector's deficit) is likely to produce an offsetting reaction among other sectors, with very little impact on the overall economy. For example, consumers or businesses may take on additional debt as an indirect result of tighter government fiscal policy.

It is impossible for *all* sectors in the economy to simultaneously reduce their deficits. If they tried to do so (perhaps following mistaken conservative advice), the end result would be a terrible recession (resulting from the sharp decline in spending). Overall balance between income and expenditure would eventually be restored, but at a much lower level of income and employment. This self-defeating outcome is called the PARADOX OF THRIFT: economic players (whether consumers, businesses, or governments) who try to increase savings by cutting back spending can end up with *lower* savings as a result of the recession which their spending cutbacks caused.

Injections and leakages

There is still another way of understanding the relationships symbolized in our complex map. Every economy needs some kind of initial spending push, just to get things going. In the simplest capitalist circle, that boost comes from investment. It creates the initial injection of spending power, which in turn generates additional income and spending (from suppliers, the company's workers, and consumer industries). The final amount of income and spending resulting from the initial injection of investment is determined by the MULTIPLIER. The multiplier exists because workers can't spend anything until they get a job; new investment which creates new jobs thereby stimulates an ongoing chain of new spending (and matching production) that's several times larger than the initial investment. This is why investment is so important – and why governments, communities, and workers all have an interest in stimulating more business investment.

In the real-world economy, however, there are other potential sources of initial spending power. The two most important come from government programs and exports. Decisions by government, or by foreign customers, to purchase domestic production can set off the same sort of economic chain-reaction that is caused by business investment. And these other forms of spending also support a total amount of economic activity far larger (that is, multiplied) than the original injection.

Table 23.3 summarizes these three major forms of spending injections: business investment, government programs, and exports. They are essential for establishing a basic level of vitality in the economy. When these forms of spending are strong and growing, the overall condition of the economy is likely to be vibrant – via a multiplied impact on overall income and spending. Policy-makers concerned with stimulating more growth and employment, therefore, will want to focus on measures which stimulate investment, government spending, and exports.

How big is the multiplier effect? The final impact of an initial spending injection on total output, income, and employment depends on a number of factors. One is how quickly the initial injection of spending "leaks out" from the chain-reaction of spending and re-spending that is sparked. On the reasonable assumption that worker households continue to spend their full incomes on consumption, there are three broad sources of this leakage. Capitalists set aside some of their income as savings (in part to repay the loans they received from bankers), rather than re-investing it or spending it on consumption. Governments siphon off a share of the new income in taxes – offsetting the cost of the programs which they provide. And consumers spend some of their income on imports. These three sources of leakage slow down (and eventually stop) the multiplier process. At a certain level of total output, the spending power lost to these leakages will perfectly offset the amount of spending power injected in the first place (by investors, governments, and exports).

What if the total GDP resulting from that balance of injections and leakages is too low, resulting in widespread unemployment? To strengthen overall spending conditions, Table 23.3 suggests two

Table 23.3 **Injections and Leakages**

Spending Injections	*Unspent Leakages*
Investment (I)	Capitalist savings $(\Pi - C_0)$
Government production (G)	Taxes $(T + T_0)$
Exports (X)	Imports (M)
Total injections:	**Total leakages:**
Investment + government + exports	**Savings + taxes + imports**

broad solutions: boost the injections, and reduce the leakages. First, overall output and employment will grow along with the spending injections: stronger investment, expanded government programs, or stronger exports. Governments can use many different tools (from direct spending, to interest rate adjustments, to export promotion measures) to stimulate these injections.

Alternatively, the multiplier effect from a given set of injections will be stronger if leakages from subsequent spending can be minimized. Limiting import penetration in domestic consumer markets, reducing income taxes, and encouraging capitalists to spend more of their profits (rather than saving them) would all enhance the stimulative power of the initial injections. Of course, these measures to reduce leakages (especially for government and capitalists) must be balanced against the simultaneous need to maintain a stable financial balance within those sectors (so that neither government nor corporate debt becomes too large).

And while governments must be concerned with encouraging strong overall income and spending conditions (to promote a greater *quantity* of production), they must also aim to enhance the *quality* and efficiency of production. For that reason, policies to stimulate injections and limit leakages must be supplemented by policies that promote productivity and innovation.

Conclusion: a complex, flexible, but fragile system

Piece by piece, our economic map has become quite complicated. At the centre of the map are the core economic relationships that define capitalism. And the vitality of that core investment-driven "circle" still determines the rise or fall of the overall system.

In our more complex portrayal, however, that core mechanism operates in a broader and more diverse context. The actions of government, the financial system, and the global economy now tailor the actions of capitalists, and help determine the overall direction of the economy. These new elements can make the system stronger or weaker, depending on whether they support or undermine spending and production. However, they certainly help to diversify the economy: crucial spending decisions now come from a wider cast of characters (not just domestic capitalists), and there are new levers that can be used to adjust economic outcomes when needed.

In this regard, modern capitalism (as portrayed in Figure 23.1) is much more stable than the one-dimensional variety described in our earlier, simpler economic map. But at the same time, these other dimensions can also introduce new sources of instability and even fragility into the system when they don't function well. The next chapter will consider the instability of capitalism in more detail.

24

The Ups and Downs
of Capitalism

The never-ending rollercoaster

Economists have always been preoccupied with the boom-and-bust pattern of the capitalist economy. And with good reason. After all, the lost opportunity, human suffering, and political instability caused by recessions and depressions demand attention from economists, business executives, and politicians alike. At times, the economy is literally bursting at the seams: investment is booming, production is expanding, incomes are rising. Yet at other times, the economy is stuck in deep mud: stagnant production, lost jobs, poverty, and pessimism.

What explains this rollercoaster, which has repeated itself many times through the history of capitalism? And what can be done to prevent these downturns and stabilize the economy around a path of steady growth?

A RECESSION occurs when a country's real GDP (adjusted for inflation) begins to shrink (see box overleaf). A very severe, long-lasting recession is called a DEPRESSION. Even a milder economic slowdown – in which GDP continues to grow, but very slowly – can create unemployment and dislocation. A RECOVERY occurs when the economy stops contracting and starts growing again.

Recessions and subsequent recoveries have diverse causes and features; each one is unique. But this rollercoaster pattern is not simply a series of occasional, random events. There is clearly a *systemic* nature to economic cycles. Even a cursory review of economic history indicates that recessions and recoveries don't just "happen" because of random and seemingly unrelated "shocks." Instead, there are inherent forces within capitalism which create and re-create this cyclical pattern.

The boom-and-bust cycle of capitalism poses a special challenge to those who defend neoclassical free-market economics. Remember, neoclassical theory predicts that the operation of competitive markets will automatically ensure that all willing workers are employed,

When is a Recession Really a Recession?

As a rule of thumb, economists officially define a recession as occurring when a country's real GDP declines for two straight quarters (that is, for six months).

However, this guideline is quite arbitrary. More broadly, it's reasonable to define a recession as any economy-wide slowdown that results in higher unemployment and falling incomes. This can occur even if real GDP continues to slowly expand. Indeed, real GDP must grow at least as fast as the sum of population growth and productivity growth, or else the unemployment rate will rise. In developed capitalist economies, this requires ongoing real GDP growth of at least 2–3 percent per year, just to keep unemployment from rising. If growth slows below this rate, then unemployment will grow and incomes will stagnate. It will "feel" like a recession, even if the economists haven't officially declared it so.

and that all available resources are fully utilized in production. The credibility of this whole theory is shaken to its core, however, during deep recessions – when millions of workers sit idly by, capital is destroyed, and investment goes nowhere.

Free-market economists try to explain away recessions as resulting either from random "shocks" or from the perverse economic interference of governments. But their explanations are not convincing. In reality, the economy has no automatic, internal ability to maintain full employment. Unemployment, as we have seen, is a normal feature of capitalism. And fluctuations in unemployment over time are also normal, reflecting the inherent dynamics of a system rooted in the profit-seeking behaviour of individual companies and investors.

How a recession starts

A recession begins with a significant downturn in some part of the economy – within any one of the links described in the "big circle" portrayed in the last chapter. It could be a particular industry, or a particular region, or a particular type of spending (investment, consumer spending, government spending, or exports). Every recession starts with some negative change that reduces spending, production, and eventually employment in one particular part of the economy.

But this initial, focused contraction is seldom large enough to cause an all-out recession in its own right. After all, to reduce the entire GDP of a large economy would require a truly massive downturn within any single sector or region (since the other sectors, generally, should still be growing). Instead, it is a chain-reaction resulting from the initial problem that creates a wider economic crisis. The downturn spreads from one sector to another, following the links that connect different industries and different kinds of spending. If conditions are right, the initial downturn cascades into a broader decline in the total economy, far beyond the initial hard-hit sector – sometimes even spreading to other countries.

As a simple example, recall the simple investment-driven economy that was described in our first economic map (back in Chapter 10). That economy depended completely on new investment spending by profit-seeking capitalists. Investment generates new production and new employment. Workers get paid. They spend their earnings on consumer goods – which in turn generates more production, more employment, and more investment.

Now suppose that something turns negative in those initial investment decisions. Investors might decide that profit rates no longer justify more investment. Or they may worry about political stability, labour peace, or other risk factors. Whatever their initial concern, investment spending declines.

What follows is an immediate contraction in industries which produce capital goods, spare parts, and other supplies for the companies which cut back investment. Eventually, those companies lay off unneeded workers. Now consumer spending begins to decline, too – since workers who are no longer earning are no longer spending, either. Thus the recession spreads into consumer goods industries. Consumer businesses also lay off workers. Total employment declines further, and consumer spending takes another hit. Meanwhile, as the recession deepens and spreads, investors become all the more pessimistic about their ability to sell new output. So investment declines even further (and not just from those companies whose initial pessimism sparked the downturn – now *every* company starts to fear the future), and the downturn is amplified.

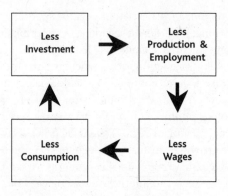

Figure 24.1   How a Recession Occurs

This chain-reaction is illustrated in Figure 24.1. Because of the dependence of production on investment, the dependence of consumption spending on employment, and the uncoordinated nature of individual investment and consumption decisions, a problem in one part of the economy – even a relatively small part of the economy – can spread and amplify until the entire economy is contracting. Importantly, the whole contagious process is rooted in some essential features of capitalism:

- Profit-seeking investments by individual companies are required to set the economy in motion.
- Workers need a job to earn wages to pay for consumption.
- Each investment decision reflects the individual judgement of that investor about the balance of risk and opportunity that's best for their own company. There's no overall coordination of the whole economy.

Its interdependent yet decentralized nature, together with its structural reliance on profit-seeking business investment, explains why capitalism is inherently prone to boom-and-bust cycles. Other economic systems (including pre-capitalist systems and planned socialist economies) also experienced periods of good times and periods of bad times – depending on the state of agriculture, technological progress, political stability, and other factors. But these systems did not demonstrate the regular, repeating, rollercoaster pattern of capitalism.

Causes of economic cycles

The preceding example describes a recession arising in an economy with only two kinds of spending: investment and consumption. In the real world, other kinds of spending are also important – like government spending and exports. A sharp downturn in any type of spending, or in the banking and financial system, can spread into full-blown recession, thanks to the inherent instability of a decentralized, profit-driven economy. Here are some of the negative events or shocks that have been important in sparking past recessions:

- **Investment instability**   Business investment spending has more influence on the direction of the overall economy than any other category of spending. As we learned in Chapter 12, investment spending depends on a complex and unstable mixture of factors: current and expected profits, capacity utilization, interest rates, a variety of potential risks, and the relative attractiveness of competing jurisdictions. Negative developments in any of these variables, if shared by enough businesses, can cause an investment-led downturn.

- **Consumer sentiment**   Consumer spending typically accounts for over half of total GDP. So by virtue of size alone, consumer spending plays an important role in the boom-and-bust cycle. However, since consumer spending tends to follow employment and wage trends very closely (rather than leading those trends), it is rare that changes in consumer spending alone will actually *cause* a recession. However, an initial negative shock in any other part of the economy can quickly cause a subsequent downturn in consumer spending. If that consumer response is large, it will tip the economy into a full downturn. In rare cases, a sudden negative shift in consumer sentiment (perhaps because of the psychological response to a catastrophe, like the 9/11 terrorist attacks) could be the initial cause of recession.

- **Supply shocks**   Major price increases or supply disruptions in key inputs used by many or most businesses may also induce an economic downturn, by undermining profitability (and hence investment), business confidence, and consumer spending. For example, volatility in global oil supplies, and skyrocketing oil prices, contributed to the global recessions of the 1970s and 1980s. Dramatic agricultural problems can also cause recessions (although these are less frequent in modern developed economies).

- **Monetary policy** Several recessions, especially under neoliberalism, have been directly caused by overzealous monetary policy. Central banks, obsessed with controlling inflation, raise interest rates too far and too fast. The economy slows down too much, and may even tip into outright recession. The major global downturn of the early 1980s was caused by anti-inflation monetary policy (see box opposite).

- **Banking cycles** As we learned in Chapter 16, private banks issue loans to businesses and households in order to profit from the resulting flow of interest payments. But banks must always balance the lure of interest income against the risk that the borrowers may default and not pay back the loans. The formation of new credit by private banks is essential to growth under capitalism. Sometimes banks are confident, and happily issue loans to new customers, at relatively low interest rates. The result is rapid economic growth. At other times, however, banks worry intensely about default. They quickly reduce new lending (causing a CREDIT SQUEEZE), and pump up interest rates. This causes slower growth or even outright recession. The inherent cause of this cycle is the profit-driven nature of the private banking system.

- **Financial instability** Speculative financial markets are inherently fragile, subject to episodes of panic, contraction, and even outright collapse. A dramatic financial downturn may have negative effects on the real economy, especially if it undermines the confidence of investors or consumers. The long global depression of the 1930s began with the American stock market collapse of 1929. In a globalized financial system, financial panic often results in the sudden flight of short-term finance away from particularly vulnerable countries (called CAPITAL FLIGHT), with devastating effects on finance, banking, and real production and employment. This mechanism caused a severe recession in southeast Asia in 1997.

- **Foreign trade** A recession can easily spread from one country to another via its impact on trade flows. Suppose one country suffers a major recession. If it has a trading partner which depends heavily on export sales to that country, it too may enter recession, as its exports decline. For example, consider the situation of Canada: its economy depends heavily on exports, almost 90 percent of which go to the US. A recession in the US, therefore, almost always causes a copycat recession in Canada, via its negative impact on American purchases of Canadian products. Imports can also cause a downturn. A major surge in import competition, if it damages too many domestic industries, can throw a trade-sensitive country into recession.

Great Recessions of the Past

The Dirty Thirties   The 1920s, like the 1990s, were a wonderful time to play the stock market. Share prices boomed, and millions of average people threw their life's savings into the market in hopes of winning a piece of the action. But like all speculative bubbles, this one collapsed – in 1929. That began a brutal decade-long recession that spread from North America to Europe and around the world. Unemployment rates reached as high as 30 percent. The downturn was made worse by persistent drought in several countries (damaging the farming sector), and by perverse fiscal and monetary policies. In this pre-Keynesian era, central bankers and finance ministers continued to fight inflation and budget deficits, even as the recession got worse.

The Volcker Recession   Paul Volcker was appointed head of the US Federal Reserve in 1979. He immediately tightened bank lending and drove up interest rates in a battle to reduce inflation. This was a shocking change after 35 years of policies which emphasized full employment over inflation control. Volcker's appointment signalled the beginning of neoliberalism. It also resulted in a steep three-year recession – by far the worst since the Dirty Thirties – that spread from America through most of the world.

Japan's Lost Decade   Japan had one of the world's most vibrant economies in the 1970s and 1980s. But it ground to a sudden halt in 1990, following a stock market and real estate crash. Then followed a decade of recession and near-recession: real GDP growth was near-zero, and at times the country experienced outright deflation (falling average prices). Even gigantic increases in government spending and zero-percent interest rates couldn't end the stagnation. Japan's experience proves that severe, long-lasting recessions can indeed still occur.

- **Government spending** A sudden downturn in government spending might also create the conditions for recession. This could result from some major change in government activity (such as the demobilization of military spending after a war), or from overly dramatic budget-cutting aimed at eliminating a deficit. Ironically, that type of budget-cutting can backfire: the government's financial situation may be worse off because of the recession than it was under the original deficit.

Clearly, there is no shortage of potential causes for a recession. What all recessions have in common, however, is that an initial downturn cascades through the consecutive links that connect investors, consumers, and industries. This is what ultimately creates the broader and more painful crisis.

Ending (and preventing) recessions

After a few months, or even years, of decline and contraction, the economy eventually shifts out of its doldrums, and growth commences once again. Various factors may contribute to the turnaround. Consumer spending may continue at some basic level, even if unemployment is high, as families dip into savings and other resources to meet basic consumption needs. Financial panics eventually run their course, allowing investors to pick up the pieces again and start searching for new bargains. The desperation arising from high unemployment and intense insecurity reduces wages, and this may encourage businesses to start hiring again. In all of these cases, spending eventually recovers in at least one major part of the economy. This then creates positive spin-off benefits and spillovers that eventually spark a wider recovery. The same chain-reactions that caused the recession now operate in a positive direction.

In modern times, however, governments try to short-circuit recessions with proactive efforts to stop the contraction and spur recovery. These measures are called COUNTER-CYCLICAL POLICIES, because they represent a deliberate effort to interrupt the boom-and-bust cycle of the economy. And the use of these counter-cyclical policies has continued under neoliberalism. In fact, if anything, these policies are more sophisticated and powerful than ever. No government is willing to tolerate the economic (and political) costs that come with prolonged recession, without at least trying to get the economy back on track.

The most common counter-cyclical tool used in modern capitalism is MONETARY POLICY. Central banks cut interest rates to speed up growth, and thus guide the economy back to a desired level of output and employment. (As we saw in Chapter 16, their goal is *not* full employment: central bankers prefer to keep a certain, ongoing level of unemployment as a cushion against workers' wage demands.) Central bankers watch economic trends very closely, gathering vast amounts of data. And they move quickly when necessary to adjust interest rates, which in turn affect growth in many ways (via investment, consumer spending, and even exports). However, interest rates take a long time to have their full effect on spending power (generally about two years). Governments can use other financial tools, in addition to interest rate adjustments, to spur growth via the monetary system – such as adjustments in banking regulations, or supplying loans directly from the central bank.

The other main tool for smoothing out economic bumps is counter-cyclical FISCAL POLICY. Governments adjust their spending (and the taxes they collect to pay for that spending), in order to strengthen (or cool down) the economy. In a recession, governments can increase public spending to spur employment and production. It can also cut taxes to spur private spending – although tax cuts are indirect and less powerful (since consumers, especially higher-income households, don't fully or immediately spend their full tax savings). In contrast, if the economy is growing too quickly, then the government can reduce spending or raise taxes to cool off growth.

There are two broad types of counter-cyclical fiscal policy. DISCRETIONARY FISCAL POLICY consists of incremental, proactive programs or projects undertaken by government in response to a recession. On the other hand, AUTOMATIC STABILIZERS are fiscal tools which act immediately to smooth out cycles – without any deliberate action by governments at all. For example, income taxes are automatically stabilizing: when incomes fall, taxes automatically fall too, and this offsets some of the contraction in spending that would otherwise have occurred. Income security programs such as unemployment insurance and welfare benefits are also automatically stabilizing: they protect a portion of lost household income (and hence a proportion of consumer spending) during a downturn.

Merely having a relatively larger public sector in the first place can itself reduce the size of economic cycles. Government programs such as education, health care, and other public services are not subject to the same profit motive, and hence the same boom-and-bust pattern, as private business production. The public sector thus tends to be an oasis of stability during recessions. It is much less vulnerable to contagious contraction than the private sector.

Unfortunately, some conservative politicians have argued in recent years for measures that undermine the stabilizing power of government programs, and in fact make government a *destabilizing* economic force. Neoliberal cutbacks to social programs (especially income security programs), and reductions in the taxes that once paid for those programs, undermines the power of automatic stabilizers, and makes the economy more vulnerable to a chain-reaction recession. Even worse are BALANCED BUDGET LAWS, which require governments to keep their budgets in balance (with no deficit) – even in a recession. Under these laws, government must either increase taxes or cut spending during recession – either of which only make the recession worse. Motivated by an ideological hatred of deficits, therefore, these policies have the perverse effect of *exaggerating* the size of economic swings that arise in the private sector.

Long waves

The preceding discussion has focused on relatively shorter-run ups and downs in economic performance – recessions that might last a year or two, followed by several years of growth, followed by another recession. Alongside these shorter-run fluctuations, however, a parallel cyclical pattern is also visible. Capitalism also demonstrates a pattern of very long-run cycles (or LONG WAVES), in which episodes of relatively vibrant growth last for several decades, followed by long periods of sluggishness and stagnation (if not outright recession).

· The postwar Golden Age (1945–75) was one such sustained expansion. So was a 30-year period in the mid-nineteenth century, when growth was spurred by massive investments in railways. The early growth of heavy industry, and the early expansion of mass-production manufacturing, stimulated another sustained expansion during the 20 years prior to World War I. These vibrant periods alternated with extended periods of slow growth, recession, or even depression.

The causes and patterns of these long waves are not fully understood by economists, although some key factors are visible in every long swing:

- **Technology** A clumping of fundamental (and profitable) technological innovations seems to be a common feature of most long upswings: railways in the 1850s; heavy industry and mass production in the early twentieth century; television, communication, and transportation in the postwar Golden Age.
- **Investment** Capitalism always depends on private investment. But investment spending is especially strong during these long upswings. This reflects an especially exuberant and long-lived conviction among capitalists that healthy profits are there for the making.
- **Politics** Every long upswing is also marked by a stable and well-functioning (from the perspective of capitalists, anyway) set of political institutions, practices, and power relationships – both within individual countries, and internationally. These institutions are needed to control labour and manage income distribution (in a manner which keeps workers satisfied, but enriches capitalists), and also to manage overall economic affairs (including international trade).

The petering out of key innovations, a consequent slowdown in investment, and a breakdown of once-stable political relationships and structures, heralds the end of a long upswing and a slide into an intervening period of conflict, uncertainty, and stagnation. Economic and political stakeholders then cast about for another set of economic and political practices that will allow a resumption of stable growth. When that recipe is found, then another long upswing may commence.

Following this analysis, some economists have concluded that the ingredients may now be in place for the commencement of a new period of sustained and relatively stable capitalist growth. After the tumultuous events of the 1980s and 1990s, when Golden Age policies were abandoned and neoliberalism was consolidated, capitalism may now be in a position to safely step on the gas pedal once again. Breakthroughs in electronic technology (like the personal computer and the internet) are stimulating investment and growth across a wide range of industries. Neoliberal policies clearly dominate the political arena. The geographical focus of expansion may have shifted somewhat – away from the industrialized countries, and toward China and other rapidly industrializing regions.

However, it's not yet clear that neoliberalism has really put in place all the conditions needed for a new long upswing. Real investment spending by business is amazingly sluggish, considering very high profits and a solidly pro-business political and economic climate. Hyperactive financial markets regularly introduce a degree of panic and chaos into the economy that is inconsistent with long-run stability. International affairs continue to be disrupted by regional wars and massive trade imbalances. Environmental problems constrain growth and living standards.

At any rate, even if neoliberalism is working profitably for capitalists, it has had negative net impacts on the living standards of most people – and sooner or later, this will throw into question the long-run political stability of the new regime. The jury is still out, therefore, on whether this modern, tough-love incarnation of capitalism has really established the conditions for a longer-run winning streak.

Part Five

Challenging Capitalism

25

Evaluating Capitalism

A report card

Back in Chapter 1, I suggested seven key criteria on which the success of an economy might be judged. Since then we've developed a comprehensive description of capitalism. Now let's go back to that initial list of criteria, and give the whole system a report card. How does modern capitalism rate, in terms of its ability to meet those seven criteria? I use the standard letter grade system: A (superior), B (good), C (adequate), D (poor), and F (failure). Here are the grades for each "subject":

Prosperity: C   When capitalism is growing vibrantly, it can improve material living standards for a significant portion of its population – although never for everyone. In the developed countries, most people (even workers) lead comfortable, reasonably prosperous lives. But even there, many people have been left behind by the prosperity bus. Poverty rates are significant, and (in some countries) growing. Across the global South, meanwhile, the system has completely abandoned vast swaths of humanity. There, capitalism has failed to even assemble the basic preconditions for development, let alone ensure that the proceeds of growth are decently shared. So the claim that capitalism is naturally and broadly associated with mass prosperity is clearly not justified.

Security: D   Even workers who have managed to win a decent material standard of living face a never-ending risk that everything could be taken away in an instant – due to individual bad luck or broader economic failure. This chronic insecurity imposes real costs on working people and their families. Even if they never actually lose their job, their home, or their pension, the fear that they *could* lose those things undermines their quality of life. More advanced social-democratic economies (like those in Scandinavia) provide comprehensive social security programs which remove much of that insecurity. But elsewhere, economic downturn or personal misfortune

Table 25.1   Capitalism's Report Card

Subject	Grade	Comments
Prosperity	C	Student has produced significant progress for some groups, but left many others behind.
Security	D	Even those with decent prosperity can lose it all in an instant.
Innovation	A–	Innovates very well, but needs to apply its talent to more important priorities.
Choice	B–	Lots of stuff in the stores, but what about constrained life choices for billions?
Equality	F	Student shows no interest whatsoever in this subject.
Sustainability	D	Failure to protect environmental standards will undermine future progress.
Democracy and accountability	D+	Corporations are governed well – but to what end? Economic inequality is deeply anti-democratic.
Overall	**C–**	**Marginal pass:** Student is definitely underperforming true economic and human potential.

ruin the life chances of millions. In the US, which lacks public health insurance, merely becoming ill can financially ruin an entire family.

Innovation: A–   Innovation is definitely capitalism's best subject. The combination of the profit motive and competitive pressure leads companies to constantly seek new products, new ways of producing them, and new markets to sell them in. Of course, this innovation isn't always *socially* useful: many of the new ways that firms devise to make money are wasteful, pointless, or destructive. Much of the system's innovative potential is misdirected to unproductive uses (from copycat prescription drugs which serve no medical purpose, to ever-more-complex financial derivatives, to increasingly annoying and intrusive ways to advertise). But there's no denying capitalism's innovative capacity.

Choice: B–   Supermarkets and retail outlets, even in poor countries, are crammed with an incredible variety of products. When consumer demand exists, private companies fall over each other racing to satisfy it, with their competing offerings. The only problem is that while companies offer a tremendous range of goods, a great many people can't afford to buy anything. This renders the glitzy "choice" of capitalist consumerism somewhat hollow. Unless you derive intrinsic pleasure from looking at store windows (and some people, indoctrinated into consumer culture, actually *do*), this kind of choice is rather phony. At the same time, we can't ignore the narrowing of life choices caused by the systemic inequality of capitalism. People with talent and ambition, who could make great economic contributions, are prevented from doing so by the artificial barriers of class, gender, race, or geography. This wasted opportunity and mass denial of true life choices is surely more important than the fact that the local supermarket sells a dozen different brands of toothpaste.

Equality: F   Capitalism was simply not cut out to pass this subject. A deep and inherent inequality is hard-wired into the system's basic programming. The inequality of wealth between those who own businesses and those who do not is stunning – and it's getting wider. Other forms of inequality are also generated by capitalism: between different groups of workers, different genders and races, different sectors, different regions, and different countries. What's more, competition tends to automatically *re-create* inequality over time. Only through deliberate efforts to reduce inequality (through taxes, transfer payments, and other tools of redistribution) can the inherent inequality of capitalism be (partially) evened out.

Sustainability: D   The profit motive creates a strong incentive for private companies to "dump" environmental costs from their operations onto others, through pollution. Moreover, the hunger for profit also creates an inherent growth imperative within capitalism. Private companies need to grow continuously to keep investors happy, and keep competitors at bay; this makes it difficult for capitalism to adapt to environmental constraints on growth. Popular concern and political pressure can force governments to defend the environment with regulations, environmental taxes, and other measures. But it's always an uphill struggle to rein in the environmental behaviour of companies whose fundamental goal is to maximize private profit.

Democracy and accountability: D+   Capitalism has developed a very sophisticated, but peculiarly one-sided, method for governing its most important institutions: large corporations. An immense amount of energy and attention is devoted to governance structures, oversight and control, and overlapping checks and balances within corporations. They are all aimed at ensuring that firms act reliably and ruthlessly to maximize the wealth of the company's shareholders. Recent corporate scandals (like the 2001 collapse of Enron Corporation, a huge but fraudulent US energy trading company) reinforced the determination of corporate governance experts to tighten these systems of account-ability. And within their very narrow mandate, these efforts have been successful: corporate behaviour is more directly and powerfully aligned toward the maximization of shareholder wealth than at any time in the history of capitalism. From the perspective of society, however, this vision of governance is painfully inadequate. Most people are not shareholders, in any significant or meaningful sense. Why wouldn't we want the most powerful institutions in the economy to respect and work toward broader goals, not just the further enrichment of shareholders? Moreover, the fact that economic and social conditions depend so much on the investment decisions of an unelected economic elite, is itself immensely anti-democratic. And private wealth exercises a highly disproportionate influence in politics.

Overall Grade: C–   In summary, I give modern capitalism a barely passing grade. Its achievements should not be ignored; its flexibility and staying power should be respected. But its failings are obvious, numerous, and monumental. Indeed, millions of human beings die prematurely every year because of capitalism's failure to devote readily available resources to meet life-and-death human needs. And the future of the planetary ecosystem is in genuine jeopardy because of the system's environmental irresponsibility.

Don't be Fooled

"This is what economics now does. It tells the young and susceptible (and also the old and vulnerable) that economic life has no content of power and politics because the firm is safely subordinate to the market and the state and for this reason it is safely at the command of the consumer and citizen. Such an economics is not neutral. It is the influential and invaluable ally of those whose exercise of power depends on an acquiescent public."

John Kenneth Galbraith, Canadian-American economist (1973).

Mapping systemic instability

This ho-hum report card indicates that capitalism is definitely under-performing in terms of meeting the concrete needs of humanity for prosperity, security, equality, sustainability, and democracy. But what about the system's performance from the perspective of its *own* ability to survive and grow? Quite apart from its failure to satisfy the needs and desires of the planet's inhabitants, is capitalism inherently and internally stable?

Let's go back to the composite economic map we developed in Part Four of this book. The core capitalist "circle" (investment, employment, production, profit, and reproduction) is at the centre, with the various complicating factors (finance, government, the global economy, and the environment) arrayed around it. Where (if anywhere) might the internal viability and stability of the whole system be fragile?

The "explosions" in Figure 25.1 highlight the main areas of potential vulnerability. Of the flows and relationships pictured, in my judgement five might present meaningful risks to the continued functioning of the overall system:

- **Financial fragility** Private finance always functions in an erratic, unpredictable, and potentially destructive manner. Financial assets are increasingly complex, interdependent, and unpredictable, and this certainly raises the possibility of financial collapse. Periodic crises (such as the Asian financial panic of 1997, or the more recent downturn in the US mortgage industry) confirm that the modern financial system is indeed unstable. However, worries about an all-out financial meltdown may not be justified. The "paper economy" rarely has a strong direct impact on real investment, production, and spending in the first place. And even when financial instability looms, policy-makers can react quickly and powerfully to try to stabilize markets and restore investor confidence. Central banks cut interest rates and inject emergency capital into financial markets; governments adjust their spending and tax policies. So the system is more robust than the meltdown scenarios assume. Nevertheless, the overdeveloped and hyperactive financial system is a constant source of instability and fragility.

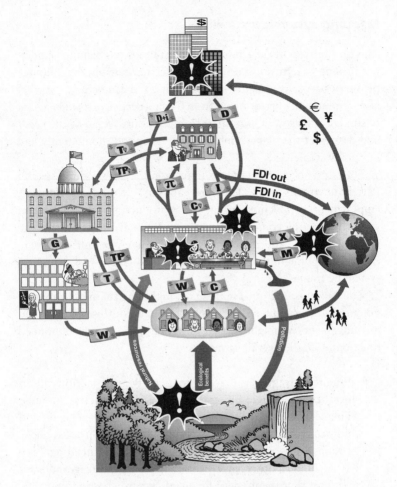

Figure 25.1   **Economic Road Map: Risks**

- **Global imbalance**   Globalization can help or hurt particular
  national or regional economies, depending on whether they
  are competitive enough to capture positive net exports and
  a positive inflow of real investment spending. Corporations
  do not particularly care about the performance of particular
  national economies, so long as their global profitability
  remains healthy. Global imbalances have become larger as
  a result of shifts in regional competitiveness, combined with
  the unparalleled ability of corporations to take advantage
  of those shifts. Most obvious in recent years has been the

unprecedented US trade deficit – and the offsetting and equally unprecedented Chinese trade surplus. How long foreign lenders (including China itself) will be willing to continue financing the US deficit, and how deeply into foreign debt the US economy can manageably sink, are both open questions. A sharp or painful adjustment of the US trade balance could cause major shock waves through the global economy. On the other hand, as the centre of global capitalism, the US retains a unique and powerful ability to tolerate international imbalances, and it's unlikely that foreign investors would ever abandon the US economy en masse.

- **Environmental limits**   There are several broad consequences of the economy's failure to sustainably manage the environment. First, the quality of life for many people is directly harmed by pollution, climate change, and the degradation of natural spaces. While deplorable, this in itself does not directly threaten the economic system. More important in economic terms will be the costs of adjustment posed by environmental challenges. In particular, global climate change will impose very large economic costs due to severe weather, rising sea levels, and other side-effects. Finally, the deterioration of the natural environment's capacity to supply needed resources and raw materials may also begin to constrain the economy. Energy shortages may be the most urgent concern in this regard. Oil prices have skyrocketed in recent years, reflecting the combination of continuing demand growth (including from China) and supply constraints. So far, the world economy has adapted to this dramatic change surprisingly smoothly, and businesses can respond to resource supply concerns with conservation measures and alternative energy sources. Whether environmental factors become truly constraining on capitalism probably depends more on how long the citizens of the world are willing to put up with deteriorating environmental quality than on any truly imminent environment-related economic crisis. In other words, the environmental constraint on capitalism may be more political in nature than economic.

- **Investment stagnation**   One curious feature of the worldwide boom in corporate profits that has occurred in the latter years of neoliberalism has been a marked failure of private firms to re-invest their abundant cashflow. Real business investment in most locations has responded sluggishly to the dramatic recovery in profits. The result has been a hoarding of corporate cash, a reduction in corporate debt, and an increase in speculative financial activity (as companies seek alternative outlets for their surplus funds). Profit-seeking investment is the key driving force of capitalism. If investment does not respond well to the historic recovery in profitability that neoliberalism has successfully engineered, it could be symptomatic of an erosion of the underlying dynamism that gives capitalism its bragging rights. Some of the problem may reflect a geographical reallocation of investment (toward super-profitable China, for example – where investment is incredibly robust). And even a more generalized weakness of investment still need not pose any inherent challenge to the continued economic survival of the system: so long as capitalists find *something* to spend their excess money on (such as their own luxury consumption), then the system can handle slower investment (and hence slower growth) without actually breaking down. However, if evidence continues to accumulate that the whole, painful neoliberal agenda has had no positive impact on real investment and economic performance, then political support for the system may be further weakened.

- **Worker compliance** Another core "achievement" of neoliberalism has been the re-creation of a more disciplined, compliant workforce. The reorientation of monetary policy (focusing on inflation control, rather than full employment), the clawback of social benefits (especially those aimed at working-age adults), and pro-employer shifts in labour standards and industrial relations, were all aimed at restoring the conditions for successful labour extraction. Now employers get a lot more bang (in the form of work effort) for their labour cost buck. This strategy has transformed labour relations and reduced unit labour costs – but is it sustainable? This depends on how long workers remain willing to work, harder than ever, for a shrinking slice of the economic pie. Again, the constraint is more political than economic.

Don't hold your breath

There is no doubt that each of these five issues raises significant question marks regarding the long-term viability of global capitalism as we know it. The internal cohesion of the whole system could be shaken by financial panic, sudden global readjustment, environmental catastrophe, investment stagnation, or a breakdown in labour relations.

But I would hesitate to conclude that any of these factors, at this point in history, pose any fundamental challenge to the whole system's continuing viability. Each one may be associated with widespread dislocation and misery. But none yet seems to imply a fundamental inability of capitalism to survive and re-create itself: that is, the ability of private businesses to invest, to produce, and to make profit.

In other words, even for these five most vulnerable links in the economic chain of capitalism, I do not see convincing evidence of an inherent, systemic vulnerability. The system is unlikely to break down of its own accord. Those of us hoping for something better from the economy cannot wait around for capitalism to self-destruct. The only factor that poses a genuine challenge to the current order is the willingness of human beings to reject the injustice and irrationality of this economy, and stand up to demand something better. Capitalism will not fall – rather, it must be pushed. Exactly what we might demand, in terms of both improving capitalism and changing it more fundamentally, is the subject of our final chapters.

26

Improving Capitalism

Room to improve

There are many obvious ways in which the economic and social performance of capitalism can and must be improved. Widespread poverty; environmental degradation; the underutilization of the talents and energies of billions of people; the misuse of so many resources. The current world economy fails the true test of efficiency (namely, does it do as much as possible to improve the living standard of humanity?) in so many glaring ways, it's hard to know where to start fixing it up.

It is evident to me that many important improvements can be made to capitalism while staying within the fundamental constraints and principles (private investment, employment, profit) that drive the whole system. While capitalism's profit motive may be the root cause of many of its failures, there is no doubt that the system can be reformed – to some degree, anyway – without changing its inherent character. There may be limits to our ability to reform capitalism (that we will start to consider in the next chapter). But those limits are not binding, in most countries and on most issues, today.

In other words, there is plenty of room to improve. Just compare the differing characteristics of existing capitalist economies. Table 26.1 summarizes key economic and social indicators for the leading country from each of the four broad "varieties" of capitalism that we defined back in Chapter 3: Anglo-Saxon (US), Continental (France), Asian (Japan), and Nordic (Sweden). All these countries are capitalist. All depend on the continuing willingness of private businesses to invest in economic activity in search of profit. But clearly, some economies do much better than others in moderating the worst effects of capitalism, and achieving more desirable human and social outcomes. The US demonstrates the highest level of GDP per capita – although this is mostly due to longer hours of work, not higher productivity (productivity per hour in the US, France, and Sweden is about the same). But the US reports much higher levels of poverty, inequality, pollution, and incarceration than the others.

Table 26.1   **Take Your Pick: Performance of Selected Capitalist Countries**

Indicator	US	France	Japan	Sweden
GDP per capita (US$, 2006)	$41,890	$30,386	$31,267	$32,525
Productivity per hour of work (US$, 2006)	$50.4	$49.9	$35.6	$44.7
Productivity growth (avg. % per year, 1996–2005)	2.1%	1.0%	1.4%	2.2%
Standardized unemployment rate (2006)	4.6%	9.2%	4.1%	7.0%
Poverty rate (% of population under half of median income, 2000–04)	17.0%	7.3%	11.8%	6.5%
Inequality (ratio of incomes of top 10% to bottom 10%)	15.9	9.1	4.5	6.2
Carbon dioxide emissions per capita (tons, 2004)	20.6	6.0	9.9	5.9
Government program spending as share of GDP (2005)	34.6%	51.4%	35.7%	56.7%
Health system	Mostly private	Mostly public	Private and public	Mostly public
Life expectancy at birth (years, 2005)	77.9	80.2	82.3	80.5
Infant mortality per 1,000 births (2005)	6	4	3	3
Incarceration rate per 1,000 people (2005)	750	85	61	79
Development aid (% gross national income, 2005)	0.22%	0.47%	0.28%	0.94%
Rank, UN Human Development Index	12	10	8	6

Sources: United Nations Development Program; Organization for Economic Cooperation and Development; International Centre for Prison Studies.

Fighting to make our respective countries more like the Nordic variant of capitalism and less like the Anglo-Saxon version (which demonstrates the worst social and environmental performance of any of these broad varieties) is a deserving and fitting challenge that rightfully deserves our first attention. Whether those improvements to capitalism end up being sufficient, in the long run, to justify its continued existence is another question (one we should think about as we go along). But in the interim, there is much to be done to alleviate suffering and injustice – right here, right now.

The reformer's shopping list

By now, every reader of this book should be able to develop their own "shopping list" of key improvements that would make the economy more humane, stable, and environmentally sustainable:

1. Improving wages, benefits, and working conditions – especially for the lowest-paid workers. Unions are crucial here.
2. Expanding overall economic activity to take up the slack currently represented by large numbers of unemployed and underemployed workers.
3. Taking targeted measures to improve the sectoral make-up of the economy, and enhancing the presence of higher-technology, higher-productivity industries. In developing countries, this is wrapped up with the broader challenge of successfully fostering all-round economic development.
4. Regulating and stabilizing financial flows, and reducing the extent to which the economy is vulnerable to financial crises.
5. Providing transfer payments to moderate inequality between rich and poor, and between gender and racial groups; and providing better economic security for people at various stages of their lives (including childhood, retirement, and periods of unemployment, ill health, or disability).
6. Providing high-quality, accessible public services to supply health care, education, and other key human services, supplementing the standard of living that can be purchased through private consumption.
7. Pushing businesses to reduce the environmental costs of their operations, and investing in environmental protection and conservation.
8. Reforming governance of the global economy, to reduce large trade imbalances, stabilize financial flows, reinforce the ability of national governments to regulate their economies in the public interest, and enhance development opportunities for poor countries.

These are eight very big changes that would, if successfully attained, dramatically enhance the human and environmental performance of capitalism.

Determined, worldwide campaigns by trade unions and social justice movements are pressing hard for change on each one of these items. And to varying degrees, reformist SOCIAL-DEMOCRATIC political parties have used this shopping list (or portions of it) as a political platform. (Unfortunately, simply electing these parties never guarantees that promised changes will occur, thanks to the continuing power of business to influence government actions; unions and movements need to force governments, even social-democratic ones, to meet their demands for progressive change.)

As we discussed in Chapter 19, governments possess a whole toolbox of policies (laws and regulations; spending and taxing power; control over interest rates and financial policies; and, when needed, the ability to step right in and do the job directly through government production). The attainment of any one of the major goals listed above would require the application of several policy measures. But as we also discussed in Chapter 19, the *political* challenge of forcing governments to use these tools in the interests of working and poor people (rather than listening only to investors and businesses) is more daunting than the more technical *policy* challenge of how to actually get the job done.

Footing the bill

The world's wealthy have made tremendous economic and political gains in the quarter-century since neoliberalism took hold. They have notably increased their share of the economic pie. They have changed the rules of the economic game – enhancing their own freedom and security, and turning back most challenges from governments, unions, and communities. They have consolidated their influence over politics and culture. Perhaps most importantly, they have succeeded in lowering mass expectations, convincing most working and poor people that their insecurity, inequality, and exploitation are inevitable facts of life (rather than injustices to be opposed and redressed).

On one hand, this constitutes a rather pessimistic scenario: efforts to reform capitalism confront the power of a well-entrenched, successful elite. But there's another way of viewing this situation. As a result of their own success, businesses have more ability to pay for the reforms we are demanding of them, than at any time in recent decades. Their pockets, in other words, are very deep.

Every trade unionist knows that an employer's ability to pay is a critical determinant of success in collective bargaining. Any company rolling in profits is far more likely grudgingly to offer a wage increase than one racking up major losses. The same logic applies at the social level, too. It is easier to demand and win broader economic and social gains when the overall system is profitable, growing, and relatively stable (although, as we have seen, capitalism is never truly stable).

Profit rates have rebounded in most developed countries to post-war highs. ▤ * As a share of GDP, business profits are at or near record levels in the US, Canada, Australia, and many other developed economies. Employers clearly have the capacity to improve wages, benefits, time off, and working conditions, without unduly harming their profitability or dominance. They can equally afford to invest in environmental protection – indeed, under certain conditions, those investments could reinforce growth and productivity.

And it's not just businesses which have the resources to meet demands for progressive reforms. In most countries, governments, too, enjoy vastly improved fiscal situations. Across the OECD, average government deficits in 2006 equalled just 2 percent of GDP – less than half as large as in the early 1990s, and low enough to reduce the debt burden and government interest costs (measured as a share of GDP). ▤ Many countries (including Canada, Australia, and the Nordic region) enjoy significant government surpluses. Invoking simple-minded fear of deficits or taxes to turn back demands for social programs and public investment is less convincing, and hence less politically effective, than in past years when deficits were large. The one developed capitalist country facing a more serious fiscal constraint is the US – the deliberate result of lopsided reductions in business and investment taxes by a right-wing government. There, more immediately than in other countries, demands for enhanced public services will need to be accompanied by proposals to raise tax revenues.

In sum, businesses and governments constitute the two major seats of power to which our shopping list of economic and social reforms must be presented. And both enjoy a stronger financial situation than they have experienced for decades. This is a silver lining in what is otherwise a dark neoliberal cloud: precisely because it has taken so much from working and poor people, neoliberalism is now in a very

* See the Economics for Everyone website for statistics, www.economicsforeveryone.com.

healthy position to give something back. This can only whet the appetite of workers and citizens for concrete, incremental gains.

One vision: a high-investment, sustainable economy

The economy needs to be reformed. The government has the tools to do it. And both government and business at present have ample resources to pay for key improvements. So far, it looks like a "no-brainer." All we need to do is motivate and organize enough people to demand the change we need, and then go out and win it.

There is a drawback, however, to pursuing a shopping list of needed reforms, one item at a time, backed by compelling moral claims and economic evidence on each issue. As we have learned, capitalism is based on a certain logic: profit-seeking private investment sets economic resources into motion, creates jobs, and generates incomes. If our goal is to improve human and environmental conditions within the framework of capitalism, then we need to keep one eye on the vitality of that underlying economic engine: investment. And even if our goal is to ultimately move beyond capitalism, understanding how business investment works will help us to better identify the limits to reform, and the specific ways in which the logic of a profit-driven economic system needs to be changed.

It may therefore be more convincing to assemble our "shopping list" into a more holistic package – one which directly addresses the challenge of the underlying dynamism of investment that is so essential to overall economic activity. In addition to demanding policies which enhance social and environmental well-being (the traditional staples of the reformist vision), we must also therefore propose measures to strengthen and stimulate investment spending (including public and non-profit investment). This will help to offset any negative effects of our reforms (such as our labour market reforms, which would clearly increase unit labour costs for employers and hence undermine profits and potentially investment) on traditional, profit-led channels of investment. And measures to boost investment will generate additional incomes (including tax revenues) that will help to fund our progressive social and environmental reforms. Pairing demands for progressive labour, social, and environmental measures with a strategy to tackle the core challenge of the capitalist economy – namely, investment – produces a more well-rounded and convincing strategy for reform.

Ironically, as we saw in earlier chapters, neoliberalism itself has not done well at stimulating investment spending, despite the painful, business-friendly measures implemented since the early 1980s. In reality, the neoliberal strategy was more concerned with redistributing the pie (in favour of business) than growing it. So there is a tremendous opportunity now to challenge the neoliberal vision of gritty, hard-nosed, highly unequal capitalism with a complete but internally consistent alternative – one that aims both to grow the pie (by investing more than neoliberalism) and to distribute it more fairly. The economic credibility of the current regime can thus be challenged on its own turf, with an agenda that reaches into the core of capitalism – the investment process – rather than limiting itself to smoothing some of the system's rougher edges. This alternative vision still depends on private investment, and takes seriously the need to keep that investment coming. It combines progressive redistributive reforms with stimulative, pro-investment policies to boost investment spending despite other changes in the package which capitalists will undoubtedly find unappealing.

Table 26.2 summarizes the major elements of this alternative vision, which I call a *high-investment, sustainable economy*. The term "high investment" highlights the importance of maintaining strong investment levels to overall economic performance. (This term was also used by Ken Livingstone, the left-wing Mayor of London, to describe some of his government's proposals to revitalize that city with large injections of private and public investment.) Our goal will be to achieve higher investment rates (with total non-residential capital spending reaching 20 percent or more of GDP) than are commonly attained under neoliberalism – but with more oversight and care in directing that investment to the most appropriate, beneficial uses. Meanwhile, the term "sustainable" highlights the necessity of managing and directing strong investment in ways which respect environmental constraints, and focus on enhancing the quality of output more than the quantity.

Private business investment spending remains at the core of the economic strategy. Aggressive measures are taken to support real business capital spending, including highly favourable tax treatment of profits which are reinvested in new capital (rather than paid out to shareholders). Other supports for business investment could include targeted fiscal policies (like an investment tax credit, tied to new capital spending), and proactive, sector-specific industrial and trade

Table 26.2 A High-Investment Sustainable Economy

Investment Measures:

Business	• Spur private business spending on real capital equipment with tax measures, subsidies, and other policies. • Use targeted measures to support investment spending in high-value industries.
Innovation	• Encourage more business R&D spending. • Use public institutions (universities, research centres) to supplement and partner with private R&D spending. • Develop business–government programs for prototypes and commercialization of new technology.
Public	• Substantially increase public investment in infrastructure and public service facilities.
Human	• Expand public spending on education at all levels (including pre-school). • Require employers to meet targeted spending levels for on-the-job training. • Expand measures to improve lifelong learning and retraining opportunities for workers of all ages.
Environmental	• Spur private investment in environmentally advanced capital equipment. • Establish very high environmental standards for new construction (private and public). • Expand public investment in environmental protection and amelioration.
Overall Goal	• Increase non-residential capital investment spending to at least 20% of GDP, supplemented by improved education and training.

Other Supportive Measures:

Monetary Policy	• Guide overall economy to very low unemployment, to maintain pressure on employers to upgrade work and incomes.
Labour and Social Policy	• Expand unionization and collective bargaining. • Improve labour standards and protections (minimum wages, health and safety laws, limits on working time, protections for precarious workers). • Work to improve pay, conditions, and productivity in low-income non-tradeable sectors (such as private services). • Expand active labour supports to assist job-seekers with training, mobility, and job retention. • Expand social and family programs to maximize labour force participation by women (child care, elder care, time off for family reasons). • Centrally or sectorally negotiate wages to seek stable growth of real wages in line with productivity.
Fiscal Policy	• Run moderate annual deficits (including paying for public capital projects). • Keep public debt within 50–75 percent of GDP.
Tax Policy	• Reform business taxes to reward real investment spending, and discourage dividend payouts. • Eliminate favourable tax treatment for financial investments. • Rely on progressive personal income taxes, and other broad taxes, to fund public programs.
Trade Policy	• Manage international trade flows to ensure a healthy share of domestic production in high-value sectors. • Oversee incoming foreign direct investment to maximize domestic technology and job spin-offs.
Financial Markets	• Regulate finance to prevent irresponsible practices, stabilize credit creation. • Eliminate tax measures and transfer programs which favour or subsidize the financial industry. • Establish public or non-profit financial institutions with capacity to expand or curtail lending power as needed.

policies to boost key sectors. But public investment plays an increasing role in setting economic resources in motion, too. An emphasis on innovation and new technology, in both private and public investment, is important; public institutions can spur pure and applied research and commercialization (sometimes in partnership with business). More spending on education, skills, and training is also needed to allow the economy to make the most of its growing stock of physical capital and its evolving technology. Throughout this ambitious pro-investment program, special emphasis is placed on environmental investments: including energy-saving capital equipment, super-efficient construction and building improvements, and public investment in environmental clean-up and conservation.

A network of supporting policies then aims to make the most of those strong injections of investment in the interests of better distributional, environmental, and trade outcomes. These include measures to improve conditions in labour markets (through collective bargaining and labour standards), manage global flows of both products and investment, and limit the risks resulting from financial instability.

This proposed high-investment, sustainable economy includes several elements reminiscent of the Nordic version of capitalism – such as intensive public spending on education, health, and labour force mobility; generous redistributive programs, financed through personal taxes; generally low business taxes; and an overarching focus on R&D and innovation. Aspects of the model also reflect the successful experience of Asian industrialization – including important roles for proactive industrial policies supporting targeted industries, and active efforts to manage foreign trade and investment flows.

This proposal, then, is not utopian or untried: all its major elements are readily visible in the real-world experience of countries which have been relatively successful at meeting social and environmental needs – while still respecting the imperative of private businesses to make a profit on their investments. For readers in the Anglo-Saxon world, this approach should be especially useful as a well-rounded, internally consistent alternative to the more extreme, unequal incarnation of capitalism which is experienced in the US, Canada, the UK, and Australia.

27

Replacing Capitalism?

Socialism: what, and why?

The key decisions in capitalism are made by private investors who try to maximize the profitability of their businesses. In this regard, the whole system is driven by private greed. Good things can happen in the course of that pursuit – sometimes by design, sometimes by accident, sometimes through political pressure. But the core motive force driving the system is not a desire to improve the human condition. It is a desire to fatten someone's pocketbook.

Yet just a cursory look at the often-sorry state of our planet indicates vast unmet needs crying out for attention: the desperate plight of billions of people in the global South, the needless deprivation of hundreds of millions more in the North, and the ongoing degradation of the environment everywhere. Surely it is possible to devote economic resources directly to tackling those crises – rather than crossing our fingers that all will be solved through the trickle-down effects of business-led growth. Imagine if we took the economic resources at our disposal (our technology, our capital equipment, our skills, our work ethic) and devoted them directly to eliminating poverty, to expanding human services (like health care and education), to protecting the environment – instead of video games, glossy advertising, and laser-guided weaponry.

This hope has led economists, and others, to imagine alternative, more humane economic systems, right from the early, dirtiest days of capitalism. The main alternative to capitalism in modern times is SOCIALISM. Under socialism, economic decisions are supposed to be guided directly by the public interest, rather than the interests of private owners.

There have been many different theories about why socialism might be necessary, and just as many different ideas about how it would work. The earliest socialists were idealistic European reformers who wanted to build cooperative communities to improve humans' physical and moral condition. Karl Marx predicted that socialism would inevitably arise due to endless class conflict between workers and capitalists, and perhaps also because of technological changes. John Maynard Keynes argued that socialism would eventually be required in order to ensure that the economy generated enough investment to keep everyone employed. His contemporary, Michal Kalecki, argued that only under socialism could full employment be combined with efficient work effort and discipline.

Common to all of these visions for explicitly managing the economy in the interest of human needs is some combination of the following two features:

- **Widespread public or non-profit ownership of enterprises** Companies under socialism might be owned directly by the state. Or they might be owned through other non-profit or collective structures – like worker or consumer cooperatives, community-owned enterprises, or non-profit agencies. In every case, the enterprises must be publicly accountable, and they must be managed to meet specified public goals (rather than just maximizing their own profit). Simply taking over private companies in the name of the public interest is not enough, in this regard. Publicly-owned enterprises must learn to effectively fulfil the same central economic roles currently performed by private firms: initiating investment, setting economic resources into motion, organizing production, and overseeing the efficiency and discipline of work. But now the *motive* for that activity has changed: to maximize public well-being, rather than private profit.

- **A larger role for economic planning** In most visions of socialism, some key economic decisions are made centrally by governments, rather than being dispersed to individual enterprises. This allows the economy to be directed toward the fulfilment of human or social goals at the macroeconomic level (not just at the level of individual firms). Exercising some collective, deliberate control over key aggregate variables (like investment, credit, key industrial developments, income distribution, inflation, and foreign trade and investment) would help to ensure that the economy meets specified social goals and targets. In light of capitalism's ongoing boom-and-bust instability, it might also help to guide the economy toward more efficient aggregate performance – reducing unemployment and ensuring that available resources are fully utilized.

Within each of these categories, differing "degrees" of socialism can be imagined. For example, public ownership could be expanded to take in virtually all companies, or it might be limited to just the largest, most important enterprises in key industries. Similarly, central planners could determine detailed production plans and price schedules right down to the level of individual industries or companies. Or planning might be limited to broad economic aggregates (setting targets for total investment, consumer spending, wage increases, foreign trade, and other key variables), with detailed decisions left to individual firms. In some versions of socialism, enterprises are publicly owned, but markets (not planning) continue to set the economy's overall direction. This system is called MARKET SOCIALISM; it was tried in a few countries, including the former Yugoslavia.

Socialism in practice: wha' 'appened?

The idea of socialism dates back two centuries. And many attempts have been made to implement that vision. Unfortunately, practical experience with socialism so far has not been very successful.

Two broad approaches have been tried in practice. First, a few countries operating within the tradition of SOCIAL DEMOCRACY explicitly aimed to transform capitalism – not just reform it. Examples of social-democratic movements with a longer-run, transformative vision include the early postwar Labour governments in Britain (which nationalized large segments of British industry), the French socialist government of the early 1980s (which nationalized most banks and many other large companies), Sweden (where a clever scheme, called the "Meidner Plan," was devised to gradually take over private business in the 1970s), and Australia (where the competitive labour market was replaced, for a while, with a centrally planned system of wage determination). In all of these cases, intense opposition from business interests, combined with difficulties encountered in the performance of publicly-owned enterprises, led these governments to abandon their more ambitious, socialist visions. Today there are no major social-democratic parties in the developed countries still committed to transforming capitalism; their only goal now is trying to *improve* capitalism (which is, needless to say, an important and legitimate task).

The second broad experiment with socialism was undertaken by various communist-led governments, which implemented widespread state and collective ownership and CENTRAL PLANNING. There was a surprising diversity of experience within this category – ranging from all-encompassing central planning (carried out under very repressive political structures) to more flexible, market-oriented systems. In every one of these countries, socialism came about in a context of war and violent upheaval, and this held back subsequent economic and democratic development. Nevertheless, central planning showed some initial promise and vitality, especially for poor countries trying to industrialize under difficult conditions. As late as the 1960s, when the USSR beat the US to put the first astronaut in space, central planning could credibly claim to pose a genuine challenge to the success of capitalism. Subsequently, however, the planned communist economies gradually lost steam.

The collapse of the Soviet Union in 1991, and the explicit adoption of pro-capitalist policies in China at about the same time, signalled the end for this version of socialism. Its failure resulted from several weaknesses, including the anti-democratic nature of the communist political system, and difficulties in designing management and incentive structures to effectively guide the actions of state-owned enterprises. On the other hand, human conditions in several former communist countries (including Russia) have visibly deteriorated since the restoration of capitalism (with declining life expectancy, growing poverty, and other negative indicators), disproving any claim that capitalism is inherently "superior."

Today there are only a handful of countries left in the world that can be called socialist – and even in those countries (like Cuba and Vietnam) the economic space occupied by private ownership and for-profit production is growing. Cuba's admirable social achievements (its education, health, and cultural indicators outrank most developing countries, and even many developed countries) demonstrate the potential of socialism to leverage the maximum possible well-being from a given amount of material production. On the other hand, Cuba continues to grapple with the failure of state-run firms to develop adequate dynamism and productivity (the 45-year US economic blockade of the island obviously hasn't helped) and concerns over democratic rights. The governments of Venezuela and Bolivia claim to be building new forms of socialism, based on the nationalization of key industries (especially natural resources and utilities) and the intense involvement of poor people in economic decision-making.

These will be interesting experiments to watch and support – all the more so because they are occurring within a mostly peaceful, democratic political context. The waning of global US influence will hopefully give these and other countries more space to pursue their efforts, free from the political and military interference which undermined past efforts to build socialism. Some equally interesting, smaller-scale experiments in non-profit economic management and development have occurred at the regional level – for example, in the Basque region of Spain or the Indian state of Kerala, where extensive networks of collectively owned enterprises (including non-profit financial institutions) have demonstrated impressive productivity, innovation, and effectiveness.

Corporations: socialists in disguise?

Contrary to the common stereotype, capitalism is not actually an *individualistic* system. A capitalist economy is not composed of economic "Lone Rangers": profit-hungry individuals making the most of their particular talents and energies, inventing, producing, and selling exciting new products. By far the most important players in the economy are large, bureaucratic institutions (namely, global corporations) – not individual entrepreneurs. Corporate actions and decision-making dominate economic affairs. Moreover, their operations are carefully *planned*. Indeed, if communist central planners could have organized the economy with as much detail, precision, and flexibility as a modern-day Toyota or Wal-Mart, communism would probably still exist! Corporations are also the major source of modern innovation. Most new ideas (for both products and processes) come from corporate-funded laboratories and research programs – where scientists and engineers work for salary (not for profit).

Curiously, therefore, corporations are actually *social* institutions. They are established to allow large numbers of people to work together, mostly cooperatively, in the pursuit of a clearly-defined goal. The problem with corporate behaviour is rooted in the nature of that goal – to maximize shareholder wealth – rather than with the institution itself.

Executives, shareholders, accountants, and economists have devoted incredible attention in recent years to the challenge of corporate governance. How do shareholders ensure that these large bureaucracies act reliably and effectively on behalf of the people who own them? And corporate governance structures continue to evolve, enhancing what is already a fairly impressive record (from the perspective of shareholders, anyway). Corporations are a highly successful, flexible, and focused institutional invention, allowing their owners to pursue the goal of private profit with unparalleled success. Unfortunately, the successful pursuit of that private goal does not translate reliably into social progress – which is why we need to think about other ways of organizing economic activity.

Table 27.1 **Ten Examples of Successful Public and Non-Profit Enterprise**

Who says that only the private sector can manage a business efficiently? Here are ten examples of public or non-profit companies which are efficient, well-managed, and guided by social and environmental goals (not just their own profit).

Company	Country	Details
Rabobank	Netherlands	Cooperative bank with 55,000 staff and €600 billion in assets; has focused recent lending on clean energy technologies.
Metsähallitus	Finland	State-owned company; engages in commercial forestry and tourism services, as well as managing public forests; has explicit conservation mandate.
Toronto Community Housing Corp.	Canada	City-owned corporation which leverages private financial resources to provide low-cost housing to 160,000 people.
Statoil	Norway	State-owned oil company; profits flow to public social investment fund; pioneered greenhouse gas reduction technologies.
Temasek Holdings	Singapore	Profitable state agency with holdings in over 50 companies in Singapore (and others abroad); has goal to qualitatively develop Singapore's economy.
Mountain Equipment Co-op	Canada	Consumer-owned co-op; largest supplier of outdoor sports equipment; commitment to environmental and labour standards.
Mondragón Cooperative Corp.	Spain	Worker-owned co-op that operates over 150 manufacturing, finance, and retail enterprises, employing over 80,000 people.
Grameen Bank	Bangladesh	Cooperative bank owned by its borrowers; provides small, low-interest loans, largely to women.
"Recovered companies"	Argentina	About 200 factories, with total employment of 10,000, seized by workers following the 2001 economic crisis, now operating on a non-profit basis.
Legacoop	Italy	Network of (mostly consumer) cooperatives across Italy, with 5 million members and 250,000 employees; also operates a cooperative financial network.

In this regard, it is my belief that socialists need to do some important research and experimentation of their own in the field of institutional governance. Publicly-owned enterprises have a bad reputation (deserved in some cases, not deserved in others) for operating in inefficient, uncreative, and even corrupt ways. Imagining ways to define clear goals, create effective incentives, impose checks and balances, and enforce accountability from public managers, constitutes in my view the central problem holding back the successful expansion of public and non-profit enterprise. Studying the experience of successful and efficient public enterprises (like those listed in Table 27.1), learning from the experience of corporate governance, and experimenting with new forms of social and non-profit entrepreneurship, is an important priority for those who still believe that the economy can indeed be run for the collective good.

These experiments will probably have to start small – in community agencies, local and regional economic development initiatives, innovative public services, and other specialized niches. We need to gradually build a culture of public and social entrepreneurship, in which the crucial role of the private investor (setting economic resources into motion, and organizing production) is supplemented and eventually replaced by the actions of publicly-motivated agencies and leaders. As these experiments succeed in resuscitating the notion that public and non-profit organizations can indeed operate in innovative, efficient, and accountable ways, then the political space for further experimentation will grow.

Corporations are large bureaucracies which ruthlessly and efficiently pursue a narrow private goal: maximum shareholder

---

All for One, or One for All?

"The first principle of economics is that every agent is actuated only by self-interest."

F.Y. Edgeworth, Irish economist, and a founder of neoclassical economics (1881).

"In no other species but *Homo sapiens* do thousands of unrelated individuals work together to accomplish a common project."

Samuel Bowles, Richard Edwards, and Frank Roosevelt, radical American economists (2005).

wealth. Can we also organize large bureaucracies which pursue (with equal determination and efficiency) some different, but clearly specified, *public* goal? Once we are able to answer that question in the affirmative, then I believe that socialists will have overcome one of the crucial problems which bedevilled both the social-democratic and communist versions of socialism.

Capitalism and human nature

There's one common objection to socialism that can more easily be disposed of, compared to these deeper challenges of governance and accountability – and that is the knee-jerk claim that since human beings are inherently "selfish," any system rooted in "sharing" is doomed to failure. Indeed, this assumption that people are motivated solely by greed is a starting assumption of neoclassical economics. Unfortunately for neoclassical economic theory, however, it is not remotely true.

There are many plausible cases in which competition and self-interest can leave all sides worse off (see box overleaf). In fact, anthropologists have discovered that the evolution of cooperative behaviour was essential to the successful emergence of early human society. And using new experimental techniques, modern economists have replicated that finding by showing that cooperative economic strategies (in which social behaviour is reciprocated, but selfish behaviour is punished) overwhelm purely competitive strategies in evolutionary competition.

Simply looking around society reveals that some of the most important and powerful human actions are motivated by something very different than greed. The firefighter entering a burning building is not doing it "for the money." Neither are the dirt-poor grandmothers in Africa who have taken on raising a whole extra generation: orphans who lost their parents to AIDS. The salaried scientists spending 60-hour weeks seeking a cure for cancer are not motivated by stock options; they are driven by a desire to improve the human condition. Even the quiet, hidden heroism of people devoting uncounted hours to caring for children and elders, after performing a full day's work in the paid labour market, is motivated by love, not money.

To be sure, economic incentives are important (even under socialism). But if everyone you encountered in your daily economic routine was truly and solely out to maximize their immediate self-

Code of Silence

Table 27.2   The Prisoners' Dilemma

Prisoner A

Prisoner B	Betrays	Doesn't Betray
Betrays	A: 5 years B: 5 years	A: 10 years B: 0 years
Doesn't Betray	A: 0 years B: 10 years	A: 1 year B: 1 year

A famous logic puzzle called the "Prisoners' Dilemma" demonstrates that selfishness can actually be *irrational*. Imagine that two criminals (named Albert and Bernard, or A and B for short) are captured by the police, and interrogated separately. The police don't have enough evidence to convict the pair for the full crime. So they offer a deal to each one: if they betray their accomplice, they'll receive a lighter sentence.

There are four possible scenarios: A betrays B, B betrays A, they both betray each other, or they both keep their mouths shut. If A betrays B but B stays silent, then B gets a full ten-year prison sentence, and A gets off free. The reverse occurs if B betrays A, and A remains silent. If the criminals betray each other, they each get five years. But if both remain silent, the police have no evidence, and each receives only one year in prison on a lesser charge. These combinations are illustrated in Table 27.2.

Now the irrationality of selfishness becomes clear. A is better off to betray B (that is, to act selfishly), whether or not B betrays A. Likewise, B is better off to betray A, whether or not A does the same to B. There is thus an apparent incentive for each prisoner to betray the other. Yet if both prisoners, following this selfish logic, do betray each other, they each get five years in prison. If they had both remained silent (an act which requires solidarity, not selfishness), they get only one year in prison. This is why hardened criminals learn quickly to keep their mouths shut during interrogation. So long as they *all* follow this rule, they *all* receive lighter sentences.

This imaginary example has many real-world (and non-criminal!) applications, explaining everything from washing your hands after using the toilet, to paying your monthly union dues. In the real world, individuals follow cooperative rules, rather than acting blindly in their immediate self-interest. Why? Because humans have learned over centuries that everyone is better off under certain forms of cooperation.

interest (at your expense), life would probably resemble occupied Iraq more than civilized society. Every person would be perpetually "on guard" against risk, theft, and danger; and the simplest economic transaction would be immensely complicated by a mutual fear that the other party was planning to exploit, steal, or assault. In reality, any practical, efficient economic system requires a level of mutual trust, safety, honesty, and morality that cannot be explained by the neoclassical vision of overarching selfishness.

At any rate, the economic case for socialism is not based on a commitment to "sharing" or "selflessness" in the first place. The idea of socialism is not that rich people should share with poor people. Rather, the goal of socialism is to consciously manage economic activity with an eye to maximizing collective economic well-being, rather than individual profit. Socialism would thus allow people to work together, to better achieve production and employment opportunities that leave virtually all of them (with the exception of the capitalists!) better off. That's a collective vision of self-interest – not a call for charity.

Keeping our options open

At this point in history, socialists have no obvious road map to guide their quest for a fundamentally more just and democratic economy. On one hand, the continuing, scandalous failure of capitalism to meet basic human needs for so many (despite the fantastic potential of modern technology) inspires the ongoing search for a better alternative. On the other hand, there is an absence of compelling real-world evidence that any other system, given our current knowledge, would reliably do better.

At any rate, socialism cannot emerge out of abstract, idealistic dreaming, imposed on society by someone who has finally discovered the "true" plan. Rather, socialism will have to arise in response to concrete human problems, and our grass-roots efforts to solve those problems. As long as those problems are there, and as long as capitalism remains unable or unwilling to address them, then socialism will exist as a potential solution. And as long as exploitation and poverty exist, then people will fight for a better economic deal.

So whether you are motivated by a bread-and-butter commitment to incrementally reforming capitalism, or by a more fiery-eyed determination to do away with it altogether, the course of action is more-or-less the same: go out and fight for that better deal. If capitalism can't or won't give it to you, consider the alternatives.

Therefore, struggles to improve capitalism in concrete, important ways must carry on. Capitalism, and capitalist governments, can well afford to undertake important reforms: redistributing income, enhancing social security, protecting the environment, promoting genuine development in the South, and addressing the other challenges that face humanity. Those reforms would make a huge difference to the lives of billions of people, and the future of the planet. And as we fight for those reforms, we can simultaneously push the envelope of the profit-led system with new forms of non-profit ownership, public entrepreneurship, and economic accountability. In short, we can keep our options open.

Conclusion

A Dozen Big Things to Remember About Economics

Congratulations! You've learned how capitalism works – from a critical, grass-roots perspective. Even though we've promised to keep things simple, the system we describe is not. And the economic map we've been building, one step at a time, has now become rather impressive. It portrays an economy that is complex, diverse, flexible, and (in some ways) fragile.

You'll never remember everything in this book, as you carry on with your work, your life, and (hopefully) your contributions to economic and social justice.

But there are a few crucial lessons that I hope you will keep in mind. These key themes will help you to analyze specific economic issues and controversies as they come up. They are key principles that help sort out what's important in the real economy, from what's not – and to distinguish reality from ideology.

So here's my personal list of the dozen top things to remember about economics:

1. **The economy depends on social relationships, not just technical relationships, and (like society) it evolves and changes over time.** There is no "natural" order to the economy. There are no inherent, unchanging laws governing its behaviour. What we call the "economy" is simply the way human beings work together, to produce goods and services, and then decide what to do with what we produce. And there's nothing permanent about it. Everything about the economy – technology, geography, social relationships – changes over time.

2. **Economics is an inherently subjective, value-laden, political discipline.** The economy is not natural, unchanging, or objective. And the study of the economy – what we call economics – is just as subjective and impermanent. The economy embodies conflicting interests between different groups, and economics closely reflects

335

those conflicting interests. No school of economics can claim to be neutral or objective. Different approaches to economics rise and fall, depending on the course of economic (and political) debates and conflicts. Every approach to economics combines an analysis of how the economy works, with a set of values and assumptions regarding how it *should* work (and in *whose* interests). Beware of economists bearing free advice – especially if the economist claims to be "objective."

3. **Productive human activity is the only force that adds value to the resources we harvest from nature.** "Work," broadly defined, includes all forms of productive human effort – including paid employment, unpaid work within households, and the managerial work of business executives. Without work, nothing happens in the economy. There are a few goods which humans can consume directly from nature (like fresh air, peace and quiet, or wild berries plucked from a bush). Everything else requires the application of human effort to transform the resources and raw materials we get from nature into goods and services we can use.

4. **Using tools makes work more productive.** Humans discovered very early on that it is much better to use tools than our bare hands. The invention, production, and accumulation of "tools" (defined broadly to include machinery, structures, infrastructure, and other kinds of physical capital) has been the central feature of economic development through human history. Developing and accumulating more advanced tools, and training people to use them effectively, must occur at the same time. However, tools themselves are *not* productive: it is the *know-how* embodied in those tools (that is, knowing to make tools first, and then use them to produce the goods and services we actually want) that is productive. Merely owning a tool is not, in itself, a productive act.

5. **In capitalism, most work consists of employment.** Employment is work that is performed for someone else, in return for the payment of wages and salaries. About 85 percent of households in developed capitalist economies rely on employment as their dominant source of income. Managing the employment relationship is a central aspect of capitalism. Employers face

a complicated challenge to try to minimize their labour costs, while simultaneously maximizing the effort and discipline of their employees. This relationship introduces an inherent conflict of interest between workers and capitalists. At the same time, there are times when workers and capitalists may choose to cooperate with each other.

6. **Unpaid work is also important.** A great deal of productive, necessary work occurs inside the household: out of sight, behind closed doors, and generally without pay. Most of that work is performed by women, whose opportunities in the "outside" economic world are constrained as a result. Remembering that this work needs to be performed, analyzing how and by whom it is performed, and making changes to it over time, are central issues in economics.

7. **Competition is a central feature of capitalism, and forces companies to behave in certain ways.** Capitalists aim to maximize the profits on their investments; one way to do that is by poaching customers, workers, resources, and capital from other capitalists. Competition therefore introduces a new constraint on the way that individual capitalists operate. It's no longer just greed that motivates them, it's also fear. That fear (of being driven from business by more successful competitors) forces executives to behave in certain ways, regardless of their personal preferences or values. Capitalism has become more competitive over time, not less (thanks to technology, globalization, privatization, and improved management skills). Even very large global companies face competition that is unforgiving and ruthless.

8. **The condition of the natural environment is crucial to our prosperity.** The environment is both a source of direct ecological benefits (fresh air, open spaces, recreation, and so on) and a source of raw materials for production. The economy cannot continually run down the quality of the environment without humans eventually paying an enormous economic price. Developing sustainable practices (to stabilize and preserve environmental quality) is an urgent economic priority.

9. **The financial industry is not, in itself, productive.** Financial institutions can play a useful role in facilitating investment and production by companies in the real economy. But this function

may be overwhelmed by pointless, wasteful, or downright destructive financial activity. Speculators seek to profit from the purchase and resale of paper assets, rather than from the production of useful goods and services.

10. **Government has played a central, supporting role since the beginning of capitalism.** Government is not the "enemy" of free-market capitalism. In fact, without government capitalism wouldn't exist at all. Government actions and programs have tended to reinforce and stabilize the basic relationships of capitalism: guaranteeing private property rights, supplying business with needed inputs (like reliable infrastructure and skilled, disciplined workers), expanding markets, and managing social relationships in a way that promotes both stability and profitability. At the same time, working people – thanks to their sheer numbers – can use democratic openings to force governments to respond to *their* needs and priorities, but only when they are sufficiently motivated and well-organized.

11. **Globalization can strengthen an economy, or it can weaken an economy.** Globalization is not new. But modern globalization is inherently biased in favour of corporations and investors. Free-trade agreements and other aspects of globalization give them more mobility and more power, while limiting the ability of national governments to regulate international flows of goods and capital. In contrast to free-trade theory (which claims globalization benefits everyone who participates), globalization may help or hurt a national economy. It can increase or decrease demand for a country's products (via the trade balance), and it can strengthen or weaken investment (via capital flows). A country's competitiveness determines whether globalization is helpful or harmful.

12. **Workers and poor people get only as much from the economy as they are able to demand, fight for, and win.** There is no reason to believe that the success of capitalists will ever naturally "trickle-down" into improved living standards for the bulk of humanity. Neoclassical theories which claim that everyone gets paid according to their productivity are theoretically inconsistent and empirically false. Income distribution is determined by power, more than markets. Demanding a fairer deal from the

system, and building the organizational and political power to back-up that demand (through unions and other social justice movements), is the only way to redivide the pie. And if those demands come up against a hard limit in the form of the system's willingness or ability to meet them, then the time will have come to look at alternatives.

On that note, this is a good time to put down this book, put on your boots – and go out to organize for a fairer share of the pie that you work so hard to produce.

Index

Terms highlighted in SMALL CAPITALS are defined in the on-line glossary downloadable at www.economicsforeveryone.com.